Mostly BASIC: Applications for Your TRS-80®

Book 2

Howard Berenbon is a graduate of Wayne State University with a Bachelor of Science in Electrical Engineering. He is currently employed in the automotive industry and spends much of his spare time developing new programs for microcomputers. He is the author of the companion to this volume, *Mostly BASIC: Applications for Your TRS-80®, Book 1;* two similar books for the Apple® II, *Mostly BASIC: Application for Your Apple® II,* Books 1 and 2; and *Mostly BASIC: Applications for Your PET®.* His articles have appeared in many of the popular electronics and microcomputer publications.

Mostly BASIC: Applications for Your TRS-80®
Book 2

by

Howard Berenbon

Howard W. Sams & Co., Inc.
4300 WEST 62ND ST. INDIANAPOLIS, INDIANA 46268 USA

FIRST EDITION
FIRST PRINTING—1981

International Standard Book Number: 0-672-21865-8
Library of Congress Catalog Card Number: 80-53269

Edited by: *Jack Davis*

Printed in the United States of America.

Preface

This book is a companion volume to *Mostly BASIC, Applications for Your TRS-80®, Book 1*. Written for the TRS-80* computer hobbyist, it consists of 32 chapters, with 37 complete computer programs written in BASIC. It can help you learn history, budget your household expenses, analyze your utility costs, and aid in stock market investment, to mention a few.

As an added feature, two types of educational fantasy games are included. The first program is a single-level dungeon called The Time Dungeon. As you wander through the maze you will be teleported to different dates in history, to answer questions relating to actual events from the past. You will receive gold for a correct response, and you will lose gold for an incorrect response. The second and similar program is called The Algebra Dungeon, where you must solve algebraic equations as you wander through a two-level dungeon.

Also included is a fantasy game called The Dungeon of Danger. Here, you must fight monsters that roam the chambers and corridors of the dungeon. Your goal is to find the way out, unharmed, with as much gold as possible.

The programs are written in Level II BASIC for the TRS-80 Model I and Model III microcomputers. Also, many of the programs will run in the TRS-80 Color Computer without modifications, and some will require minor modifications.

Note portions of some of the programs are identical. However, to avoid confusion, especially for the beginning operator, the complete program listing is given for each version. Thus, there is no need to input part of a program from one listing and then skip to another to complete the desired program.

Many of the programs are easily modified to run in other microcomputer BASICs. In some cases the programs contain additional lines to ensure some compatibility with the many dialects of BASIC.

I hope that this book will help stimulate your imagination and aid you in the development of some of your own applications for your home computer.

HOWARD BERENBON

---

* TRS-80 is a registered trademark of Tandy Corporation

To my parents, Fay and Irving Berenbon.
To my family and friends who helped with their encouragement and constructive criticism.

Contents

SECTION I

Educational Programs

SECTION II

Home Applications

SECTION III

Money and Investment

SECTION I

Educational Programs

An important application for the home computer is its use as an educational aid. This section consists of eleven chapters, with sixteen educational programs written in BASIC.

The section begins with an educational fantasy game called The Time Dungeon. Here, the player is teleported to different dates in history, to answer questions relating to actual events from the past. There are six separate programs including American History, 1607 to 1850; American History, 1848 to 1914; American History, 1916 to 1975; World History, World War I; World History, World War II; and Ancient History, Middle East, 4000 B.C. to 6 B.C. All six programs are identical except for the subject and date at line 100 and the question DATA sets at lines 483 to 532. After entering one complete program, you need only change line 100 and the DATA set to complete the entry of all six games. But each program is listed separately to avoid confusion.

Next is an algebra educational fantasy game called The Algebra Dungeon. The word association program is a test for children. The algebra test program generates simple algebra problems. There are two memory test games: one that generates random letters and another that displays words. There is the Presidents test program that tests for dates in office, and the State Capitals test that tests your knowledge of the capitals. The Student Grader is an aid for teachers. Finally, there is a Relativistic Mass Simulation for physics students.

CHAPTER 1

The Time Dungeon

The Time Dungeon is an educational fantasy game where you must answer history questions while wandering through the chambers and corridors of the 64-chamber dungeon. When you enter an active time portal, you will be teleported to an event in history. There, you will be asked a question. There are six complete programs in this chapter. They are written in BASIC for your microcomputer. See Program 1-1 for American History, 1607 to 1850; Program 1-2 for American History, 1848 to 1914; Program 1-3 for American History, 1916 to 1975; Program 1-4 for World History, World War I; Program 1-5 for World History, World War II; and Program 1-6 for Ancient History, Middle East, 4000 B.C. to 6 B.C.

THE PROGRAM

You are given 1000 gold pieces and then teleported to a random location in the dungeon. Your goal is to find your way out, with as much gold as possible. Gold pieces are acquired by correctly answering questions about events in history. When you enter a chamber that is an active time portal, you will be teleported to a specific year. Then a question relating to that year is displayed. You will receive a random amount of gold if a correct answer is entered, and you will lose gold for an incorrect response. See Fig. 1-1 for a sample run.

ACTIONS OR MOVES

In your trip through the dungeon you will encounter active time portals, alien travelers, inactive time portals, time traps, secret doors leading to north-south or east-west corridors, maps, a crystal key, and exit portals.

After you run the program, enter your name, or your favorite fantasy character's name, for your trip into history. Then enter the present year. In a few seconds you will be teleported to an inactive time portal, somewhere in the dungeon.

You now have a choice of six actions. Enter the letter in parentheses for the following actions or moves in the dungeon:

(N)ORTH movement (up)
(E)AST movement (right)
(S)OUTH movement (down)
(W)EST movement (left)
E(X)IT (when you are at an exit portal and have the crystal key)
(G)OLD pieces left

Mapping the Dungeon

Before you proceed, it is a good idea to begin mapping out the dungeon. Find your way to a corner, to orient yourself. Draw an eight (8) by eight (8) checkerboard, and make a note of the contents of each square using the following symbols:

0 = inactive portal
AP = active portal
NS = north-south corridor
EW = east-west corridor
A = alien traveler
X = exit portal
T = time trap
=P= = your location in the dungeon

It must be noted that after you answer a question correctly (in an active time portal) that portal becomes inactive. But an incorrect answer leaves the portal active for future use. Also, after encountering an alien traveler, that chamber becomes an inactive portal. But the alien can reappear elsewhere in the dungeon.

Mapping the dungeon will allow you to find all the active time portals, keep track of time traps (so you can avoid them), and identify exit portal locations. On occasion, maps can be found on glowing screens within corridors. But this will be discussed later in the text.

North Movement (UP)

Entering an N allows you to move north through the dungeon. You may not move north under the following conditions:

1. If you reach the North Wall, you cannot pass through it.

```
THE TIME DUNGEON: AMERICAN HISTORY
COPYRIGHT (C) 1980 BY HOWARD BERENBON

AN EDUCATIONAL FANTASY GAME




YOU WILL BE TELEPORTED TO . . .

THE TIME DUNGEON . . . .
TO STUDY AMERICAN HISTORY

ENTER YOUR CHARACTER'S NAME?
? SARGON
ENTER PRESENT YEAR
? 1981

SARGON . . . YOU ARE ON YOUR WAY


YOU HAVE ARRIVED AT . . . .

THE TIME DUNGEON: AMERICAN HISTORY
FOR THE YEARS:    1916 TO 1975

YOU CARRY 1000 GOLD PIECES

YOU WILL ENCOUNTER . . .
TIME PORTALS WHICH TELEPORT
YOU TO EVENTS IN AMERICAN HISTORY


YOU ARE IN A GLOWING TIME PORTAL

THE LIGHT FADES . . . . . .
THE PORTAL IS INACTIVE . . . .

SARGON,  WHAT IS YOUR ACTION OR MOVE?

(N)ORTH, (E)AST, (S)OUTH
(W)EST, E(X)IT, (G)OLD
? N

YOU ENTER INTO A BLUE HAZY . . .
. . . . . . . TIME PORTAL . . .

A PULSATING GLOW . . . . . . .
. . . . INDICATES ACTIVATION

PRESENT YEAR . . .   1981


    P O R T A L   Y E A R   .   .   .   1 9 7 4


P O R T A L   Y E A R   .   .   .   1 9 6 5
A R R I V A L   .   .   .   .   .   A T
D E S T I N A T I O N   Y E A R   .   .   .   .   1 9 6 5


YOU HAVE ARRIVED AT THE YEAR  1965
. . . . . . IN AMERICAN HISTORY

YOU MUST ANSWER THIS QUESTION . . TO CONTINUE YOUR JOURNEY
--------------------------------------------------------------
THE YEAR IS:  1965

RACE RIOTS ERUPTED IN THE .... SECTION OF LOS ANGELES?:
WHITE             POOR
OLD               WATTS
--------------------------------------------------------------
QUESTION TYPE: *** MULTIPLE CHOICE ?
ENTER CORRECT ANSWER?
? WATTS


CORRECT
YOU WIN  237  GOLD PIECES

SARGON,  WHAT IS YOUR ACTION OR MOVE?

(N)ORTH, (E)AST, (S)OUTH
(W)EST, E(X)IT, (G)OLD
? E


YOU ENTER INTO A BLUE HAZY . . .
. . . . . . . TIME PORTAL . . .

A PULSATING GLOW . . . . . . .
. . . . INDICATES ACTIVATION

PRESENT YEAR . . .   1965


 .. P O R T A L   Y E A R   .   .   .   1 9 7 0


 .. P O R T A L   Y E A R   .   .   .   1 9 7 0
A R R I V A L   .   .   .   .   .   A T
D E S T I N A T I O N   Y E A R   .   .   .   .   1 9 7 0


YOU HAVE ARRIVED AT THE YEAR  1970
. . . . . . IN AMERICAN HISTORY

YOU MUST ANSWER THIS QUESTION . . TO CONTINUE YOUR JOURNEY
--------------------------------------------------------------
THE YEAR IS:  1970

U.S. AND S. VIETNAMESE TROOPS ENTERED WHAT CITY
--------------------------------------------------------------
QUESTION TYPE: PEOPLE, PLACES, OR THINGS ?
ENTER CORRECT ANSWER?
? CAMBODIA


CORRECT
YOU WIN  260  GOLD PIECES

SARGON,  WHAT IS YOUR ACTION OR MOVE?

(N)ORTH, (E)AST, (S)OUTH
(W)EST, E(X)IT, (G)OLD
? S
```

Fig. 1-1. The Time Dungeon

```
YOU ENTER A NORTH-SOUTH CORRIDOR
THRU A SECRET DOOR

THE DOOR CLOSES AND LOCKS BEHIND YOU

ON THE WALL IS A GLOWING SCREEN
BELOW THE SCREEN IS A RED BUTTON


DO YOU WISH TO PUSH THE BUTTON?
ENTER  (Y)ES  OR  (N)O
? Y


THE TIME DUNGEON * * * MAP

?   AP  O   O   O   ?   O   ?
NS  O   O   ?   ?   AP  ?   AP
X   AP  NS  NS  AP  AP  AP  O
EW  EW  AP  X   ?   AP  NS  NS
O   O   O   AP  O   AP  O   AP
AP  NS  AP  ?   NS  EW  NS  AP
EW  O   AP  AP  O   O   O   O
EW  NS  O   O   O   O   =P= AP


YOU ENTER INTO A BLUE HAZY . . .
. . . . . . . TIME PORTAL . . .

A PULSATING GLOW . . . . . . .
. . . . INDICATES ACTIVATION

PRESENT YEAR . . .   1942


  .   P O R T A L   Y E A R .. ..  .   1 9 4 3


  .   P O R T A L   Y E A R .. ..  .   1 9 4 4
A R R I V A L   .   .   .  .   A T
D E S T I N A T I O N   Y E A R   .   .   .   .   1 9 4 4


YOU HAVE ARRIVED AT THE YEAR  1944
. . . . . . . IN AMERICAN HISTORY

YOU MUST ANSWER THIS QUESTION . . TO CONTINUE YOUR JOURNEY
-----------------------------------------------------------------
THE YEAR IS:  1944

THE .... INVADED EUROPE AND FREED FRANCE-BELGIUM-& LUXEMBOURG
-----------------------------------------------------------------
QUESTION TYPE: PEOPLE, PLACES, OR THINGS ?
ENTER CORRECT ANSWER?
? ALLIES


CORRECT
YOU WIN  308  GOLD PIECES

SARGON,  WHAT IS YOUR ACTION OR MOVE?

(N)ORTH, (E)AST, (S)OUTH
(W)EST, E(X)IT, (G)OLD
? N


YOU ENTER INTO A BLUE HAZY . . .
. . . . . . . TIME PORTAL . . .

A PULSATING GLOW . . . . . . .
. . . . INDICATES ACTIVATION

PRESENT YEAR . . .   1944


  . P O R T A L   Y E A R  .  .  .   1 9 4 1


  . P O R T A L   Y E A R  .  .  .   1 9 4 1
A R R I V A L   .   .   .   A T
D E S T I N A T I O N   Y E A R   .   .   .   .   1 9 4 1


YOU HAVE ARRIVED AT THE YEAR  1941
. . . . . . . IN AMERICAN HISTORY

YOU MUST ANSWER THIS QUESTION . . TO CONTINUE YOUR JOURNEY
-----------------------------------------------------------------
THE YEAR IS:  1941

ROOSEVELT AND CHURCHILL ISSUED THE .... CHARTER OF POSTWAR ARMS?
:
PACIFIC          FREEDOM
ATLANTIC         WESTERN
-----------------------------------------------------------------
QUESTION TYPE: *** MULTIPLE CHOICE ?
ENTER CORRECT ANSWER?
? ATLANTIC

CORRECT
YOU WIN  248  GOLD PIECES

YOU SEARCH THE CHAMBER . . . AND
FIND . . . . THE CRYSTAL KEY

SARGON,  WHAT IS YOUR ACTION OR MOVE?

(N)ORTH, (E)AST, (S)OUTH
(W)EST, E(X)IT, (G)OLD
? W


YOU ARE AT AN EXIT PORTAL

(A KEY IS REQUIRED)

SARGON,  WHAT IS YOUR ACTION OR MOVE?

(N)ORTH, (E)AST, (S)OUTH
(W)EST, E(X)IT, (G)OLD
? X


YOU ENTER THE EXIT PORTAL AND
INSERT THE CRYSTAL KEY INTO THE SLOT

THE MACHINE BEGINS TO HUM . . . .


    P O R T A L   Y E A R  .  ..  .   1 9 5 2
```

sample run.

```
      PORTAL YEAR . . .  1981
ARRIVAL . . . . AT
DESTINATION YEAR . . . .  1981
```

```
YOU FOUND YOUR WAY . . . . .
. . . . BACK TO THE PRESENT

YOU HAVE ACQUIRED  3511  GOLD PIECES

GAME RATING IS  447

YOU TOOK  57  TURNS TO FIND THE WAY OUT
AND ANSWERED  9  QUESTION(S) CORRECTLY,
OUT OF  9  QUESTIONS ASKED.

ANOTHER GAME?
ENTER '1'-YES  '0'-NO
? 1
```

Fig. 1-1—cont. The Time Dungeon sample run.

2. If you enter an east-west corridor (through a secret door), movement north is not allowed.

East Movement (RIGHT)

Entering an E allows you to move east. You may not move east under the following conditions:

1. If you reach the East Wall, you cannot pass through it.
2. If you enter a north-south corridor (through a secret door), movement east is not allowed.

South Movement (DOWN)

Entering an S allows you to move south. You may not move south under the following conditions:

1. If you reach the South Wall, you cannot pass through it.
2. If you enter an east-west corridor (through a secret door), movement south is not allowed.

West Movement (LEFT)

Entering a W allows you to move west. You may not move west under the following conditions:

1. If you reach the West Wall, you cannot pass through it.
2. If you enter a north-south corridor (through a secret door), movement west is not allowed.

Exiting the Dungeon

Entering an X, when you are at an exit portal and have the crystal key, allows you to be teleported back to the present. If you haven't found the key, or you are not at an exit portal, you may not exit the dungeon.

To find the crystal key, you must correctly answer a random number of history questions. But, on occasion, you may find the key when encountering unfriendly alien travelers.

Gold Pieces Left

Entering a G will display the number of gold pieces you have with you. You will start out with 1000 and can gain or lose gold during your trip. But if you lose all your gold pieces, you will lose the game.

Active Portals

When you encounter an active time portal, the year in which you currently are will be displayed, and then a star background will be generated, indicating activation. The portal year will be displayed at the center of the screen as it decrements or increments from the present year to your new destination year. When approaching the destination year this action will slow down, and it will stop when the year is reached.

The question is displayed along with the year that you were teleported to. It is chosen randomly from a list of 50 and will not be repeated until all other questions are asked (for at least two or three games).

A correct answer wins you a random amount of gold, up to 625 pieces, then the portal becomes inactive. If your answer is incorrect, then the correct answer is displayed and you lose a random amount of gold (up to 425 pieces). But the time portal remains active for future use.

The questions are high-school and college level.

Question Types

There are four types of questions possible:

1. People, places, or things.
2. True or false.
3. Who am I (name).
4. Multiple choice.

Type 1 questions may be on any subject relating to the portal destination year. Enter the word or group of words that apply. It can be a fill-in-the-blank type or just a question.

Type 2 requires a true or false response. Enter the letter T for true, or F for false, when requested.

Type 3 requires a last-name entry. Enter the last name only.

Type 4 is a multiple-choice question. It will display a question with four possible answers, one of which is correct. Enter the correct answer.

Question types 1, 3, and 4 require that your answer be spelled correctly, otherwise an incorrect response will be indicated.

The Crystal Key

You will find the crystal key after you answer a random number of questions correctly (you need the key to exit the dungeon).

ALIEN TRAVELERS

When you encounter an alien traveler, he may be friendly or unfriendly. The friendly alien will give you a random number of gold pieces as he leaves. The unfriendly alien will take some of your gold. In this encounter, however, there is a chance that you may find the crystal key.

When the alien leaves, the chamber becomes an inactive portal, but the alien may reappear elsewhere in the dungeon.

TIME TRAPS

Some of the chambers contain time traps, which may, or may not, activate. If they activate, then you will be teleported to an unknown location in the dungeon and lose all but 100 gold pieces. When you discover time traps, avoid them.

NORTH-SOUTH AND EAST-WEST CORRIDORS

North-south and east-west corridors may be entered from any direction (through secret doors), but will limit your next move to the corridor direction displayed.

Corridor Objects

It is possible to find maps or gold inside a corridor. On occasion you will discover a glowing screen on the wall, with a red button below the screen. Depressing this button will result in one of three happenings:

1. A map of the dungeon will be displayed for a random number of seconds. The following symbols will be printed for the 64-chamber dungeon:

   0 = inactive portal
   AP = active portal
   NS = north-south corridor
   EW = east-west corridor
   ? = unknown contents (either an alien traveler or time trap)
   X = exit portal
   =P= = your location in the dungeon
2. Nothing happens.
3. You will receive gold pieces each time you push the button, but the corridor narrows at the same time. There is a possibility of getting stuck in the corridor. If that happens, you lose the game.

See Fig. 1-2 for a sample map.

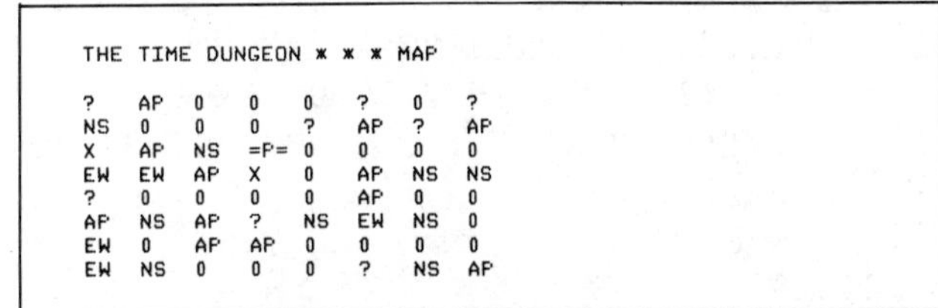

```
THE TIME DUNGEON * * * MAP

?   AP  0   0   0   ?   0   ?
NS  0   0   0   ?   AP  ?   AP
X   AP  NS  =P= 0   0   0   0
EW  EW  AP  X   0   AP  NS  NS
?   0   0   0   0   AP  0   0
AP  NS  AP  ?   NS  EW  NS  0
EW  0   AP  AP  0   0   0   0
EW  NS  0   0   0   ?   NS  AP
```

Fig. 1-2. The Time Dungeon sample map.

INACTIVE PORTALS

Inactive portals are, normally, empty chambers. Occasionally, however, you will find a door inside the chamber. Trying the door will result in one of three happenings:

1. The door opens, and you find gold inside the closet.
2. The door won't open.
3. The door opens, and the chamber begins to spin. You are teleported, momentarily, into another dimension, where you can lose up to half of your gold and waste up to 20 moves.

GAME RATING

After you complete the game, a game rating is displayed along with the number of gold pieces acquired, the number of history questions answered correctly out of the number of questions asked, and the number of turns (moves) taken. The rating is a number from approximately −600 to +2000, depending on the above statistics. The higher the rating number, the better is the game rating. A negative number indicates a poor rating.

Program 1-1. The Time Dungeon: American History, 1607 to 1850, Program Listing

```
100 CLS:CLEAR400:BZ$="AMERICAN HISTORY":BW$="1607 TO 1850"
101 PRINT"THE TIME DUNGEON: ";BZ$
102 PRINT"COPYRIGHT (C) 1980 BY HOWARD BERENBON"
103 PRINT"TRS-80 VERSION"
104 PRINT
105 PRINT"AN EDUCATIONAL FANTASY GAME"
106 GT=5:GOSUB134:Q3=0
107 CLS:DIMA(9,9),B(50):GOSUB451
108 PRINT"YOU WILL BE TELEPORTED TO . . ."
109 PRINT
110 PRINT"THE TIME DUNGEON . . . ."
111 PRINT"TO STUDY ";BZ$
112 PRINT
113 RANDOM
114 CA=0:G=1000:M1=1:K=0:KL=1:TT=0:TR=0
115 PRINT"ENTER YOUR CHARACTER'S NAME?"
116 INPUTA$
117 PRINT"ENTER PRESENT YEAR"
118 INPUTY2:YY=Y2:IFY2>2000THEN117
119 PRINT:PRINTA$;" . . . YOU ARE ON YOUR WAY"
120 GT=2:GOSUB134
121 GOSUB143
122 CLS
123 PRINT"YOU HAVE ARRIVED AT . . . ."
124 PRINT
125 PRINT"THE TIME DUNGEON: ";BZ$
126 PRINT"FOR THE YEARS:     ";BW$
127 PRINT
128 PRINT"YOU CARRY 1000 GOLD PIECES":PRINT
129 PRINT"YOU WILL ENCOUNTER . . ."
130 PRINT"TIME PORTALS WHICH TELEPORT"
131 PRINT"YOU TO EVENTS IN ";BZ$
132 GT=8:GOSUB134
133 GOTO199
134 FORZZ=1TO400*GT
135 NEXTZZ
136 RETURN
137 PRINT"0   ";:RETURN
138 PRINT"AP  ";:RETURN
139 PRINT"?   ";:RETURN
140 PRINT"NS  ";:RETURN
141 PRINT"EW  ";:RETURN
142 PRINT"X   ";:RETURN
143 REM SET UP DUNGEON
144 FORX=1TO8
145 FORY=1TO8
146 A(X,Y)=RND(7)
147 NEXTY
148 NEXTX
149 REM TRAPS
150 H=RND(3)+1
151 FORN=1TOH
152 X=RND(8)
```

```
153 Y=RND(8)
154 A(X,Y)=8
155 NEXTN
156 REM EXITS
157 S=RND(4)+1
158 FORN=1TOS
159 X=RND(8)
160 Y=RND(8)
161 A(X,Y)=9
162 NEXTN
163 RETURN
164 R6=RND(4):PRINTQD$;"?:"
165 ONR6GOSUB167,168,169,170
166 GOTO433
167 PRINTAD$,I1$:PRINTI2$,I3$:RETURN
168 PRINTI2$,AD$:PRINTI1$,I3$:RETURN
169 PRINTI1$,I2$:PRINTAD$,I3$:RETURN
170 PRINTI3$,I1$:PRINTI2$,AD$:RETURN
171 CLS
172 PRINTCHR$(23)
173 GT=1
174 GOSUB134
175 FORB=1TO70:B4=RND(1020)
176 PRINT@B4,".";
177 NEXTB
178 GT=.005:Y5=25
179 IFY3=YYTHENPRINT"ALREADY AT . . . .":GOTO196
180 IFY3<YYTHEN188
181 IF(Y3-YY)<=50THEN185
182 Y3=Y3-Y5
183 GOSUB382
184 IFY3=YYTHEN195
185 IF(Y3-YY)<=50THENY5=1
186 IF(Y3-YY)<=5THENGT=.4
187 GOTO182
188 IF(YY-Y3)<=50THEN192
189 Y3=Y3+Y5
190 GOSUB382
191 IFY3=YYTHEN195
192 IF(YY-Y3)<=50THENY5=1
193 IF(YY-Y3)<=5THENGT=.4
194 GOTO189
195 PRINT"ARRIVAL . . . . AT"
196 PRINT"DESTINATION YEAR . . . . ";YY
197 GT=4:GOSUB134
198 CLS:RETURN
199 C=RND(8):D=RND(8):A(C,D)=1
200 K4=RND(4)+3
201 CLS:A=A(C,D):GT=1:GOSUB134
202 ONAGOSUB292,300,410,410,306,330,335,338,362
203 IFKL=0THEN567
204 PRINT:IFTT=1THENTT=0:GOTO201
205 IFG<=0THEN264
```

```
206 PRINTA$;",  WHAT IS YOUR ACTION OR MOVE?"
207 PRINT
208 PRINT"(N)ORTH, (E)AST, (S)OUTH"
209 PRINT"(W)EST, E(X)IT, (G)OLD
210 INPUTM1$
211 M1=M1+1:IFK=0ANDM1>70THEN371
212 IFM1$="N"THEN220
213 IFM1$="E"THEN225
214 IFM1$="S"THEN230
215 IFM1$="W"THEN235
216 IFM1$="X"THEN240
217 IFM1$="G"THEN251
218 PRINT
219 GOTO204
220 REM NORTH
221 IFA=7THEN255
222 IF(D-1)=0THEN281
223 D=D-1
224 GOTO201
225 REM EAST
226 IFA=6THEN260
227 IF(C+1)=9THEN286
228 C=C+1
229 GOTO201
230 REM SOUTH
231 IFA=7THEN255
232 IF(D+1)=9THEN288
233 D=D+1
234 GOTO201
235 REM WEST
236 IFA=6THEN260
237 IF(C-1)=0THEN290
238 C=C-1
239 GOTO201
240 CLS
241 IFA<>9THEN248
242 IFK=1THEN387
243 PRINT"YOU CANNOT EXIT THE TIME DUNGEON"
244 PRINT"YOU DON'T HAVE THE CRYSTAL KEY"
245 GT=2:GOSUB134
246 PRINT
247 GOTO204
248 PRINT"YOU ARE NOT AT AN EXIT PORTAL"
249 GT=2:GOSUB134
250 GOTO204
251 REM GOLD
252 CLS:PRINT"YOU HAVE ";G;" GOLD PIECES WITH YOU"
253 PRINT
254 GOTO204
255 REM EW
256 CLS:PRINT"YOU ARE IN AN EAST-WEST CORRIDOR"
257 PRINT"YOU CAN ONLY GO EAST OR WEST"
258 PRINT
```

```
259 GOTO204
260 REM NS
261 CLS:PRINT"YOU ARE IN A NORTH-SOUTH CORRIDOR"
262 PRINT"YOU CAN ONLY GO NORTH OR SOUTH"
263 GOTO258
264 REM GOLD ZERO
265 GT=2:GOSUB134
266 PRINT
267 PRINT"YOU LOST ALL YOUR GOLD AND YOU WERE"
268 PRINT" . . . UNABLE TO MEET THE DEMANDS OF"
269 PRINT" . . . THE TIME DUNGEON . . . . ."
270 PRINT
271 PRINT
272 GT=3:GOSUB134
273 GOSUB402
274 PRINT
275 PRINT"ANOTHER GAME?"
276 PRINT"ENTER '1'-YES  '0'-NO"
277 INPUTAA
278 IFAA<>1THEN280
279 CLS:GOTO108
280 END
281 CLS:PRINT"YOU ARE AT THE NORTH WALL"
282 PRINT"YOU CANNOT PASS THROUGH"
283 PRINT
284 PRINT"TRY ANOTHER DIRECTION?"
285 GOTO204
286 CLS:PRINT"YOU ARE AT THE EAST WALL"
287 GOTO282
288 CLS:PRINT"YOU ARE AT THE SOUTH WALL"
289 GOTO282
290 CLS:PRINT"YOU ARE AT THE WEST WALL"
291 GOTO282
292 KT=RND(9)
293 PRINT"YOU ARE IN A GLOWING TIME PORTAL"
294 GT=1:GOSUB134
295 PRINT
296 PRINT"THE LIGHT FADES . . . . . ."
297 PRINT"THE PORTAL IS INACTIVE . . . ."
298 IFA=1ANDKT>=8THEN570
299 RETURN
300 PRINT"YOU ARE IN A DUST FILLED PORTAL"
301 GT=1:GOSUB134
302 PRINT
303 PRINT"A BRIGHT LIGHT IS ACTIVATED AND . ."
304 PRINT
305 GOTO296
306 CLS
307 PRINT"AN ALIEN TRAVELER IS IN THIS CHAMBER"
308 A(C,D)=RND(2):GOSUB478
309 GT=1:GOSUB134
310 TD=RND(10)
311 G4=RND(350)
```

```
312 Y=RND(8)
313 IFY<=5THEN320
314 PRINT:IF(G-G4)<0THENG4=G
315 PRINT"HE IS UNFRIENDLY . . . . AND AS HE"
316 PRINT"LEAVES . . . HE TAKES ";G4;" GOLD PIECES"
317 PRINT:G=G-G4
318 IFTD=5ANDK=0THEN325
319 RETURN
320 PRINT
321 PRINT"HE IS FRIENDLY . . . . . AND GIVES YOU"
322 PRINT". . ";G4;" GOLD PIECES, WHICH YOU ACCEPT"
323 PRINT:G=G+G4
324 GOTO318
325 PRINT:GT=2:GOSUB134
326 PRINT"YOU SEARCH THE CHAMBER . . . AND"
327 GT=1:GOSUB134
328 PRINT"FIND . . . . THE CRYSTAL KEY"
329 K=1:RETURN
330 CLS
331 PRINT"YOU ENTER A NORTH-SOUTH CORRIDOR"
332 PRINT"THRU A SECRET DOOR":PRINT:GOSUB380
333 KT=RND(9):IFKT>=7THEN545
334 RETURN
335 CLS
336 PRINT"YOU ENTER AN EAST-WEST CORRIDOR"
337 GOTO332
338 REM TRAP
339 PRINT"YOU ENCOUNTER . . . A TIME TRAP"
340 PRINT". . . . . . . . . IN THIS CHAMBER":GT=1:GOSUB134
341 TD=RND(9)
342 IFTD>=7THEN347
343 PRINT
344 PRINT"BUT YOU'RE LUCKY . . . . ."
345 PRINT". . . IT DIDN'T ACTIVATE"
346 RETURN
347 TT=1:PRINT"AND IT ACTIVATED . . . . .":GT=2:GOSUB134
348 FORA=1TO250
349 PRINT"*        %";
350 NEXTA
351 C=RND(8):D=RND(8)
352 PRINT
353 PRINT:G=100
354 PRINT"YOU HAVE BEEN TELEPORTED TO . . . ."
355 PRINT". . . . AN UNKNOWN LOCATION . . . ."
356 PRINT
357 PRINT"AND YOU LOST MOST OF YOUR GOLD"
358 PRINT
359 PRINT"YOU HAVE . . . ";G;" GOLD PIECES LEFT"
360 GT=6:GOSUB134
361 RETURN
362 PRINT"YOU ARE AT AN EXIT PORTAL"
363 PRINT
364 PRINT"(A KEY IS REQUIRED)"
```

```
365 PRINT
366 RETURN
367 H=1:O=9:W=8
368 B=0:E=5:R=14
369 C=0:PR=0
370 GOTO216
371 PRINT:GT=2:GOSUB134
372 PRINT"BUT BEFORE YOU PROCEED . ."
373 PRINT"YOU LOOK TO THE GROUND AND . . ."
374 PRINT" . . . FIND THE CRYSTAL KEY . .":K=1
375 GT=3:GOSUB134
376 GOTO212
377 PRINT"YOU ANSWERED ";CA;" QUESTION(S) CORRECTLY"
378 PRINT" . . . . . IN ";M1;" TURNS,"
379 GOTO409
380 PRINT"THE DOOR CLOSES AND LOCKS BEHIND YOU":GT=1:GOSUB134
381 RETURN
382 REM TIME DISPLAY
383 PRINT@390,"PORTAL YEAR . . . ";Y3
384 PRINT@448,STRING$(64,191)
385 GOSUB134
386 RETURN
387 CLS:REM EXIT PORTAL
388 PRINT"YOU ENTER THE EXIT PORTAL AND"
389 PRINT"INSERT THE CRYSTAL KEY INTO THE SLOT"
390 PRINT:GT=4:GOSUB134
391 PRINT"THE MACHINE BEGINS TO HUM . . . ."
392 PRINT:GT=2:GOSUB134
393 YY=Y2:GOSUB171
394 PRINT
395 PRINT"YOU FOUND YOUR WAY . . . . ."
396 PRINT". . . . BACK TO THE PRESENT"
397 PRINT
398 PRINT"YOU HAVE ACQUIRED ";G;" GOLD PIECES"
399 PRINT
400 GOSUB402
401 GOTO274
402 GG=G+100
403 R=INT((GG*CA-7000+1)/M1)
404 PRINT
405 PRINT"GAME RATING IS ";R
406 PRINT:IFG<=0ORKL=0THEN377
407 PRINT"YOU TOOK ";M1;" TURNS TO FIND THE WAY OUT"
408 PRINT"AND ANSWERED ";CA;" QUESTION(S) CORRECTLY,"
409 PRINT"OUT OF ";TR;" QUESTIONS ASKED.":RETURN
410 CLS:Y3=YY
411 GOSUB444
412 Q3=Q3+1
413 IFQ3>50THENQ3=0:GOTO415
414 GOTO416
415 GOSUB451
416 Q=RND(50)
417 IFB(Q)=1THEN416
```

```
418 B(Q)=1
419 PRINT
420 FORAB=1TOQ
421 READ YY,QD$,ID,AD$,I1$,I2$,I3$
422 NEXTAB
423 RESTORE
424 GOSUB171
425 CLS:TR=TR+1
426 PRINT"YOU HAVE ARRIVED AT THE YEAR ";YY
427 PRINT". . . . . . IN ";BZ$:PRINT
428 PRINT"YOU MUST ANSWER THIS QUESTION";
429 PRINT" . . TO CONTINUE YOUR JOURNEY"
430 PRINT"------------------------------------------------------------"
431 PRINT"THE YEAR IS: ";YY:PRINT:IFID=4THEN164
432 PRINTQD$
433 PRINT"------------------------------------------------------------"
434 PRINT"QUESTION TYPE: ";
435 ON ID GOSUB 455,456,457,458
436 GOSUB459
437 IFE$=AD$THEN441
438 PRINT"INCORRECT"
439 GOSUB471
440 RETURN
441 PRINT"CORRECT"
442 GOSUB463
443 RETURN
444 PRINT"YOU ENTER INTO A BLUE HAZY . . ."
445 PRINT". . . . . . . TIME PORTAL . . . "
446 PRINT:GT=1:GOSUB134
447 PRINT"A PULSATING GLOW . . . . . . ."
448 PRINT". . . . INDICATES ACTIVATION":PRINT
449 PRINT"PRESENT YEAR . . .  ";Y3:GT=3:GOSUB134
450 RETURN
451 FORI=1TO50
452 B(I)=0
453 NEXTI
454 RETURN
455 PRINT"PEOPLE, PLACES, OR THINGS ?":RETURN
456 PRINT"*** (T)RUE OR (F)ALSE  ?":RETURN
457 PRINT"*** WHO AM I (LAST NAME) ?":RETURN
458 PRINT"*** MULTIPLE CHOICE ?":RETURN
459 PRINT"ENTER CORRECT ANSWER?"
460 INPUTE$
461 G4=RND(500)+125
462 RETURN
463 G=G+G4
464 PRINT"YOU WIN ";G4;" GOLD PIECES"
465 A(C,D)=RND(2)
466 CA=CA+1:IFK=1THENRETURN
467 IFCA=K4THEN469
468 RETURN
469 GOSUB325
470 RETURN
```

Program 1-1—cont. The Time Dungeon: American History, 1607 to 1850, Program Listing

```
471 PRINT:G4=RND(400)+25
472 PRINT"THE CORRECT ANSWER IS '";AD$;"'"
473 PRINT:IF(G-G4)<0THENG4=G
474 G=G-G4
475 GT=1:GOSUB134
476 PRINT"YOU LOSE ";G4;" GOLD PIECES"
477 RETURN
478 ZT=5
479 X=RND(8):Y=RND(8)
480 IFA(X,Y)<=2THENA(X,Y)=5:RETURN
481 ZT=ZT-1:IFZT=0THENRETURN
482 GOTO479
483 DATA 1619,IN WHAT COLONY BEGAN THE SALE OF SLAVES FROM AFRICA,4,VIRGINIA,NEW
 HAMPSHIRE,PLYMOUTH,CONNECTICUT
484 DATA 1620,WHAT GROUP OF PEOPLE FOUNDED THE PLYMOUTH COLONY,4,SEPARATISTS,MOR
MONS,ENGLISH,CONFORMISTS
485 DATA 1607,THE LONDON CO. EXPEDITION SENT 3 SHIPS-GODSPEED-SARAH CONSTANT-& .
...,4,DISCOVERY,ENTERPRISE,BRITAIN,NEW WORLD
486 DATA 1607,CAPT. CHRISTOPHER .... COMMANDED THE 1ST LONDON CO. EXPEDITION,4,N
EWPORT,PIKE,SMITH,WILLIAMS
487 DATA 1607,JAMESTOWN IS NAMED AFTER THE ENGLISH KING-JAMES I,2,T,0,0,0
488 DATA 1630,WHAT GROUP BEGAN THE COLONY OF MASSACHUSETTS BAY,4,PURITANS,SEPARA
TISTS,MORMONS,LOYALISTS
489 DATA 1630,THE PURITANS WERE NOT WELL EQUIPPED TO SETTLE IN MASSACHUSETTS,2,F
,0,0,0
490 DATA 1635,WHAT COLONY DID REVEREND THOMAS HOOK HELP ESTABLISH,4,CONNECTICUT,
VIRGINIA,PLYMOUTH,MASSACHUSETTS
491 DATA 1635,I WAS BANISHED FROM MASSACHUSETTS BAY FOR MY RELIGIOUS BELIEFS,3,W
ILLIAMS,0,0,0
492 DATA 1783,WHAT DOCUMENT ENDED THE WAR OF INDEPENDENCE?,1,TREATY OF PARIS,0,0
,0
493 DATA 1781,I SURRENDERED MY ENTIRE ARMY DURING THE WAR OF INDEPENDENCE,3,CORN
WALLIS,0,0,0
494 DATA 1766,WHAT COLONIAL TAX DID THE BRITISH REPEAL,4,STAMP ACT,WOOLEN ACT,SH
IP TAX,FOOD TAX
495 DATA 1690,BRITISH PASSED THE .... ACT TO STOP THE MANUFACTURE OF TEXTILES,4,
WOOLEN,COTTON,RAYON,CLOTHS
496 DATA 1782,AT WHAT CITY WAS THE AMERICAN VICTORY THAT SHOCKED THE BRITISH,4,Y
ORKTOWN,JAMESTOWN,NEW YORK,SARATOGA
497 DATA 1786,AT WHAT CITY BEGAN THE ALTERING OF THE ARTICLES OF CONFEDERATION,4
,ANNAPOLIS,SARATOGA,NEW YORK,ALBANY
498 DATA 1636,I FOUNDED THE SETTLEMENT CALLED PROVIDENCE,3,WILLIAMS,0,0,0
499 DATA 1638,NEW HAMPSHIRE WAS BUILT BY OVERFLOW OF PEOPLE FROM MASSACHUSETTS,2
,T,0,0,0
500 DATA 1679,IN 1679-WHAT COLONY RECEIVED A CHARTER FROM THE KING,4,NEW HAMPSHI
RE,PLYMOUTH,VIRGINIA,CONNECTICUT
501 DATA 1649,LORD BALTIMORE PERSUADED THE VIRGINIA COLONY TO PASS A TOLERATION
ACT,2,F,0,0,0
502 DATA 1649,.... AND WILLIAMS ESTABLISHED THE TOLERATION ACT,4,BALTIMORE,WASHI
NGTON,JEFFERSON,FRANKLIN
503 DATA 1649,TOLERATION ACT ALLOWS CATHOLICS & PROTESTANTS RELIGIOUS FREEDOM,2,
T,0,0,0
```

```
504 DATA 1624,NEW YORK HAD BEEN FOUNDED AS NEW NETHERLAND-A DUTCH COLONY,2,T,0,0
,0
505 DATA 1760,I WAS KNOWN FOR MY EXPERIMENTS WITH ELECTRICITY,3,FRANKLIN,0,0,0
506 DATA 1760,I WROTE THE BOOK CALLED 'NOTES ON VIRGINIA',3,JEFFERSON,0,0,0
507 DATA 1763,THE FRENCH & INDIAN WAR ENDED WITH THE SIGNING OF WHAT DOCUMENT,1,
PEACE OF PARIS,0,0,0
508 DATA 1777,MAIN BATTLE BETWEEN CONTINENTALS & BURGOYNE'S FORCES WAS NEAR?,4,S
ARATOGA,NEW YORK,YORKTOWN,ANNAPOLIS
509 DATA 1785,CONFEDERATIONS 1ST LAND ORDINANCE WAS CALLED-LAND ORDINANCE OF 178
5,2,T,0,0,0
510 DATA 1787,NORTHWEST ORDINANCE ALLOWED CREATION OF NEW STATES IN THE WEST,2,T
,0,0,0
511 DATA 1787,THE CONSTITUTION OF THE UNITED STATES WAS COMPLETED IN 1785,2,F,0,
0,0
512 DATA 1791,WHAT WERE THE 1ST 10 AMENDMENTS TO THE CONSTITUTION CALLED,1,BILL
OF RIGHTS,0,0,0
513 DATA 1790,THOMAS JEFFERSON AND JAMES MADISON FOUNDED THE .... PARTY,1,REPUBL
ICAN,0,0,0
514 DATA 1812,WAR OF 1812 RESULTED FROM BRITISH VIOLATING AMERICAN TRADE RIGHTS,
2,T,0,0,0
515 DATA 1807,WHAT AMERICAN SHIP DID THE BRITISH OPEN FIRE UPON,4,CHESAPEAKE,SAR
ATOGA,DISCOVERY,GODSPEED
516 DATA 1812,WHO COMMANDED THE BATTLE OF NEW ORLEANS,4,JACKSON,BALTIMORE,LINCOL
N,WASHINGTON
517 DATA 1806,HE FOLLOWED THE MISSISSIPPI RIVER NORTHWARD TO ITS SOURCE,4,PIKE,S
MITH,ROGERS,JAMES
518 DATA 1845,WHAT GROUP OF PEOPLE MIGRATED TO THE GREAT SALT LAKE,4,MORMONS,SEP
ARATISTS,LOYALISTS,INDIANS
519 DATA 1845,I LEAD THE MORMON MIGRATION TO THE UTAH TERRITORY,3,YOUNG,0,0,0
520 DATA 1850,BETWEEN 1830 AND 1850-2 MILLION EUROPEONS IMMIGRATED TO THE U.S.,2
,T,0,0,0
521 DATA 1807,I INVENTED THE STEAMBOAT-WHICH MADE WATER TRANSPORTATION EASIER,3,
FULTON,0,0,0
522 DATA 1812,BY 1812-STEAMBOATS SERVED ON THE OHIO AND MISSISSIPPI RIVERS,2,T,0
,0,0
523 DATA 1816,I CREATED THE 'ERA OF GOOD FEELING' IN POLITICS,3,MONROE,0,0,0
524 DATA 1832,I FEARED THE BANK OF THE UNITED STATES AS TOO POWERFUL,3,JACKSON,0
,0,0
525 DATA 1830,I SPOKE BEFORE THE SENATE IN SUPPORT OF 'UNIONS',3,WEBSTER,0,0,0
526 DATA 1812,THE WAR OF 1812 WAS OFTEN CALLED THE SECOND WAR FOR INDEPENDENCE,2
,T,0,0,0
527 DATA 1803,.... PURCHASE WAS AN ACHIEVEMENT OF JEFFERSON'S ADMINISTRATION,4,L
OUISIANA,NORTHWEST,SOUTHERN,VIRGINIAN
528 DATA 1825,THE GREATEST NUMBER OF PEOPLE MIGRATED TO NORTHERN-MOHAWK VALLEY,2
,T,0,0,0
529 DATA 1790,IN 1790-THERE WERE 8 MILLION PEOPLE IN THE UNITED STATES,2,F,0,0,0

530 DATA 1850,THERE WERE 8 MILLION PEOPLE BEYOND THE APPALACHIAN MOUNTAINS,2,T,0
,0,0
531 DATA 1825,THE .... CANAL-CONNECTING ALBANY WITH THE GREAT LAKES-WAS OPENED,4
,ERIE,NEW YORK,MICHIGAN,ST CLARE
532 DATA 1810,THE MACON BILL NO. 2 ALLOWED TRADE WITH FRANCE AND ENGLAND,2,T,0,0
,0
```

```
533 CLS:PRINT"THE TIME DUNGEON * * * MAP"
534 PRINT
535 FORQ=1TO8
536 FORN=1TO8
537 IFC=NANDD=QTHENPRINT"=P= ";:GOTO540
538 S1=A(N,Q)
539 ONS1GOSUB137,137,138,138,139,140,141,139,142
540 NEXTN
541 PRINT
542 NEXTQ
543 GT=RND(8)+RND(CA+5):GOSUB134
544 CLS:RETURN
545 PRINT:PRINT"ON THE WALL IS A GLOWING SCREEN"
546 PRINT"BELOW THE SCREEN IS A RED BUTTON":PRINT
547 KT=RND(9):KL=RND(15)+2
548 GOSUB565
549 INPUTK$
550 IFK$="Y"THEN552
551 RETURN
552 IFKT>=6THEN533
553 IFKT<=4THEN562
554 PRINT:G4=RND(100)+25:G=G+G4
555 PRINT"YOU RECEIVE ";G4;" GOLD PIECES . . ."
556 PRINT"BUT . . . . . . THE CORRIDOR NARROWS":GT=3:GOSUB134
557 KL=KL-1:IFKL=0THENRETURN
558 GOSUB565
559 INPUTK$
560 IFK$="Y"THEN554
561 RETURN
562 PRINT:PRINT"NOTHING HAPPENS"
563 GT=1:GOSUB134
564 RETURN
565 PRINT:PRINT"DO YOU WISH TO PUSH THE BUTTON?"
566 PRINT"ENTER  (Y)ES  OR  (N)O":RETURN
567 CLS:PRINT"YOU ARE STUCK IN THE NARROW CORRIDOR"
568 PRINT". . . . . . . . . . . AND . . .":PRINT:GT=3:GOSUB134
569 GOTO264
570 PRINT:PRINT"YOU NOTICE A DOOR TO YOUR RIGHT"
571 PRINT
572 KT=RND(9)
573 PRINT"DO YOU WISH TO OPEN THE DOOR?"
574 PRINT"ENTER  (Y)ES  OR  (N)O"
575 INPUTK$
576 IFK$="Y"THEN578
577 RETURN
578 PRINT:PRINT"YOU TRY THE DOOR . . . . .":GT=1:GOSUB134
579 IFKT>=7THEN589
580 IFKT<=4THEN587
581 PRINT:G4=RND(100)+25
582 PRINT"THE DOOR OPENS . . . . . . ."
583 PRINT"REVEALING A CLOSET . . . ."
584 PRINT:G=G+G4
585 PRINT"WHERE YOU FIND ";G4;" GOLD PIECES"
```

```
586 PRINT:RETURN
587 PRINT"BUT THE DOOR WON'T OPEN . . . ."
588 PRINT". . . . IT MUST BE LOCKED":RETURN
589 PRINT:PRINT"THE DOOR OPENS . . . AND SUDDENLY"
590 PRINT"THE CHAMBER BEGINS TO . . . SPIN"
591 G7=INT(G/2):G4=RND(G7):MM=RND(20)
592 GT=4:GOSUB134:G=G-G4
593 FORK9=1TO250
594 PRINT"+    =    +";
595 NEXTK9
596 CLS:PRINT"YOU WERE TELEPORTED INTO . . . ."
597 PRINT". . . . ANOTHER DIMENSION . . . ."
598 PRINT". . AND RETURNED IN AN INSTANT . ."
599 PRINT:PRINT"BUT YOU DROPPED ";G4;" GOLD PIECES"
600 PRINT". . . AND WASTED ";MM;" MOVES . . ."
601 M1=M1+MM
602 GT=4:GOSUB134
603 RETURN
```

Program 1-2. The Time Dungeon: American History, 1848 to 1914, Program Listing

```
100 CLS:CLEAR400:BZ$="AMERICAN HISTORY":BW$="1848 TO 1914"
101 PRINT"THE TIME DUNGEON: ";BZ$
102 PRINT"COPYRIGHT (C) 1980 BY HOWARD BERENBON"
103 PRINT"TRS-80 VERSION"
104 PRINT
105 PRINT"AN EDUCATIONAL FANTASY GAME"
106 GT=5:GOSUB134:Q3=0
107 CLS:DIMA(9,9),B(50):GOSUB451
108 PRINT"YOU WILL BE TELEPORTED TO . . ."
109 PRINT
110 PRINT"THE TIME DUNGEON . . . ."
111 PRINT"TO STUDY ";BZ$
112 PRINT
113 RANDOM
114 CA=0:G=1000:M1=1:K=0:KL=1:TT=0:TR=0
115 PRINT"ENTER YOUR CHARACTER'S NAME?"
116 INPUTA$
117 PRINT"ENTER PRESENT YEAR"
118 INPUTY2:YY=Y2:IFY2>2000THEN117
119 PRINT:PRINTA$;" . . . YOU ARE ON YOUR WAY"
120 GT=2:GOSUB134
121 GOSUB143
122 CLS
123 PRINT"YOU HAVE ARRIVED AT . . . ."
124 PRINT
125 PRINT"THE TIME DUNGEON: ";BZ$
126 PRINT"FOR THE YEARS:    ";BW$
127 PRINT
128 PRINT"YOU CARRY 1000 GOLD PIECES":PRINT
129 PRINT"YOU WILL ENCOUNTER . . ."
130 PRINT"TIME PORTALS WHICH TELEPORT"
131 PRINT"YOU TO EVENTS IN ";BZ$
132 GT=8:GOSUB134
133 GOTO199
134 FORZZ=1TO400*GT
135 NEXTZZ
136 RETURN
137 PRINT"O   ";:RETURN
138 PRINT"AP  ";:RETURN
139 PRINT"?   ";:RETURN
140 PRINT"NS  ";:RETURN
141 PRINT"EW  ";:RETURN
142 PRINT"X   ";:RETURN
143 REM SET UP DUNGEON
144 FORX=1TO8
145 FORY=1TO8
146 A(X,Y)=RND(7)
147 NEXTY
148 NEXTX
149 REM TRAPS
150 H=RND(3)+1
151 FORN=1TOH
152 X=RND(8)
```

```
153 Y=RND(8)
154 A(X,Y)=8
155 NEXTN
156 REM EXITS
157 S=RND(4)+1
158 FORN=1TOS
159 X=RND(8)
160 Y=RND(8)
161 A(X,Y)=9
162 NEXTN
163 RETURN
164 R6=RND(4):PRINTQD$;"?:"
165 ONR6GOSUB167,168,169,170
166 GOTO433
167 PRINTAD$,I1$:PRINTI2$,I3$:RETURN
168 PRINTI2$,AD$:PRINTI1$,I3$:RETURN
169 PRINTI1$,I2$:PRINTAD$,I3$:RETURN
170 PRINTI3$,I1$:PRINTI2$,AD$:RETURN
171 CLS
172 PRINTCHR$(23)
173 GT=1
174 GOSUB134
175 FORB=1TO70:B4=RND(1020)
176 PRINT@B4,".";
177 NEXTB
178 GT=.005:Y5=25
179 IFY3=YYTHENPRINT"ALREADY AT . . . .":GOTO196
180 IFY3<YYTHEN188
181 IF(Y3-YY)<=50THEN185
182 Y3=Y3-Y5
183 GOSUB382
184 IFY3=YYTHEN195
185 IF(Y3-YY)<=50THENY5=1
186 IF(Y3-YY)<=5THENGT=.4
187 GOTO182
188 IF(YY-Y3)<=50THEN192
189 Y3=Y3+Y5
190 GOSUB382
191 IFY3=YYTHEN195
192 IF(YY-Y3)<=50THENY5=1
193 IF(YY-Y3)<=5THENGT=.4
194 GOTO189
195 PRINT"ARRIVAL . . . . AT"
196 PRINT"DESTINATION YEAR . . . . ";YY
197 GT=4:GOSUB134
198 CLS:RETURN
199 C=RND(8):D=RND(8):A(C,D)=1
200 K4=RND(4)+3
201 CLS:A=A(C,D):GT=1:GOSUB134
202 ONAGOSUB292,300,410,410,306,330,335,338,362
203 IFKL=0THEN567
204 PRINT:IFTT=1THENTT=0:GOTO201
205 IFG<=0THEN264
```

```
206 PRINTA$;",  WHAT IS YOUR ACTION OR MOVE?"
207 PRINT
208 PRINT"(N)ORTH, (E)AST, (S)OUTH"
209 PRINT"(W)EST, E(X)IT, (G)OLD
210 INPUTM1$
211 M1=M1+1:IFK=0ANDM1>70THEN371
212 IFM1$="N"THEN220
213 IFM1$="E"THEN225
214 IFM1$="S"THEN230
215 IFM1$="W"THEN235
216 IFM1$="X"THEN240
217 IFM1$="G"THEN251
218 PRINT
219 GOTO204
220 REM NORTH
221 IFA=7THEN255
222 IF(D-1)=0THEN281
223 D=D-1
224 GOTO201
225 REM EAST
226 IFA=6THEN260
227 IF(C+1)=9THEN286
228 C=C+1
229 GOTO201
230 REM SOUTH
231 IFA=7THEN255
232 IF(D+1)=9THEN288
233 D=D+1
234 GOTO201
235 REM WEST
236 IFA=6THEN260
237 IF(C-1)=0THEN290
238 C=C-1
239 GOTO201
240 CLS
241 IFA<>9THEN248
242 IFK=1THEN387
243 PRINT"YOU CANNOT EXIT THE TIME DUNGEON"
244 PRINT"YOU DON'T HAVE THE CRYSTAL KEY"
245 GT=2:GOSUB134
246 PRINT
247 GOTO204
248 PRINT"YOU ARE NOT AT AN EXIT PORTAL"
249 GT=2:GOSUB134
250 GOTO204
251 REM GOLD
252 CLS:PRINT"YOU HAVE ";G;" GOLD PIECES WITH YOU"
253 PRINT
254 GOTO204
255 REM EW
256 CLS:PRINT"YOU ARE IN AN EAST-WEST CORRIDOR"
257 PRINT"YOU CAN ONLY GO EAST OR WEST"
258 PRINT
```

```
259 GOTO204
260 REM NS
261 CLS:PRINT"YOU ARE IN A NORTH-SOUTH CORRIDOR"
262 PRINT"YOU CAN ONLY GO NORTH OR SOUTH"
263 GOTO258
264 REM GOLD ZERO
265 GT=2:GOSUB134
266 PRINT
267 PRINT"YOU LOST ALL YOUR GOLD AND YOU WERE"
268 PRINT" . . . UNABLE TO MEET THE DEMANDS OF"
269 PRINT" . . . THE TIME DUNGEON . . . . ."
270 PRINT
271 PRINT
272 GT=3:GOSUB134
273 GOSUB402
274 PRINT
275 PRINT"ANOTHER GAME?"
276 PRINT"ENTER '1'-YES  '0'-NO"
277 INPUTAA
278 IFAA<>1THEN280
279 CLS:GOTO108
280 END
281 CLS:PRINT"YOU ARE AT THE NORTH WALL"
282 PRINT"YOU CANNOT PASS THROUGH"
283 PRINT
284 PRINT"TRY ANOTHER DIRECTION?"
285 GOTO204
286 CLS:PRINT"YOU ARE AT THE EAST WALL"
287 GOTO282
288 CLS:PRINT"YOU ARE AT THE SOUTH WALL"
289 GOTO282
290 CLS:PRINT"YOU ARE AT THE WEST WALL"
291 GOTO282
292 KT=RND(9)
293 PRINT"YOU ARE IN A GLOWING TIME PORTAL"
294 GT=1:GOSUB134
295 PRINT
296 PRINT"THE LIGHT FADES . . . . . ."
297 PRINT"THE PORTAL IS INACTIVE . . . ."
298 IFA=1ANDKT>=8THEN570
299 RETURN
300 PRINT"YOU ARE IN A DUST FILLED PORTAL"
301 GT=1:GOSUB134
302 PRINT
303 PRINT"A BRIGHT LIGHT IS ACTIVATED AND . ."
304 PRINT
305 GOTO296
306 CLS
307 PRINT"AN ALIEN TRAVELER IS IN THIS CHAMBER"
308 A(C,D)=RND(2):GOSUB478
309 GT=1:GOSUB134
310 TD=RND(10)
311 G4=RND(350)
```

```
312 Y=RND(8)
313 IFY<=5THEN320
314 PRINT:IF(G-G4)<0THENG4=G
315 PRINT"HE IS UNFRIENDLY . . . . AND AS HE"
316 PRINT"LEAVES . . . HE TAKES ";G4;" GOLD PIECES"
317 PRINT:G=G-G4
318 IFTD=5ANDK=0THEN325
319 RETURN
320 PRINT
321 PRINT"HE IS FRIENDLY . . . . . AND GIVES YOU"
322 PRINT". . ";G4;" GOLD PIECES, WHICH YOU ACCEPT"
323 PRINT:G=G+G4
324 GOTO318
325 PRINT:GT=2:GOSUB134
326 PRINT"YOU SEARCH THE CHAMBER . . . AND"
327 GT=1:GOSUB134
328 PRINT"FIND . . . . THE CRYSTAL KEY"
329 K=1:RETURN
330 CLS
331 PRINT"YOU ENTER A NORTH-SOUTH CORRIDOR"
332 PRINT"THRU A SECRET DOOR":PRINT:GOSUB380
333 KT=RND(9):IFKT>=7THEN545
334 RETURN
335 CLS
336 PRINT"YOU ENTER AN EAST-WEST CORRIDOR"
337 GOTO332
338 REM TRAP
339 PRINT"YOU ENCOUNTER . . . A TIME TRAP"
340 PRINT". . . . . . . . IN THIS CHAMBER":GT=1:GOSUB134
341 TD=RND(9)
342 IFTD>=7THEN347
343 PRINT
344 PRINT"BUT YOU'RE LUCKY . . . . ."
345 PRINT". . . IT DIDN'T ACTIVATE"
346 RETURN
347 TT=1:PRINT"AND IT ACTIVATED . . . . .":GT=2:GOSUB134
348 FORA=1TO250
349 PRINT"*        %";
350 NEXTA
351 C=RND(8):D=RND(8)
352 PRINT
353 PRINT:G=100
354 PRINT"YOU HAVE BEEN TELEPORTED TO . . . ."
355 PRINT". . . . AN UNKNOWN LOCATION . . . ."
356 PRINT
357 PRINT"AND YOU LOST MOST OF YOUR GOLD"
358 PRINT
359 PRINT"YOU HAVE . . . ";G;" GOLD PIECES LEFT"
360 GT=6:GOSUB134
361 RETURN
362 PRINT"YOU ARE AT AN EXIT PORTAL"
363 PRINT
364 PRINT"(A KEY IS REQUIRED)"
```

```
365 PRINT
366 RETURN
367 H=1:O=9:W=8
368 B=0:E=5:R=14
369 C=0:PR=0
370 GOTO216
371 PRINT:GT=2:GOSUB134
372 PRINT"BUT BEFORE YOU PROCEED . ."
373 PRINT"YOU LOOK TO THE GROUND AND . . ."
374 PRINT" . . . FIND THE CRYSTAL KEY . .":K=1
375 GT=3:GOSUB134
376 GOTO212
377 PRINT"YOU ANSWERED ";CA;" QUESTION(S) CORRECTLY"
378 PRINT" . . . . . IN ";M1;" TURNS,"
379 GOTO409
380 PRINT"THE DOOR CLOSES AND LOCKS BEHIND YOU":GT=1:GOSUB134
381 RETURN
382 REM TIME DISPLAY
383 PRINT@390,"PORTAL YEAR . . . ";Y3
384 PRINT@448,STRING$(64,191)
385 GOSUB134
386 RETURN
387 CLS:REM EXIT PORTAL
388 PRINT"YOU ENTER THE EXIT PORTAL AND"
389 PRINT"INSERT THE CRYSTAL KEY INTO THE SLOT"
390 PRINT:GT=4:GOSUB134
391 PRINT"THE MACHINE BEGINS TO HUM . . . ."
392 PRINT:GT=2:GOSUB134
393 YY=Y2:GOSUB171
394 PRINT
395 PRINT"YOU FOUND YOUR WAY . . . . ."
396 PRINT". . . . BACK TO THE PRESENT"
397 PRINT
398 PRINT"YOU HAVE ACQUIRED ";G;" GOLD PIECES"
399 PRINT
400 GOSUB402
401 GOTO274
402 GG=G+100
403 R=INT((GG*CA-7000+1)/M1)
404 PRINT
405 PRINT"GAME RATING IS ";R
406 PRINT:IFG<=0ORKL=0THEN377
407 PRINT"YOU TOOK ";M1;" TURNS TO FIND THE WAY OUT"
408 PRINT"AND ANSWERED ";CA;" QUESTION(S) CORRECTLY,"
409 PRINT"OUT OF ";TR;" QUESTIONS ASKED.":RETURN
410 CLS:Y3=YY
411 GOSUB444
412 Q3=Q3+1
413 IFQ3>50THENQ3=0:GOTO415
414 GOTO416
415 GOSUB451
416 Q=RND(50)
417 IFB(Q)=1THEN416
```

```
418 B(Q)=1
419 PRINT
420 FORAB=1TOQ
421 READ YY,QD$,ID,AD$,I1$,I2$,I3$
422 NEXTAB
423 RESTORE
424 GOSUB171
425 CLS
426 PRINT"YOU HAVE ARRIVED AT THE YEAR ";YY
427 PRINT". . . . . . IN ";BZ$:PRINT
428 PRINT"YOU MUST ANSWER THIS QUESTION";
429 PRINT" . . TO CONTINUE YOUR JOURNEY"
430 PRINT"----------------------------------------------------------------"
431 PRINT"THE YEAR IS: ";YY:PRINT:IFID=4THEN164
432 PRINTQD$
433 PRINT"----------------------------------------------------------------"
434 PRINT"QUESTION TYPE: ";
435 ON ID GOSUB 455,456,457,458
436 GOSUB459
437 IFE$=AD$THEN441
438 PRINT"INCORRECT"
439 GOSUB471
440 RETURN
441 PRINT"CORRECT"
442 GOSUB463
443 RETURN
444 PRINT"YOU ENTER INTO A BLUE HAZY . . ."
445 PRINT". . . . . . . TIME PORTAL . . . "
446 PRINT:GT=1:GOSUB134
447 PRINT"A PULSATING GLOW . . . . . . ."
448 PRINT". . . . INDICATES ACTIVATION":PRINT
449 PRINT"PRESENT YEAR . . .  ";Y3:GT=3:GOSUB134
450 RETURN
451 FORI=1TO50
452 B(I)=0
453 NEXTI
454 RETURN
455 PRINT"PEOPLE, PLACES, OR THINGS ?":RETURN
456 PRINT"*** (T)RUE OR (F)ALSE  ?":RETURN
457 PRINT"*** WHO AM I (LAST NAME) ?":RETURN
458 PRINT"*** MULTIPLE CHOICE ?":RETURN
459 PRINT"ENTER CORRECT ANSWER?"
460 INPUTE$
461 G4=RND(500)+125
462 RETURN
463 G=G+G4
464 PRINT"YOU WIN ";G4;" GOLD PIECES"
465 A(C,D)=RND(2)
466 CA=CA+1:IFK=1THENRETURN
467 IFCA=K4THEN469
468 RETURN
469 GOSUB325
470 RETURN
```

```
471 PRINT:G4=RND(400)+25
472 PRINT"THE CORRECT ANSWER IS '";AD$;"'"
473 PRINT:IF(G-G4)<0THENG4=G
474 G=G-G4
475 GT=1:GOSUB134
476 PRINT"YOU LOSE ";G4;" GOLD PIECES"
477 RETURN
478 ZT=5
479 X=RND(8):Y=RND(8)
480 IFA(X,Y)<=2THENA(X,Y)=5:RETURN
481 ZT=ZT-1:IFZT=0THENRETURN
482 GOTO479
483 DATA 1850,SLAVE TRADE WAS ABOLISHED IN WASHINGTON DC,2,T,0,0,0
484 DATA 1848,THE .... RUSH STARTED IN CALIFORNIA,4,GOLD,SILVER,TIN,BRASS
485 DATA 1852,I PUBLISHED 'UNCLE TOM'S CABIN',3,STOWE,0,0,0
486 DATA 1853,WHAT ALLOWED PURCHASE OF LAND FROM MEXICO,1,GADSDEN PURCHASE,0,0,0
487 DATA 1854,I ENACTED THE KANSAS & NEBRASKA ACT,3,DOUGLAS,0,0,0
488 DATA 1856,WHAT POLITICAL PARTY WAS FORMED THIS YEAR,4,REPUBLICAN,DEMOCRATIC,
WHIGS,PROGRESSIVE
489 DATA 1857,THE SUPREME COURT RULED THE MISSOURI COMPROMISE CONSTITUTIONAL,2,F
,0,0,0
490 DATA 1858,HE DEBATED SENATOR DOUGLAS ON SLAVERY,4,LINCOLN,PLESSY,STOWE,LEE
491 DATA 1859,I TRIED TO SEIZE THE FEDERAL ARSENAL AT HARPERS FERRY,3,BROWN,0,0,
0
492 DATA 1860,LINCOLN WAS ELECTED PRESIDENT IN THIS YEAR,2,T,0,0,0
493 DATA 1861,WHO WAS PRESIDENT OF THE 'CONFEDERATE STATES OF AMERICA',4,DAVIS,L
EE,BROWN,LINCOLN
494 DATA 1861,S. CAROLINA TROOPS FIRED ON FORT .....-STARTING THE CIVIL WAR,1,SU
MTER,0,0,0
495 DATA 1861,NORTH CAROLINA WAS A CONFEDERATE STATE,2,T,0,0,0
496 DATA 1862,THE EMANCIPATION PROCLAMATION WAS TO TAKE EFFECT IN JANUARY-1863,2
,T,0,0,0
497 DATA 1863,GENERAL MEADE'S UNION FORCES DEFEATS GENERAL LEE'S AT?,4,GETTYSBUR
G,NEW YORK,APPOMATTOX,WASHINGTON
498 DATA 1864,HE BECAME COMMANDER OF THE UNION ARMIES,4,GRANT,LEE,DAVIS,JACKSON
499 DATA 1865,THE .... AMENDMENT-ABOLISHING SLAVERY-WAS RATIFIED,4,13TH,2ND,20TH
,5TH
500 DATA 1865,WHO ASSASSINATED LINCOLN-ON APRIL 14TH,1,BOOTH,0,0,0
501 DATA 1865,GENERAL LEE SURRENDERED AT ..... COURT HOUSE,1,APPOMATTOX,0,0,0
502 DATA 1866,IN WHAT STATE WAS THE KU KLUX KLAN FORMED,4,TENNESSEE,VIRGINIA,TEX
AS,GEORGIA
503 DATA 1867,WHAT LAND WAS PURCHASED FROM RUSSIA THIS YEAR,4,ALASKA,HAWAII,OREG
ON,TEXAS
504 DATA 1867,WHAT WERE THE NORTHERNERS CALLED WHO HELPED TO REBUILD THE SOUTH,1
,CARPETBAGGERS,0,0,0
505 DATA 1870,THE 15TH AMENDMENT GAVE 'BLACKS' THE RIGHT TO ....,1,VOTE,0,0,0
506 DATA 1871,A DISASTROUS FIRE DESTROYED WHAT CITY,4,CHICAGO,DETROIT,NEW YORK,B
OSTON
507 DATA 1875,CIVIL RIGHTS ACT PASSED AGAINST PUBLIC DISCRIMINATION OF BLACKS,2,
T,0,0,0
508 DATA 1876,MY TROOPS WERE MASSACRED BY SITTING BULL-AT LITTLE BIGHORN,3,CUSTE
R,0,0,0
509 DATA 1881,WHAT PRESIDENT WAS SHOT THIS YEAR,4,GARFIELD,LINCOLN,TAFT,DAVIS
```

```
510 DATA 1886,HE WAS PRESIDENT OF THE AMERICAN FEDERATION OF LABOR,4,GOMPERS,MON
ROE,TAFT,FRICK
511 DATA 1883,THE ..... ACT ESTABLISHED THE CIVIL SERVICE SYSTEM,4,PENDLETON,LAB
OR,TRADE,WORKERS
512 DATA 1890,THE ..... ANTI-TRUST ACT BECAME LAW THIS YEAR,4,SHERMAN,PULLMAN,PE
NDLETON,TAFT
513 DATA 1894,WHAT STRIKE BROUGHT FEDERAL INTERVENTION,4,PULLMAN,COAL,FARMERS,GR
AIN
514 DATA 1895,SOUTHERN STATES USED .... CLAUSES-DEPRIVE BLACKS VOTING RIGHTS,1,G
RANDFATHER,0,0,0
515 DATA 1896,SUPREME COURT-PLESSY V. FERGUSON-UPHELD LOUISIANA SEGRAGATION LAW,
2,T,0,0,0
516 DATA 1897,KLONDIKE .... RUSH BEGAN THIS YEAR,4,GOLD,SILVER,URANIUM,DIAMOND
517 DATA 1898,SPANISH-AMERICAN WAR BEGAN WHEN WHAT SHIP EXPLODED-HAVANA HARBOR,4
,MAINE,UNION,YORK,ATLANTIC
518 DATA 1898,THE UNITED STATES ANNEXED THE ..... ISLANDS,1,HAWAIIAN,0,0,0
519 DATA 1899,THE UNITED STATES PARTICIPATED IN THE 1ST ..... CONFERENCE,1,HAGUE
,0,0,0
520 DATA 1900,SAMOAN ISLANDS WERE DIVIDED BETWEEN THE UNITED STATES & ....,4,GER
MANY,RUSSIA,FRANCE,ITALY
521 DATA 1901,I BECAME PRESIDENT AFTER MCKINLEY WAS SHOT,3,ROOSEVELT,0,0,0
522 DATA 1902,WHAT DID ROOSEVELT PLEDGE FOR BOTH LABOR & INDUSTRY,1,SQUARE DEAL,
0,0,0
523 DATA 1903,THE ..... BROTHERS FLEW THE 1ST SUCCESSFUL AIRPLANE FLIGHT,1,WRIGH
T,0,0,0
524 DATA 1906,EARTHQUAKE AND FIRE DESTROYED WHAT CITY,4,SAN FRANCISCO,CHICAGO,BO
STON,RICHMOND
525 DATA 1907,GENTLEMANS AGREEMENT-WITH JAPAN-ALLOWED LABORERS TO MIGRATE HERE,2
,F,0,0,0
526 DATA 1908,I WAS ELECTED PRESIDENT THIS YEAR,3,TAFT,0,0,0
527 DATA 1909,HE DISCOVERED THE NORTH POLE THIS YEAR,4,PEARY,LOUIS,SMITH,PIKE
528 DATA 1912,ROOSEVELT WAS WHAT PARTY'S CANDIDATE FOR PRESIDENT,1,PROGRESSIVE,0
,0,0
529 DATA 1913,THE FEDERAL .... SYSTEM WAS ESTABLISHED THIS YEAR,1,RESERVE,0,0,0
530 DATA 1914,THE FEDERAL .... COMMISSION WAS ESTABLISHED THIS YEAR,1,TRADE,0,0,
0
531 DATA 1914,THE UNITED STATES CLAIMED NEUTRALITY TO WORLD WAR I,2,T,0,0,0
532 DATA 1913,WILSON WON A REDUCTION OF THE .... AFTER A HARD FIGHT,1,TARIFF,0,0
,0
533 CLS:PRINT"THE TIME DUNGEON * * * MAP"
534 PRINT
535 FORQ=1TO8
536 FORN=1TO8
537 IFC=NANDD=QTHENPRINT"=P= ";:GOTO540
538 S1=A(N,Q)
539 ONS1GOSUB137,137,138,138,139,140,141,139,142
540 NEXTN
541 PRINT
542 NEXTQ
543 GT=RND(8)+RND(CA+5):GOSUB134
544 CLS:RETURN
545 PRINT:PRINT"ON THE WALL IS A GLOWING SCREEN"
546 PRINT"BELOW THE SCREEN IS A RED BUTTON":PRINT
```

```
547 KT=RND(9):KL=RND(15)+2
548 GOSUB565
549 INPUTK$
550 IFK$="Y"THEN552
551 RETURN
552 IFKT>=6THEN533
553 IFKT<=4THEN562
554 PRINT:G4=RND(100)+25:G=G+G4
555 PRINT"YOU RECEIVE ";G4;" GOLD PIECES . . ."
556 PRINT"BUT . . . . . . THE CORRIDOR NARROWS":GT=3:GOSUB134
557 KL=KL-1:IFKL=0THENRETURN
558 GOSUB565
559 INPUTK$
560 IFK$="Y"THEN554
561 RETURN
562 PRINT:PRINT"NOTHING HAPPENS"
563 GT=1:GOSUB134
564 RETURN
565 PRINT:PRINT"DO YOU WISH TO PUSH THE BUTTON?"
566 PRINT"ENTER  (Y)ES  OR  (N)O":RETURN
567 CLS:PRINT"YOU ARE STUCK IN THE NARROW CORRIDOR"
568 PRINT". . . . . . . . . . . AND . . .":PRINT:GT=3:GOSUB134
569 GOTO264
570 PRINT:PRINT"YOU NOTICE A DOOR TO YOUR RIGHT"
571 PRINT
572 KT=RND(9)
573 PRINT"DO YOU WISH TO OPEN THE DOOR?"
574 PRINT"ENTER  (Y)ES  OR  (N)O"
575 INPUTK$
576 IFK$="Y"THEN578
577 RETURN
578 PRINT:PRINT"YOU TRY THE DOOR . . . . .":GT=1:GOSUB134
579 IFKT>=7THEN589
580 IFKT<=4THEN587
581 PRINT:G4=RND(100)+25
582 PRINT"THE DOOR OPENS . . . . . . ."
583 PRINT"REVEALING A CLOSET . . . ."
584 PRINT:G=G+G4
585 PRINT"WHERE YOU FIND ";G4;" GOLD PIECES"
586 PRINT:RETURN
587 PRINT"BUT THE DOOR WON'T OPEN . . . ."
588 PRINT". . . . IT MUST BE LOCKED":RETURN
589 PRINT:PRINT"THE DOOR OPENS . . . AND SUDDENLY"
590 PRINT"THE CHAMBER BEGINS TO . . . SPIN"
591 G7=INT(G/2):G4=RND(G7):MM=RND(20)
592 GT=4:GOSUB134:G=G-G4
593 FORK9=1TO250
594 PRINT"+    =    +";
595 NEXTK9
596 CLS:PRINT"YOU WERE TELEPORTED INTO . . . ."
597 PRINT". . . . ANOTHER DIMENSION . . . ."
598 PRINT". . AND RETURNED IN AN INSTANT . ."
599 PRINT:PRINT"BUT YOU DROPPED ";G4;" GOLD PIECES"
```

```
600 PRINT". . . AND WASTED ";MM;" MOVES . . ."
601 M1=M1+MM
602 GT=4:GOSUB134
603 RETURN
```

Program 1-3. The Time Dungeon: American History, 1916 to 1975, Program Listing

```
100 CLS:CLEAR400:BZ$="AMERICAN HISTORY":BW$="1916 TO 1975"
101 PRINT"THE TIME DUNGEON: ";BZ$
102 PRINT"COPYRIGHT (C) 1980 BY HOWARD BERENBON"
103 PRINT"TRS-80 VERSION"
104 PRINT
105 PRINT"AN EDUCATIONAL FANTASY GAME"
106 GT=5:GOSUB134:Q3=0
107 CLS:DIMA(9,9),B(50):GOSUB451
108 PRINT"YOU WILL BE TELEPORTED TO . . ."
109 PRINT
110 PRINT"THE TIME DUNGEON . . . ."
111 PRINT"TO STUDY ";BZ$
112 PRINT
113 RANDOM
114 CA=0:G=1000:M1=1:K=0:KL=1:TT=0:TR=0
115 PRINT"ENTER YOUR CHARACTER'S NAME?"
116 INPUTA$
117 PRINT"ENTER PRESENT YEAR"
118 INPUTY2:YY=Y2:IFY2>2000THEN117
119 PRINT:PRINTA$;" . . . YOU ARE ON YOUR WAY"
120 GT=2:GOSUB134
121 GOSUB143
122 CLS
123 PRINT"YOU HAVE ARRIVED AT . . . ."
124 PRINT
125 PRINT"THE TIME DUNGEON: ";BZ$
126 PRINT"FOR THE YEARS:    ";BW$
127 PRINT
128 PRINT"YOU CARRY 1000 GOLD PIECES":PRINT
129 PRINT"YOU WILL ENCOUNTER . . ."
130 PRINT"TIME PORTALS WHICH TELEPORT"
131 PRINT"YOU TO EVENTS IN ";BZ$
132 GT=8:GOSUB134
133 GOTO199
134 FORZZ=1TO400*GT
135 NEXTZZ
136 RETURN
137 PRINT"O   ";:RETURN
138 PRINT"AP  ";:RETURN
139 PRINT"?   ";:RETURN
140 PRINT"NS  ";:RETURN
141 PRINT"EW  ";:RETURN
142 PRINT"X   ";:RETURN
143 REM SET UP DUNGEON
144 FORX=1TO8
145 FORY=1TO8
146 A(X,Y)=RND(7)
147 NEXTY
148 NEXTX
149 REM TRAPS
150 H=RND(3)+1
151 FORN=1TOH
152 X=RND(8)
```

```
153 Y=RND(8)
154 A(X,Y)=8
155 NEXTN
156 REM EXITS
157 S=RND(4)+1
158 FORN=1TOS
159 X=RND(8)
160 Y=RND(8)
161 A(X,Y)=9
162 NEXTN
163 RETURN
164 R6=RND(4):PRINTQD$;"?:"
165 ONR6GOSUB167,168,169,170
166 GOTO433
167 PRINTAD$,I1$:PRINTI2$,I3$:RETURN
168 PRINTI2$,AD$:PRINTI1$,I3$:RETURN
169 PRINTI1$,I2$:PRINTAD$,I3$:RETURN
170 PRINTI3$,I1$:PRINTI2$,AD$:RETURN
171 CLS
172 PRINTCHR$(23)
173 GT=1
174 GOSUB134
175 FORB=1TO70:B4=RND(1020)
176 PRINT@B4,".";
177 NEXTB
178 GT=.005:Y5=25
179 IFY3=YYTHENPRINT"ALREADY AT . . . .":GOTO196
180 IFY3<YYTHEN188
181 IF(Y3-YY)<=50THEN185
182 Y3=Y3-Y5
183 GOSUB382
184 IFY3=YYTHEN195
185 IF(Y3-YY)<=50THENY5=1
186 IF(Y3-YY)<=5THENGT=.4
187 GOTO182
188 IF(YY-Y3)<=50THEN192
189 Y3=Y3+Y5
190 GOSUB382
191 IFY3=YYTHEN195
192 IF(YY-Y3)<=50THENY5=1
193 IF(YY-Y3)<=5THENGT=.4
194 GOTO189
195 PRINT"ARRIVAL . . . . AT"
196 PRINT"DESTINATION YEAR . . . . ";YY
197 GT=4:GOSUB134
198 CLS:RETURN
199 C=RND(8):D=RND(8):A(C,D)=1
200 K4=RND(4)+3
201 CLS:A=A(C,D):GT=1:GOSUB134
202 ONAGOSUB292,300,410,410,306,330,335,338,362
203 IFKL=0THEN567
204 PRINT:IFTT=1THENTT=0:GOTO201
205 IFG<=0THEN264
```

```
206 PRINTA$;",  WHAT IS YOUR ACTION OR MOVE?"
207 PRINT
208 PRINT"(N)ORTH, (E)AST, (S)OUTH"
209 PRINT"(W)EST, E(X)IT, (G)OLD
210 INPUTM1$
211 M1=M1+1:IFK=0ANDM1>70THEN371
212 IFM1$="N"THEN220
213 IFM1$="E"THEN225
214 IFM1$="S"THEN230
215 IFM1$="W"THEN235
216 IFM1$="X"THEN240
217 IFM1$="G"THEN251
218 PRINT
219 GOTO204
220 REM NORTH
221 IFA=7THEN255
222 IF(D-1)=0THEN281
223 D=D-1
224 GOTO201
225 REM EAST
226 IFA=6THEN260
227 IF(C+1)=9THEN286
228 C=C+1
229 GOTO201
230 REM SOUTH
231 IFA=7THEN255
232 IF(D+1)=9THEN288
233 D=D+1
234 GOTO201
235 REM WEST
236 IFA=6THEN260
237 IF(C-1)=0THEN290
238 C=C-1
239 GOTO201
240 CLS
241 IFA<>9THEN248
242 IFK=1THEN387
243 PRINT"YOU CANNOT EXIT THE TIME DUNGEON"
244 PRINT"YOU DON'T HAVE THE CRYSTAL KEY"
245 GT=2:GOSUB134
246 PRINT
247 GOTO204
248 PRINT"YOU ARE NOT AT AN EXIT PORTAL"
249 GT=2:GOSUB134
250 GOTO204
251 REM GOLD
252 CLS:PRINT"YOU HAVE ";G;" GOLD PIECES WITH YOU"
253 PRINT
254 GOTO204
255 REM EW
256 CLS:PRINT"YOU ARE IN AN EAST-WEST CORRIDOR"
257 PRINT"YOU CAN ONLY GO EAST OR WEST"
258 PRINT
```

```
259 GOTO204
260 REM NS
261 CLS:PRINT"YOU ARE IN A NORTH-SOUTH CORRIDOR"
262 PRINT"YOU CAN ONLY GO NORTH OR SOUTH"
263 GOTO258
264 REM GOLD ZERO
265 GT=2:GOSUB134
266 PRINT
267 PRINT"YOU LOST ALL YOUR GOLD AND YOU WERE"
268 PRINT" . . . UNABLE TO MEET THE DEMANDS OF"
269 PRINT" . . . THE TIME DUNGEON . . . . ."
270 PRINT
271 PRINT
272 GT=3:GOSUB134
273 GOSUB402
274 PRINT
275 PRINT"ANOTHER GAME?"
276 PRINT"ENTER '1'-YES  '0'-NO"
277 INPUTAA
278 IFAA<>1THEN280
279 CLS:GOTO108
280 END
281 CLS:PRINT"YOU ARE AT THE NORTH WALL"
282 PRINT"YOU CANNOT PASS THROUGH"
283 PRINT
284 PRINT"TRY ANOTHER DIRECTION?"
285 GOTO204
286 CLS:PRINT"YOU ARE AT THE EAST WALL"
287 GOTO282
288 CLS:PRINT"YOU ARE AT THE SOUTH WALL"
289 GOTO282
290 CLS:PRINT"YOU ARE AT THE WEST WALL"
291 GOTO282
292 KT=RND(9)
293 PRINT"YOU ARE IN A GLOWING TIME PORTAL"
294 GT=1:GOSUB134
295 PRINT
296 PRINT"THE LIGHT FADES . . . . . ."
297 PRINT"THE PORTAL IS INACTIVE . . . ."
298 IFA=1ANDKT>=8THEN570
299 RETURN
300 PRINT"YOU ARE IN A DUST FILLED PORTAL"
301 GT=1:GOSUB134
302 PRINT
303 PRINT"A BRIGHT LIGHT IS ACTIVATED AND . ."
304 PRINT
305 GOTO296
306 CLS
307 PRINT"AN ALIEN TRAVELER IS IN THIS CHAMBER"
308 A(C,D)=RND(2):GOSUB478
309 GT=1:GOSUB134
310 TD=RND(10)
311 G4=RND(350)
```

```
312 Y=RND(8)
313 IFY<=5THEN320
314 PRINT:IF(G-G4)<0THENG4=G
315 PRINT"HE IS UNFRIENDLY . . . . AND AS HE"
316 PRINT"LEAVES . . . HE TAKES ";G4;" GOLD PIECES"
317 PRINT:G=G-G4
318 IFTD=5ANDK=0THEN325
319 RETURN
320 PRINT
321 PRINT"HE IS FRIENDLY . . . . . AND GIVES YOU"
322 PRINT". . ";G4;" GOLD PIECES, WHICH YOU ACCEPT"
323 PRINT:G=G+G4
324 GOTO318
325 PRINT:GT=2:GOSUB134
326 PRINT"YOU SEARCH THE CHAMBER . . . AND"
327 GT=1:GOSUB134
328 PRINT"FIND . . . . THE CRYSTAL KEY"
329 K=1:RETURN
330 CLS
331 PRINT"YOU ENTER A NORTH-SOUTH CORRIDOR"
332 PRINT"THRU A SECRET DOOR":PRINT:GOSUB380
333 KT=RND(9):IFKT>=7THEN545
334 RETURN
335 CLS
336 PRINT"YOU ENTER AN EAST-WEST CORRIDOR"
337 GOTO332
338 REM TRAP
339 PRINT"YOU ENCOUNTER . . . A TIME TRAP"
340 PRINT". . . . . . . . IN THIS CHAMBER":GT=1:GOSUB134
341 TD=RND(9)
342 IFTD>=7THEN347
343 PRINT
344 PRINT"BUT YOU'RE LUCKY . . . . ."
345 PRINT". . . IT DIDN'T ACTIVATE"
346 RETURN
347 TT=1:PRINT"AND IT ACTIVATED . . . . .":GT=2:GOSUB134
348 FORA=1TO250
349 PRINT"*        %";
350 NEXTA
351 C=RND(8):D=RND(8)
352 PRINT
353 PRINT:G=100
354 PRINT"YOU HAVE BEEN TELEPORTED TO . . . ."
355 PRINT". . . . AN UNKNOWN LOCATION . . . ."
356 PRINT
357 PRINT"AND YOU LOST MOST OF YOUR GOLD"
358 PRINT
359 PRINT"YOU HAVE . . . ";G;" GOLD PIECES LEFT"
360 GT=6:GOSUB134
361 RETURN
362 PRINT"YOU ARE AT AN EXIT PORTAL"
363 PRINT
364 PRINT"(A KEY IS REQUIRED)"
```

```
365 PRINT
366 RETURN
367 H=1:O=9:W=8
368 B=0:E=5:R=14
369 C=0:PR=0
370 GOTO216
371 PRINT:GT=2:GOSUB134
372 PRINT"BUT BEFORE YOU PROCEED . ."
373 PRINT"YOU LOOK TO THE GROUND AND . . ."
374 PRINT" . . . FIND THE CRYSTAL KEY . .":K=1
375 GT=3:GOSUB134
376 GOTO212
377 PRINT"YOU ANSWERED ";CA;" QUESTION(S) CORRECTLY"
378 PRINT" . . . . . IN ";M1;" TURNS,"
379 GOTO409
380 PRINT"THE DOOR CLOSES AND LOCKS BEHIND YOU":GT=1:GOSUB134
381 RETURN
382 REM TIME DISPLAY
383 PRINT@390,"PORTAL YEAR . . . ";Y3
384 PRINT@448,STRING$(64,191)
385 GOSUB134
386 RETURN
387 CLS:REM EXIT PORTAL
388 PRINT"YOU ENTER THE EXIT PORTAL AND"
389 PRINT"INSERT THE CRYSTAL KEY INTO THE SLOT"
390 PRINT:GT=4:GOSUB134
391 PRINT"THE MACHINE BEGINS TO HUM . . . ."
392 PRINT:GT=2:GOSUB134
393 YY=Y2:GOSUB171
394 PRINT
395 PRINT"YOU FOUND YOUR WAY . . . . ."
396 PRINT". . . . BACK TO THE PRESENT"
397 PRINT
398 PRINT"YOU HAVE ACQUIRED ";G;" GOLD PIECES"
399 PRINT
400 GOSUB402
401 GOTO274
402 GG=G+100
403 R=INT((GG*CA-7000+1)/M1)
404 PRINT
405 PRINT"GAME RATING IS ";R
406 PRINT:IFG<=0ORKL=0THEN377
407 PRINT"YOU TOOK ";M1;" TURNS TO FIND THE WAY OUT"
408 PRINT"AND ANSWERED ";CA;" QUESTION(S) CORRECTLY,"
409 PRINT"OUT OF ";TR;" QUESTIONS ASKED.":RETURN
410 CLS:Y3=YY
411 GOSUB444
412 Q3=Q3+1
413 IFQ3>50THENQ3=0:GOTO415
414 GOTO416
415 GOSUB451
416 Q=RND(50)
417 IFB(Q)=1THEN416
```

```
418 B(Q)=1
419 PRINT
420 FORAB=1TOQ
421 READ YY,QD$,ID,AD$,I1$,I2$,I3$
422 NEXTAB
423 RESTORE
424 GOSUB171
425 CLS:TR=TR+1
426 PRINT"YOU HAVE ARRIVED AT THE YEAR ";YY
427 PRINT". . . . . . IN ";BZ$:PRINT
428 PRINT"YOU MUST ANSWER THIS QUESTION";
429 PRINT" . . TO CONTINUE YOUR JOURNEY"
430 PRINT"------------------------------------------------------------"
431 PRINT"THE YEAR IS: ";YY:PRINT:IFID=4THEN164
432 PRINTQD$
433 PRINT"------------------------------------------------------------"
434 PRINT"QUESTION TYPE: ";
435 ON ID GOSUB 455,456,457,458
436 GOSUB459
437 IFE$=AD$THEN441
438 PRINT"INCORRECT"
439 GOSUB471
440 RETURN
441 PRINT"CORRECT"
442 GOSUB463
443 RETURN
444 PRINT"YOU ENTER INTO A BLUE HAZY . . ."
445 PRINT". . . . . . . TIME PORTAL . . . "
446 PRINT:GT=1:GOSUB134
447 PRINT"A PULSATING GLOW . . . . . . ."
448 PRINT". . . . INDICATES ACTIVATION":PRINT
449 PRINT"PRESENT YEAR . . .  ";Y3:GT=3:GOSUB134
450 RETURN
451 FORI=1TO50
452 B(I)=0
453 NEXTI
454 RETURN
455 PRINT"PEOPLE, PLACES, OR THINGS ?":RETURN
456 PRINT"*** (T)RUE OR (F)ALSE  ?":RETURN
457 PRINT"*** WHO AM I (LAST NAME) ?":RETURN
458 PRINT"*** MULTIPLE CHOICE ?":RETURN
459 PRINT"ENTER CORRECT ANSWER?"
460 INPUTE$
461 G4=RND(500)+125
462 RETURN
463 G=G+G4
464 PRINT"YOU WIN ";G4;" GOLD PIECES"
465 A(C,D)=RND(2)
466 CA=CA+1:IFK=1THENRETURN
467 IFCA=K4THEN469
468 RETURN
469 GOSUB325
470 RETURN
```

```
471 PRINT:G4=RND(400)+25
472 PRINT"THE CORRECT ANSWER IS '";AD$;"'"
473 PRINT:IF(G-G4)<0THENG4=G
474 G=G-G4
475 GT=1:GOSUB134
476 PRINT"YOU LOSE ";G4;" GOLD PIECES"
477 RETURN
478 ZT=5
479 X=RND(8):Y=RND(8)
480 IFA(X,Y)<=2THENA(X,Y)=5:RETURN
481 ZT=ZT-1:IFZT=0THENRETURN
482 GOTO479
483 DATA 1917,UNITED STATES SEVERED RELATIONS WITH WHAT COUNTRY,4,GERMANY,CANADA
,RUSSIA,FRANCE
484 DATA 1916,HE PURSUED PANCHO VILLA INTO MEXICO-WITHOUT SUCCESS,4,PERSHING,YOR
K,HILL,SINCLAIR
485 DATA 1917,CONGRESS DECLARED WAR ON GERMANY-APRIL 6-1917,2,T,0,0,0
486 DATA 1920,HE ORDERED MASS ARRESTS DURING THE 'RED SCARE' PERIOD,4,PALMER,SCO
PES,MARSHALL,MCCARTHY
487 DATA 1920,THE 19TH AMENDMENT-WOMEN'S ....-WAS RATIFIED THIS YEAR,1,SUFFRAGE,
0,0,0
488 DATA 1923,I BECAME PRESIDENT AFTER HARDING DIED,3,COOLIDGE,0,0,0
489 DATA 1925,I WAS CONVICTED FOR TEACHING EVOLUTION IN TENNESSEE,3,SCOPES,0,0,0

490 DATA 1923,WHAT SWINDLE ENVOLVED OIL RESERVES LEASED TO SINCLAIR BY SEC. FALL
,1,TEAPOT DOME,0,0,0
491 DATA 1927,I MADE THE 1ST NONSTOP SOLO FLIGHT FROM NEW YORK TO PARIS,3,LINDBE
RGH,0,0,0
492 DATA 1929,WHAT CRASH GREW INTO THE 'GREAT DEPRESSON',1,STOCK MARKET,0,0,0
493 DATA 1933,ROOSEVELT ADOPTED WHAT POLICIES FOR ECONOMIC & SOCIAL WELFARE,1,NE
W DEAL,0,0,0
494 DATA 1933,A SEVERE DROUGHT CONVERTED THE GREAT PLAINS INTO WHAT,1,DUST BOWL,
0,0,0
495 DATA 1934,THE FBI KILLED WHAT WELL KNOWN GANGSTER-IN CHICAGO,1,DILLINGER,0,0
,0
496 DATA 1939,SCIENTISTS-INCLUDING EINSTEIN-TOLD ROOSEVELT THAT AN ATOMIC BOMB W
AS POSSIBLE,2,T,0,0,0
497 DATA 1939,U.S. PLEDGED NEUTRALITY AFTER THE WAR BEGAN IN EUROPE,2,T,0,0,0
498 DATA 1940,WHAT ACT MADE IT UNLAWFUL TO ADVOCATE THE OVERTHROW OF THE U.S.,4,
SMITH,TRUMAN,TAFT,GUN
499 DATA 1941,JAPANESE ATTACKED .... HARBOR-ON DECEMBER 7-1941,1,PEARL,0,0,0
500 DATA 1941,ROOSEVELT AND CHURCHILL ISSUED THE .... CHARTER OF POSTWAR ARMS,4,
ATLANTIC,PACIFIC,FREEDOM,WESTERN
501 DATA 1941,THE UNITED STATES DECLARED WAR ON WHAT COUNTRY,1,JAPAN,0,0,0
502 DATA 1942,JAPANESE-AMERICANS WERE RELOCATED TO WESTERN .... CAMPS IN 1942,4,
DETENTION,SAFETY,SECURITY,FREEDOM
503 DATA 1944,THE .... INVADED EUROPE AND FREED FRANCE-BELGIUM-& LUXEMBOURG,1,AL
LIES,0,0,0
504 DATA 1945,THE U.S. DROPPED ATOMIC BOMBS ON HIROSHIMA AND .....,1,NAGASAKI,0,
0,0
505 DATA 1947,I PROPOSED A PLAN FOR EUROPEAN RECOVERY-THIS YEAR,3,MARSHALL,0,0,0
506 DATA 1948,HE ACCUSED ALGER HISS OF GIVING DOCUMENTS TO THE RUSSIANS,4,CHAMBE
RS,TRUMAN,MCCARTHY,ROOSEVELT
```

```
507 DATA 1947,THE ....-HARTLY ACT LIMITED POWER OF LABOR,4,TAFT,SMITH,SHERMAN,BR
OWN
508 DATA 1949,THE NORTH .... TREATY ORGANIZATION WAS APPROVED THIS YEAR,4,ATLANT
IC,PACIFIC,WEST,AMERICAN
509 DATA 1950,TRUMAN SENT U.S. TROOPS TO WHAT COUNTRY,4,KOREA,ISRAEL,TURKEY,ITAL
Y
510 DATA 1950,SENATOR .... CHARGED THAT THE STATE DEPT. WAS INFILTRATED BY COMMU
NISTS,4,MCCARTHY,BROWN,MARSHALL,TAFT
511 DATA 1954,THE SUPREME COURT OUTLAWED .... SEGREGATION IN PUBLIC SCHOOLS,1,RA
CIAL,0,0,0
512 DATA 1955,THE AFL AND .... MERGED INTO ONE LABOR ORGANIZATION,4,CIO,NRA,CIA,
FBI
513 DATA 1956,I REFUSED TO GIVE MY BUS SEAT TO A WHITE MAN-IN MONTGOMERY,3,PARKS
,0,0,0
514 DATA 1957,THE TRUMAN DOCTRINE WAS EXTENDED TO AID WHAT MIDDLE EAST COUNTRY,4
,JORDAN,ISRAEL,IRAN,EGYPT
515 DATA 1957,THE .... RIGHTS ACT WAS PASSED-DEALING WITH MINORITIES,1,CIVIL,0,0
,0
516 DATA 1959,THE STATES OF .... AND HAWAII WERE ADMITTED TO THE UNION,1,ALASKA,
0,0,0
517 DATA 1960,I FLEW THE U-2 SPY PLANE THAT WAS SHOT DOWN OVER RUSSIA,3,POWERS,0
,0,0
518 DATA 1961,THE ANTI-CASTRO INVASION AT 'BAY OF PIGS' WAS SUCCESSFUL,2,F,0,0,0
519 DATA 1962,HE WAS THE 1ST AMERICAN TO ORBIT THE EARTH,4,GLENN,POWERS,ARMSTRON
G,ALDRIN
520 DATA 1963,IN WHAT CITY WAS PRESIDENT KENNEDY ASSASSINATED,4,DALLAS,WASHINGTO
N,BOSTON,CHICAGO
521 DATA 1964,WHAT AMENDMENT-ABOLISHING POLL TAX-WAS RATIFIED,4,24TH,20TH,31ST,2
9TH
522 DATA 1965,U.S. TROOP BUILD-UP IN VIETNAM CAUSED ANTI-WAR DEMONSTRATIONS,2,T,
0,0,0
523 DATA 1965,RACE RIOTS ERUPTED IN THE .... SECTION OF LOS ANGELES,4,WATTS,POOR
,OLD,WHITE
524 DATA 1968,REV. MARTIN LUTHER .... WAS ASSASSINATED THIS YEAR,1,KING,0,0,0
525 DATA 1968,SENATOR ROBERT F. .... WAS ASSASSINATED THIS YEAR,1,KENNEDY,0,0,0
526 DATA 1967,HE WAS THE 1ST BLACK ELECTED TO THE SUPREME COURT,3,MARSHALL,COSBY
,CARVER,KING
527 DATA 1969,ARMSTRONG AND ALDRIN WERE THE 1ST TO LAND ON THE MOON,2,T,0,0,0
528 DATA 1970,U.S. AND S. VIETNAMESE TROOPS ENTERED WHAT CITY,1,CAMBODIA,0,0,0
529 DATA 1971,THE 26TH AMENDMENT ALLOWED VOTING RIGHTS TO .... YEAR OLDS,4,18,20
,17,16
530 DATA 1972,WHAT SCANDLE WAS 'COVERED UP' BY NIXON,1,WATERGATE,0,0,0
531 DATA 1975,THE WAR IN .... ENDED THIS YEAR,1,VIETNAM,0,0,0
532 DATA 1974,PRESIDENT NIXON RESIGNED BECAUSE OF THE .... SCANDLE,1,WATERGATE,0
,0,0
533 CLS:PRINT"THE TIME DUNGEON * * * MAP"
534 PRINT
535 FORQ=1TO8
536 FORN=1TO8
537 IFC=NANDD=QTHENPRINT"=P= ";:GOTO540
538 S1=A(N,Q)
539 ONS1GOSUB137,137,138,138,139,140,141,139,142
540 NEXTN
```

```
541 PRINT
542 NEXTQ
543 GT=RND(8)+RND(CA+5):GOSUB134
544 CLS:RETURN
545 PRINT:PRINT"ON THE WALL IS A GLOWING SCREEN"
546 PRINT"BELOW THE SCREEN IS A RED BUTTON":PRINT
547 KT=RND(9):KL=RND(15)+2
548 GOSUB565
549 INPUTK$
550 IFK$="Y"THEN552
551 RETURN
552 IFKT>=6THEN533
553 IFKT<=4THEN562
554 PRINT:G4=RND(100)+25:G=G+G4
555 PRINT"YOU RECEIVE ";G4;" GOLD PIECES . . ."
556 PRINT"BUT . . . . . . THE CORRIDOR NARROWS":GT=3:GOSUB134
557 KL=KL-1:IFKL=0THENRETURN
558 GOSUB565
559 INPUTK$
560 IFK$="Y"THEN554
561 RETURN
562 PRINT:PRINT"NOTHING HAPPENS"
563 GT=1:GOSUB134
564 RETURN
565 PRINT:PRINT"DO YOU WISH TO PUSH THE BUTTON?"
566 PRINT"ENTER  (Y)ES  OR  (N)O":RETURN
567 CLS:PRINT"YOU ARE STUCK IN THE NARROW CORRIDOR"
568 PRINT". . . . . . . . . . . AND . . .":PRINT:GT=3:GOSUB134
569 GOTO264
570 PRINT:PRINT"YOU NOTICE A DOOR TO YOUR RIGHT"
571 PRINT
572 KT=RND(9)
573 PRINT"DO YOU WISH TO OPEN THE DOOR?"
574 PRINT"ENTER  (Y)ES  OR  (N)O"
575 INPUTK$
576 IFK$="Y"THEN578
577 RETURN
578 PRINT:PRINT"YOU TRY THE DOOR . . . . .":GT=1:GOSUB134
579 IFKT>=7THEN589
580 IFKT<=4THEN587
581 PRINT:G4=RND(100)+25
582 PRINT"THE DOOR OPENS . . . . . . ."
583 PRINT"REVEALING A CLOSET . . . ."
584 PRINT:G=G+G4
585 PRINT"WHERE YOU FIND ";G4;" GOLD PIECES"
586 PRINT:RETURN
587 PRINT"BUT THE DOOR WON'T OPEN . . . ."
588 PRINT". . . . IT MUST BE LOCKED":RETURN
589 PRINT:PRINT"THE DOOR OPENS . . . AND SUDDENLY"
590 PRINT"THE CHAMBER BEGINS TO . . . SPIN"
591 G7=INT(G/2):G4=RND(G7):MM=RND(20)
592 GT=4:GOSUB134:G=G-G4
593 FORK9=1TO250
```

```
594 PRINT"+     =     +";
595 NEXTK9
596 CLS:PRINT"YOU WERE TELEPORTED INTO . . . ."
597 PRINT". . . . ANOTHER DIMENSION . . . ."
598 PRINT". . AND RETURNED IN AN INSTANT . ."
599 PRINT:PRINT"BUT YOU DROPPED ";G4;" GOLD PIECES"
600 PRINT". . . AND WASTED ";MM;" MOVES . . ."
601 M1=M1+MM
602 GT=4:GOSUB134
603 RETURN
```

Program 1-4. The Time Dungeon: World History, World War I, Program Listing

```
100 CLS:CLEAR400:BZ$="WORLD HISTORY-WW I":BW$="1894 TO 1919"
101 PRINT"THE TIME DUNGEON: ";BZ$
102 PRINT"COPYRIGHT (C) 1980 BY HOWARD BERENBON"
103 PRINT"TRS-80 VERSION"
104 PRINT
105 PRINT"AN EDUCATIONAL FANTASY GAME"
106 GT=5:GOSUB134:Q3=0
107 CLS:DIMA(9,9),B(50):GOSUB451
108 PRINT"YOU WILL BE TELEPORTED TO . . ."
109 PRINT
110 PRINT"THE TIME DUNGEON . . . ."
111 PRINT"TO STUDY ";BZ$
112 PRINT
113 RANDOM
114 CA=0:G=1000:M1=1:K=0:KL=1:TT=0:TR=0
115 PRINT"ENTER YOUR CHARACTER'S NAME?"
116 INPUTA$
117 PRINT"ENTER PRESENT YEAR"
118 INPUTY2:YY=Y2:IFY2>2000THEN117
119 PRINT:PRINTA$;" . . . YOU ARE ON YOUR WAY"
120 GT=2:GOSUB134
121 GOSUB143
122 CLS
123 PRINT"YOU HAVE ARRIVED AT . . . ."
124 PRINT
125 PRINT"THE TIME DUNGEON: ";BZ$
126 PRINT"FOR THE YEARS:    ";BW$
127 PRINT
128 PRINT"YOU CARRY 1000 GOLD PIECES":PRINT
129 PRINT"YOU WILL ENCOUNTER . . ."
130 PRINT"TIME PORTALS WHICH TELEPORT"
131 PRINT"YOU TO EVENTS IN ";BZ$
132 GT=8:GOSUB134
133 GOTO199
134 FORZZ=1TO400*GT
135 NEXTZZ
136 RETURN
137 PRINT"O   ";:RETURN
138 PRINT"AP  ";:RETURN
139 PRINT"?   ";:RETURN
140 PRINT"NS  ";:RETURN
141 PRINT"EW  ";:RETURN
142 PRINT"X   ";:RETURN
143 REM SET UP DUNGEON
144 FORX=1TO8
145 FORY=1TO8
146 A(X,Y)=RND(7)
147 NEXTY
148 NEXTX
149 REM TRAPS
150 H=RND(3)+1
151 FORN=1TOH
```

```
152 X=RND(8)
153 Y=RND(8)
154 A(X,Y)=8
155 NEXTN
156 REM EXITS
157 S=RND(4)+1
158 FORN=1TOS
159 X=RND(8)
160 Y=RND(8)
161 A(X,Y)=9
162 NEXTN
163 RETURN
164 R6=RND(4):PRINTQD$;"?:"
165 ONR6GOSUB167,168,169,170
166 GOTO433
167 PRINTAD$,I1$:PRINTI2$,I3$:RETURN
168 PRINTI2$,AD$:PRINTI1$,I3$:RETURN
169 PRINTI1$,I2$:PRINTAD$,I3$:RETURN
170 PRINTI3$,I1$:PRINTI2$,AD$:RETURN
171 CLS
172 PRINTCHR$(23)
173 GT=1
174 GOSUB134
175 FORB=1TO70:B4=RND(1020)
176 PRINT@B4,".";
177 NEXTB
178 GT=.005:Y5=25
179 IFY3=YYTHENPRINT"ALREADY AT . . . .":GOTO196
180 IFY3<YYTHEN188
181 IF(Y3-YY)<=50THEN185
182 Y3=Y3-Y5
183 GOSUB382
184 IFY3=YYTHEN195
185 IF(Y3-YY)<=50THENY5=1
186 IF(Y3-YY)<=5THENGT=.4
187 GOTO182
188 IF(YY-Y3)<=50THEN192
189 Y3=Y3+Y5
190 GOSUB382
191 IFY3=YYTHEN195
192 IF(YY-Y3)<=50THENY5=1
193 IF(YY-Y3)<=5THENGT=.4
194 GOTO189
195 PRINT"ARRIVAL . . . . AT"
196 PRINT"DESTINATION YEAR . . . . ";YY
197 GT=4:GOSUB134
198 CLS:RETURN
199 C=RND(8):D=RND(8):A(C,D)=1
200 K4=RND(4)+3
201 CLS:A=A(C,D):GT=1:GOSUB134
202 ONAGOSUB292,300,410,410,306,330,335,338,362
203 IFKL=0THEN567
```

```
204 PRINT:IFTT=1THENTT=0:GOTO201
205 IFG<=0THEN264
206 PRINTA$;",  WHAT IS YOUR ACTION OR MOVE?"
207 PRINT
208 PRINT"(N)ORTH, (E)AST, (S)OUTH"
209 PRINT"(W)EST, E(X)IT, (G)OLD
210 INPUTM1$
211 M1=M1+1:IFK=0ANDM1>70THEN371
212 IFM1$="N"THEN220
213 IFM1$="E"THEN225
214 IFM1$="S"THEN230
215 IFM1$="W"THEN235
216 IFM1$="X"THEN240
217 IFM1$="G"THEN251
218 PRINT
219 GOTO204
220 REM NORTH
221 IFA=7THEN255
222 IF(D-1)=0THEN281
223 D=D-1
224 GOTO201
225 REM EAST
226 IFA=6THEN260
227 IF(C+1)=9THEN286
228 C=C+1
229 GOTO201
230 REM SOUTH
231 IFA=7THEN255
232 IF(D+1)=9THEN288
233 D=D+1
234 GOTO201
235 REM WEST
236 IFA=6THEN260
237 IF(C-1)=0THEN290
238 C=C-1
239 GOTO201
240 CLS
241 IFA<>9THEN248
242 IFK=1THEN387
243 PRINT"YOU CANNOT EXIT THE TIME DUNGEON"
244 PRINT"YOU DON'T HAVE THE CRYSTAL KEY"
245 GT=2:GOSUB134
246 PRINT
247 GOTO204
248 PRINT"YOU ARE NOT AT AN EXIT PORTAL"
249 GT=2:GOSUB134
250 GOTO204
251 REM GOLD
252 CLS:PRINT"YOU HAVE ";G;" GOLD PIECES WITH YOU"
253 PRINT
254 GOTO204
255 REM EW
```

```
256 CLS:PRINT"YOU ARE IN AN EAST-WEST CORRIDOR"
257 PRINT"YOU CAN ONLY GO EAST OR WEST"
258 PRINT
259 GOTO204
260 REM NS
261 CLS:PRINT"YOU ARE IN A NORTH-SOUTH CORRIDOR"
262 PRINT"YOU CAN ONLY GO NORTH OR SOUTH"
263 GOTO258
264 REM GOLD ZERO
265 GT=2:GOSUB134
266 PRINT
267 PRINT"YOU LOST ALL YOUR GOLD AND YOU WERE"
268 PRINT" . . . UNABLE TO MEET THE DEMANDS OF"
269 PRINT" . . . THE TIME DUNGEON . . . . ."
270 PRINT
271 PRINT
272 GT=3:GOSUB134
273 GOSUB402
274 PRINT
275 PRINT"ANOTHER GAME?"
276 PRINT"ENTER '1'-YES  '0'-NO"
277 INPUTAA
278 IFAA<>1THEN280
279 CLS:GOTO108
280 END
281 CLS:PRINT"YOU ARE AT THE NORTH WALL"
282 PRINT"YOU CANNOT PASS THROUGH"
283 PRINT
284 PRINT"TRY ANOTHER DIRECTION?"
285 GOTO204
286 CLS:PRINT"YOU ARE AT THE EAST WALL"
287 GOTO282
288 CLS:PRINT"YOU ARE AT THE SOUTH WALL"
289 GOTO282
290 CLS:PRINT"YOU ARE AT THE WEST WALL"
291 GOTO282
292 KT=RND(9)
293 PRINT"YOU ARE IN A GLOWING TIME PORTAL"
294 GT=1:GOSUB134
295 PRINT
296 PRINT"THE LIGHT FADES . . . . . ."
297 PRINT"THE PORTAL IS INACTIVE . . . ."
298 IFA=1ANDKT>=8THEN570
299 RETURN
300 PRINT"YOU ARE IN A DUST FILLED PORTAL"
301 GT=1:GOSUB134
302 PRINT
303 PRINT"A BRIGHT LIGHT IS ACTIVATED AND . ."
304 PRINT
305 GOTO296
306 CLS
307 PRINT"AN ALIEN TRAVELER IS IN THIS CHAMBER"
```

```
308 A(C,D)=RND(2):GOSUB478
309 GT=1:GOSUB134
310 TD=RND(10)
311 G4=RND(350)
312 Y=RND(8)
313 IFY<=5THEN320
314 PRINT:IF(G-G4)<0THENG4=G
315 PRINT"HE IS UNFRIENDLY . . . . AND AS HE"
316 PRINT"LEAVES . . . HE TAKES ";G4;" GOLD PIECES"
317 PRINT:G=G-G4
318 IFTD=5ANDK=0THEN325
319 RETURN
320 PRINT
321 PRINT"HE IS FRIENDLY . . . . . AND GIVES YOU"
322 PRINT". . ";G4;" GOLD PIECES, WHICH YOU ACCEPT"
323 PRINT:G=G+G4
324 GOTO318
325 PRINT:GT=2:GOSUB134
326 PRINT"YOU SEARCH THE CHAMBER . . . AND"
327 GT=1:GOSUB134
328 PRINT"FIND . . . . THE CRYSTAL KEY"
329 K=1:RETURN
330 CLS
331 PRINT"YOU ENTER A NORTH-SOUTH CORRIDOR"
332 PRINT"THRU A SECRET DOOR":PRINT:GOSUB380
333 KT=RND(9):IFKT>=7THEN545
334 RETURN
335 CLS
336 PRINT"YOU ENTER AN EAST-WEST CORRIDOR"
337 GOTO332
338 REM TRAP
339 PRINT"YOU ENCOUNTER . . . A TIME TRAP"
340 PRINT". . . . . . . . IN THIS CHAMBER":GT=1:GOSUB134
341 TD=RND(9)
342 IFTD>=7THEN347
343 PRINT
344 PRINT"BUT YOU'RE LUCKY . . . . ."
345 PRINT". . . IT DIDN'T ACTIVATE"
346 RETURN
347 TT=1:PRINT"AND IT ACTIVATED . . . . .":GT=2:GOSUB134
348 FORA=1TO250
349 PRINT"*        %";
350 NEXTA
351 C=RND(8):D=RND(8)
352 PRINT
353 PRINT:G=100
354 PRINT"YOU HAVE BEEN TELEPORTED TO . . . ."
355 PRINT". . . . AN UNKNOWN LOCATION . . . ."
356 PRINT
357 PRINT"AND YOU LOST MOST OF YOUR GOLD"
358 PRINT
359 PRINT"YOU HAVE . . . ";G;" GOLD PIECES LEFT"
```

```
360 GT=6:GOSUB134
361 RETURN
362 PRINT"YOU ARE AT AN EXIT PORTAL"
363 PRINT
364 PRINT"(A KEY IS REQUIRED)"
365 PRINT
366 RETURN
367 H=1:O=9:W=8
368 B=0:E=5:R=14
369 C=0:PR=0
370 GOTO216
371 PRINT:GT=2:GOSUB134
372 PRINT"BUT BEFORE YOU PROCEED . ."
373 PRINT"YOU LOOK TO THE GROUND AND . . ."
374 PRINT" . . . FIND THE CRYSTAL KEY . .":K=1
375 GT=3:GOSUB134
376 GOTO212
377 PRINT"YOU ANSWERED ";CA;" QUESTION(S) CORRECTLY"
378 PRINT" . . . . . IN ";M1;" TURNS,"
379 GOTO409
380 PRINT"THE DOOR CLOSES AND LOCKS BEHIND YOU":GT=1:GOSUB134
381 RETURN
382 REM TIME DISPLAY
383 PRINT@390,"PORTAL YEAR . . . ";Y3
384 PRINT@448,STRING$(64,191)
385 GOSUB134
386 RETURN
387 CLS:REM EXIT PORTAL
388 PRINT"YOU ENTER THE EXIT PORTAL AND"
389 PRINT"INSERT THE CRYSTAL KEY INTO THE SLOT"
390 PRINT:GT=4:GOSUB134
391 PRINT"THE MACHINE BEGINS TO HUM . . . ."
392 PRINT:GT=2:GOSUB134
393 YY=Y2:GOSUB171
394 PRINT
395 PRINT"YOU FOUND YOUR WAY . . . . ."
396 PRINT". . . . BACK TO THE PRESENT"
397 PRINT
398 PRINT"YOU HAVE ACQUIRED ";G;" GOLD PIECES"
399 PRINT
400 GOSUB402
401 GOTO274
402 GG=G+100
403 R=INT((GG*CA-7000+1)/M1)
404 PRINT
405 PRINT"GAME RATING IS ";R
406 PRINT:IFG<=0ORKL=0THEN377
407 PRINT"YOU TOOK ";M1;" TURNS TO FIND THE WAY OUT"
408 PRINT"AND ANSWERED ";CA;" QUESTION(S) CORRECTLY,"
409 PRINT"OUT OF ";TR;" QUESTIONS ASKED.":RETURN
410 CLS:Y3=YY
411 GOSUB444
```

```
412 Q3=Q3+1
413 IFQ3>50THENQ3=0:GOTO415
414 GOTO416
415 GOSUB451
416 Q=RND(50)
417 IFB(Q)=1THEN416
418 B(Q)=1
419 PRINT
420 FORAB=1TOQ
421 READ YY,QD$,ID,AD$,I1$,I2$,I3$
422 NEXTAB
423 RESTORE
424 GOSUB171
425 CLS:TR=TR+1
426 PRINT"YOU HAVE ARRIVED AT THE YEAR ";YY
427 PRINT". . . . . . IN ";BZ$:PRINT
428 PRINT"YOU MUST ANSWER THIS QUESTION";
429 PRINT" . . TO CONTINUE YOUR JOURNEY"
430 PRINT"--------------------------------------------------------------"
431 PRINT"THE YEAR IS: ";YY:PRINT:IFID=4THEN164
432 PRINTQD$
433 PRINT"--------------------------------------------------------------"
434 PRINT"QUESTION TYPE: ";
435 ON ID GOSUB 455,456,457,458
436 GOSUB459
437 IFE$=AD$THEN441
438 PRINT"INCORRECT"
439 GOSUB471
440 RETURN
441 PRINT"CORRECT"
442 GOSUB463
443 RETURN
444 PRINT"YOU ENTER INTO A BLUE HAZY . . ."
445 PRINT". . . . . . . TIME PORTAL . . . "
446 PRINT:GT=1:GOSUB134
447 PRINT"A PULSATING GLOW . . . . . . ."
448 PRINT". . . . INDICATES ACTIVATION":PRINT
449 PRINT"PRESENT YEAR . . .  ";Y3:GT=3:GOSUB134
450 RETURN
451 FORI=1TO50
452 B(I)=0
453 NEXTI
454 RETURN
455 PRINT"PEOPLE, PLACES, OR THINGS ?":RETURN
456 PRINT"*** (T)RUE OR (F)ALSE  ?":RETURN
457 PRINT"*** WHO AM I (LAST NAME) ?":RETURN
458 PRINT"*** MULTIPLE CHOICE ?":RETURN
459 PRINT"ENTER CORRECT ANSWER?"
460 INPUTE$
461 G4=RND(500)+125
462 RETURN
463 G=G+G4
```

```
464 PRINT"YOU WIN ";G4;" GOLD PIECES"
465 A(C,D)=RND(2)
466 CA=CA+1:IFK=1THENRETURN
467 IFCA=K4THEN469
468 RETURN
469 GOSUB325
470 RETURN
471 PRINT:G4=RND(400)+25
472 PRINT"THE CORRECT ANSWER IS '";AD$;"'"
473 PRINT:IF(G-G4)<0THENG4=G
474 G=G-G4
475 GT=1:GOSUB134
476 PRINT"YOU LOSE ";G4;" GOLD PIECES"
477 RETURN
478 ZT=5
479 X=RND(8):Y=RND(8)
480 IFA(X,Y)<=2THENA(X,Y)=5:RETURN
481 ZT=ZT-1:IFZT=0THENRETURN
482 GOTO479
483 DATA 1894,FRANCE AND .... FORMED A MILITARY ALLIANCE,4,RUSSIA,ITALY,GERMANY,
SPAIN
484 DATA 1904,THE AGREEMENT BETWEEN ENGLAND & FRANCE WAS CALLED ....,4,ENTENTE C
ORDIALE,NEW EUROPE,FREE EUROPE,AMI ICI
485 DATA 1902,GREAT BRITAIN AND .... FORMED AN ALLIANCE THIS YEAR,4,JAPAN,U.S.,C
ANADA,GERMANY
486 DATA 1905,ENGLAND BUILT THE .... BATTLESHIP THIS YEAR,4,DREADNOUGHT,DISCOVER
Y,FREEDOM,BRITAIN
487 DATA 1899,THE 1ST PEACE CONFERENCE WAS HELD AT THE ....,1,HAGUE,0,0,0
488 DATA 1907,THE HAGUE PEACE CONFERENCES WERE NOT EFFECTIVE,2,T,0,0,0
489 DATA 1905,FRANCE TRIED TO OCCUPY .... THIS YEAR,4,MOROCCO,HOLLAND,TURKEY,SPA
IN
490 DATA 1911,ITALY DECLARED WAR ON ....-AND SIZED TRIPOLI,4,TURKEY,SPAIN,JAPAN,
RUMANIA
491 DATA 1912,THE BALKAN WARS PREPARED EUROPE FOR WW I,2,T,0,0,0
492 DATA 1914,JUNE 28-THE ARCHDUKE FRANCIS .... WAS ASSASSINATED,1,FERDINAND,0,0
,0
493 DATA 1914,ARCHDUKE FERDINAND WAS SHOT IN WHAT CITY,1,SARAJEVO,0,0,0
494 DATA 1914,JULY 28-AUSTRIA-HUNGARY DECLARED WAR ON ....,4,SERBIA,U.S.,SPAIN,I
TALY
495 DATA 1914,AUG 1-GERMANY DECLARED WAR ON ....,1,RUSSIA,0,0,0
496 DATA 1914,AUG 4-ENGLAND DECLARED WAR ON ....,1,GERMANY,0,0,0
497 DATA 1914,AUG 3-GERMANY DECLARED WAR ON ....,1,FRANCE,0,0,0
498 DATA 1914,THE CENTRAL POWERS WERE STRONGER THAN THE ALLIES,2,F,0,0,0
499 DATA 1914,SEPT 6-THE 1ST BATTLE OF THE .... RIVER,4,MARNE,SEINE,TEMPS,HAGUE
500 DATA 1914,GERMANS TRY TO CAPTURE PARIS-BUT FAIL,2,T,0,0,0
501 DATA 1914,AUG-RUSSIANS LOST THE BATTLE OF ....,4,TANNENBERG,SEINE,HINDENBURG
,AUSTRIA
502 DATA 1914,I COMMANDED THE GERMANS AT THE BATTLE OF TANNENBERG,3,HINDENBURG,0
,0,0
503 DATA 1915,ALLIES HOPED TO TIGHTEN THE ....-TO LIMIT SUPPLIES TO THE ENEMY,1,
BLOCKADE,0,0,0
```

```
504 DATA 1915,SPRING-GERMANS LAUNCHED A HEAVY OFFENSIVE ON THE EASTERN FRONT,2,T
,0,0,0
505 DATA 1915,THE BRITISH CAMPAIGN IN THE MIDDLE EAST WAS A SUCCESS,2,F,0,0,0
506 DATA 1916,RUSSIAN FORCES HIT AUSTRIA-& TOOK ABOUT 300000 PRISONERS,2,T,0,0,0
507 DATA 1916,MOST OF RUMANIA WAS OCCUPIED BY THE CENTRAL POWERS,2,T,0,0,0
508 DATA 1915,GERMANS DECLARED THE SEAS AROUND THE BRITISH ISLES A ...,4,WAR ZON
E,HAZARD,NEUTRAL ZONE,BOMB ZONE
509 DATA 1915,MAY-BRITISH LINER .... WAS TORPEDOED BY THE GERMANS,4,LUSITANIA,CO
NCORD,BRITAIN,ALLENBY
510 DATA 1916,DEC 12-GERMANY CONTACTED THE ALLIES TO SUGGEST PEACE TALKS,2,T,0,0
,0
511 DATA 1916,DEC 30-ALLIES AGREE TO MAKE PEACE WITH GERMANY,2,F,0,0,0
512 DATA 1917,APRIL 6-U.S. DECLARED WAR ON ....,1,GERMANY,0,0,0
513 DATA 1916,MY SLOGAN WAS 'HE KEPT US OUT OF WAR',3,WILSON,0,0,0
514 DATA 1917,JAN 19-GERMANY BEGINS .... WARFARE-UNRESTRICTED,4,SUBMARINE,LAND,A
IR,ALL OUT
515 DATA 1917,I COMMANDED THE AMERICAN EXPEDITIONARY FORCE,3,PERSHING,0,0,0
516 DATA 1917,BRITISH GENERAL .... WON THE HOLY LAND,4,ALLENBY,THOMAS,SMYTH,ROGE
RS
517 DATA 1918,WILSON'S '14 POINTS' OUTLINED A LASTING PEACE,2,T,0,0,0
518 DATA 1918,THE AMERICAN 2ND DIVISION STOPPED THE GERMANS AT ....-FRANCE,4,CHA
TEAUTHIERRY,HAGUE,NICE,CAAN
519 DATA 1918,JULY-2ND BATTLE OF THE MARNE PUSHED BACK THE GERMANS,2,T,0,0,0
520 DATA 1918,OCT-THE .... LINE WAS BROKEN IN MANY PLACES,4,HINDENBURG,EASTERN,F
RONT,WESTERN
521 DATA 1918,OCT-GENERAL ALLENBY CONQUERED ....,4,TURKEY,IRAN,JORDAN,EGYPT
522 DATA 1918,NOV 3-AUSTRIA ASKED FOR AN ARMISTICE,2,T,0,0,0
523 DATA 1919,JAN 18-THE .... PEACE CONFERENCE OPENED THIS DAY,4,PARIS,LONDON,NE
W YORK,HAGUE
524 DATA 1919,THE PARIS CONFERENCE PRODUCED FIVE PEACE ....,1,TREATIES,0,0,0
525 DATA 1919,THE TREATY OF .... WAS SIGNED BETWEEN GERMANY & THE ALLIES,1,VERSA
ILLES,0,0,0
526 DATA 1919,TREATY OF VERSAILLES WAS SIGNED IN THE ....,1,HALL OF MIRRORS,0,0,
0
527 DATA 1918,NOV-KAISER WILLIAM II WAS FORCED TO ....,1,ABDICATE,0,0,0
528 DATA 1918,NOV 11-GERMANS SIGNED AN ARMISTICE IN A RAILROAD CAR,2,T,0,0,0
529 DATA 1918,TOTAL COST OF THE WAR WAS ABOUT 300 BILLION DOLLARS,2,T,0,0,0
530 DATA 1919,ALL OF WILSON'S '14 POINTS' WERE ACCEPTED,2,F,0,0,0
531 DATA 1919,CLEMINCEAU OF FRANCE WANTED TO KEEP GERMANY ....,4,WEAK,UNDIVIDED,
DIVIDED,STRONG
532 DATA 1919,WILSON'S POINT 14 GAVE RISE TO THE 'LEAGUE OF NATIONS',2,T,0,0,0
533 CLS:PRINT"THE TIME DUNGEON * * * MAP"
534 PRINT
535 FORQ=1TO8
536 FORN=1TO8
537 IFC=NANDD=QTHENPRINT"=P= ";:GOTO540
538 S1=A(N,Q)
539 ONS1GOSUB137,137,138,138,139,140,141,139,142
540 NEXTN
541 PRINT
542 NEXTQ
543 GT=RND(8)+RND(CA+5):GOSUB134
```

```
544 CLS:RETURN
545 PRINT:PRINT"ON THE WALL IS A GLOWING SCREEN"
546 PRINT"BELOW THE SCREEN IS A RED BUTTON":PRINT
547 KT=RND(9):KL=RND(15)+2
548 GOSUB565
549 INPUTK$
550 IFK$="Y"THEN552
551 RETURN
552 IFKT>=6THEN533
553 IFKT<=4THEN562
554 PRINT:G4=RND(100)+25:G=G+G4
555 PRINT"YOU RECEIVE ";G4;" GOLD PIECES . . ."
556 PRINT"BUT . . . . . . THE CORRIDOR NARROWS":GT=3:GOSUB134
557 KL=KL-1:IFKL=0THENRETURN
558 GOSUB565
559 INPUTK$
560 IFK$="Y"THEN554
561 RETURN
562 PRINT:PRINT"NOTHING HAPPENS"
563 GT=1:GOSUB134
564 RETURN
565 PRINT:PRINT"DO YOU WISH TO PUSH THE BUTTON?"
566 PRINT"ENTER  (Y)ES  OR  (N)O":RETURN
567 CLS:PRINT"YOU ARE STUCK IN THE NARROW CORRIDOR"
568 PRINT". . . . . . . . . . AND . . .":PRINT:GT=3:GOSUB134
569 GOTO264
570 PRINT:PRINT"YOU NOTICE A DOOR TO YOUR RIGHT"
571 PRINT
572 KT=RND(9)
573 PRINT"DO YOU WISH TO OPEN THE DOOR?"
574 PRINT"ENTER  (Y)ES  OR  (N)O"
575 INPUTK$
576 IFK$="Y"THEN578
577 RETURN
578 PRINT:PRINT"YOU TRY THE DOOR . . . . .":GT=1:GOSUB134
579 IFKT>=7THEN589
580 IFKT<=4THEN587
581 PRINT:G4=RND(100)+25
582 PRINT"THE DOOR OPENS . . . . . . ."
583 PRINT"REVEALING A CLOSET . . . ."
584 PRINT:G=G+G4
585 PRINT"WHERE YOU FIND ";G4;" GOLD PIECES"
586 PRINT:RETURN
587 PRINT"BUT THE DOOR WON'T OPEN . . . ."
588 PRINT". . . . IT MUST BE LOCKED":RETURN
589 PRINT:PRINT"THE DOOR OPENS . . . AND SUDDENLY"
590 PRINT"THE CHAMBER BEGINS TO . . . SPIN"
591 G7=INT(G/2):G4=RND(G7):MM=RND(20)
592 GT=4:GOSUB134:G=G-G4
593 FORK9=1TO250
594 PRINT"+     =     +";
595 NEXTK9
```

```
596 CLS:PRINT"YOU WERE TELEPORTED INTO . . . ."
597 PRINT". . . . ANOTHER DIMENSION . . . ."
598 PRINT". . AND RETURNED IN AN INSTANT . ."
599 PRINT:PRINT"BUT YOU DROPPED ";G4;" GOLD PIECES"
600 PRINT". . . AND WASTED ";MM;" MOVES . . ."
601 M1=M1+MM
602 GT=4:GOSUB134
603 RETURN
```

Program 1-5. The Time Dungeon: World History, World War II, Program Listing

```
100 CLS:CLEAR400:BZ$="WORLD HISTORY-WW II":BW$="1933 TO 1945"
101 PRINT"THE TIME DUNGEON: ";BZ$
102 PRINT"COPYRIGHT (C) 1980 BY HOWARD BERENBON"
103 PRINT"TRS-80 VERSION"
104 PRINT
105 PRINT"AN EDUCATIONAL FANTASY GAME"
106 GT=5:GOSUB134:Q3=0
107 CLS:DIMA(9,9),B(50):GOSUB451
108 PRINT"YOU WILL BE TELEPORTED TO . . ."
109 PRINT
110 PRINT"THE TIME DUNGEON . . . ."
111 PRINT"TO STUDY ";BZ$
112 PRINT
113 RANDOM
114 CA=0:G=1000:M1=1:K=0:KL=1:TT=0:TR=0
115 PRINT"ENTER YOUR CHARACTER'S NAME?"
116 INPUTA$
117 PRINT"ENTER PRESENT YEAR"
118 INPUTY2:YY=Y2:IFY2>2000THEN117
119 PRINT:PRINTA$;" . . . YOU ARE ON YOUR WAY"
120 GT=2:GOSUB134
121 GOSUB143
122 CLS
123 PRINT"YOU HAVE ARRIVED AT . . . ."
124 PRINT
125 PRINT"THE TIME DUNGEON: ";BZ$
126 PRINT"FOR THE YEARS:    ";BW$
127 PRINT
128 PRINT"YOU CARRY 1000 GOLD PIECES":PRINT
129 PRINT"YOU WILL ENCOUNTER . . ."
130 PRINT"TIME PORTALS WHICH TELEPORT"
131 PRINT"YOU TO EVENTS IN ";BZ$
132 GT=8:GOSUB134
133 GOTO199
134 FORZZ=1TO400*GT
135 NEXTZZ
136 RETURN
137 PRINT"O   ";:RETURN
138 PRINT"AP  ";:RETURN
139 PRINT"?   ";:RETURN
140 PRINT"NS  ";:RETURN
141 PRINT"EW  ";:RETURN
142 PRINT"X   ";:RETURN
143 REM SET UP DUNGEON
144 FORX=1TO8
145 FORY=1TO8
146 A(X,Y)=RND(7)
147 NEXTY
148 NEXTX
149 REM TRAPS
150 H=RND(3)+1
151 FORN=1TOH
```

```
152 X=RND(8)
153 Y=RND(8)
154 A(X,Y)=8
155 NEXTN
156 REM EXITS
157 S=RND(4)+1
158 FORN=1TOS
159 X=RND(8)
160 Y=RND(8)
161 A(X,Y)=9
162 NEXTN
163 RETURN
164 R6=RND(4):PRINTQD$;"?:"
165 ONR6GOSUB167,168,169,170
166 GOTO433
167 PRINTAD$,I1$:PRINTI2$,I3$:RETURN
168 PRINTI2$,AD$:PRINTI1$,I3$:RETURN
169 PRINTI1$,I2$:PRINTAD$,I3$:RETURN
170 PRINTI3$,I1$:PRINTI2$,AD$:RETURN
171 CLS
172 PRINTCHR$(23)
173 GT=1
174 GOSUB134
175 FORB=1TO70:B4=RND(1020)
176 PRINT@B4,".";
177 NEXTB
178 GT=.005:Y5=25
179 IFY3=YYTHENPRINT"ALREADY AT . . . .":GOTO196
180 IFY3<YYTHEN188
181 IF(Y3-YY)<=50THEN185
182 Y3=Y3-Y5
183 GOSUB382
184 IFY3=YYTHEN195
185 IF(Y3-YY)<=50THENY5=1
186 IF(Y3-YY)<=5THENGT=.4
187 GOTO182
188 IF(YY-Y3)<=50THEN192
189 Y3=Y3+Y5
190 GOSUB382
191 IFY3=YYTHEN195
192 IF(YY-Y3)<=50THENY5=1
193 IF(YY-Y3)<=5THENGT=.4
194 GOTO189
195 PRINT"ARRIVAL . . . . AT"
196 PRINT"DESTINATION YEAR . . . . ";YY
197 GT=4:GOSUB134
198 CLS:RETURN
199 C=RND(8):D=RND(8):A(C,D)=1
200 K4=RND(4)+3
201 CLS:A=A(C,D):GT=1:GOSUB134
202 ONAGOSUB292,300,410,410,306,330,335,338,362
203 IFKL=0THEN567
```

```
204 PRINT:IFTT=1THENTT=0:GOTO201
205 IFG<=0THEN264
206 PRINTA$;",  WHAT IS YOUR ACTION OR MOVE?"
207 PRINT
208 PRINT"(N)ORTH, (E)AST, (S)OUTH"
209 PRINT"(W)EST, E(X)IT, (G)OLD
210 INPUTM1$
211 M1=M1+1:IFK=0ANDM1>70THEN371
212 IFM1$="N"THEN220
213 IFM1$="E"THEN225
214 IFM1$="S"THEN230
215 IFM1$="W"THEN235
216 IFM1$="X"THEN240
217 IFM1$="G"THEN251
218 PRINT
219 GOTO204
220 REM NORTH
221 IFA=7THEN255
222 IF(D-1)=0THEN281
223 D=D-1
224 GOTO201
225 REM EAST
226 IFA=6THEN260
227 IF(C+1)=9THEN286
228 C=C+1
229 GOTO201
230 REM SOUTH
231 IFA=7THEN255
232 IF(D+1)=9THEN288
233 D=D+1
234 GOTO201
235 REM WEST
236 IFA=6THEN260
237 IF(C-1)=0THEN290
238 C=C-1
239 GOTO201
240 CLS
241 IFA<>9THEN248
242 IFK=1THEN387
243 PRINT"YOU CANNOT EXIT THE TIME DUNGEON"
244 PRINT"YOU DON'T HAVE THE CRYSTAL KEY"
245 GT=2:GOSUB134
246 PRINT
247 GOTO204
248 PRINT"YOU ARE NOT AT AN EXIT PORTAL"
249 GT=2:GOSUB134
250 GOTO204
251 REM GOLD
252 CLS:PRINT"YOU HAVE ";G;" GOLD PIECES WITH YOU"
253 PRINT
254 GOTO204
255 REM EW
```

```
256 CLS:PRINT"YOU ARE IN AN EAST-WEST CORRIDOR"
257 PRINT"YOU CAN ONLY GO EAST OR WEST"
258 PRINT
259 GOTO204
260 REM NS
261 CLS:PRINT"YOU ARE IN A NORTH-SOUTH CORRIDOR"
262 PRINT"YOU CAN ONLY GO NORTH OR SOUTH"
263 GOTO258
264 REM GOLD ZERO
265 GT=2:GOSUB134
266 PRINT
267 PRINT"YOU LOST ALL YOUR GOLD AND YOU WERE"
268 PRINT" . . . UNABLE TO MEET THE DEMANDS OF"
269 PRINT" . . . THE TIME DUNGEON . . . . ."
270 PRINT
271 PRINT
272 GT=3:GOSUB134
273 GOSUB402
274 PRINT
275 PRINT"ANOTHER GAME?"
276 PRINT"ENTER '1'-YES  '0'-NO"
277 INPUTAA
278 IFAA<>1THEN280
279 CLS:GOTO108
280 END
281 CLS:PRINT"YOU ARE AT THE NORTH WALL"
282 PRINT"YOU CANNOT PASS THROUGH"
283 PRINT
284 PRINT"TRY ANOTHER DIRECTION?"
285 GOTO204
286 CLS:PRINT"YOU ARE AT THE EAST WALL"
287 GOTO282
288 CLS:PRINT"YOU ARE AT THE SOUTH WALL"
289 GOTO282
290 CLS:PRINT"YOU ARE AT THE WEST WALL"
291 GOTO282
292 KT=RND(9)
293 PRINT"YOU ARE IN A GLOWING TIME PORTAL"
294 GT=1:GOSUB134
295 PRINT
296 PRINT"THE LIGHT FADES . . . . . ."
297 PRINT"THE PORTAL IS INACTIVE . . . ."
298 IFA=1ANDKT>=8THEN570
299 RETURN
300 PRINT"YOU ARE IN A DUST FILLED PORTAL"
301 GT=1:GOSUB134
302 PRINT
303 PRINT"A BRIGHT LIGHT IS ACTIVATED AND . ."
304 PRINT
305 GOTO296
306 CLS
307 PRINT"AN ALIEN TRAVELER IS IN THIS CHAMBER"
```

```
308 A(C,D)=RND(2):GOSUB478
309 GT=1:GOSUB134
310 TD=RND(10)
311 G4=RND(350)
312 Y=RND(8)
313 IFY<=5THEN320
314 PRINT:IF(G-G4)<0THENG4=G
315 PRINT"HE IS UNFRIENDLY . . . . AND AS HE"
316 PRINT"LEAVES . . . HE TAKES ";G4;" GOLD PIECES"
317 PRINT:G=G-G4
318 IFTD=5ANDK=0THEN325
319 RETURN
320 PRINT
321 PRINT"HE IS FRIENDLY . . . . . AND GIVES YOU"
322 PRINT". . ";G4;" GOLD PIECES, WHICH YOU ACCEPT"
323 PRINT:G=G+G4
324 GOTO318
325 PRINT:GT=2:GOSUB134
326 PRINT"YOU SEARCH THE CHAMBER . . . AND"
327 GT=1:GOSUB134
328 PRINT"FIND . . . . THE CRYSTAL KEY"
329 K=1:RETURN
330 CLS
331 PRINT"YOU ENTER A NORTH-SOUTH CORRIDOR"
332 PRINT"THRU A SECRET DOOR":PRINT:GOSUB380
333 KT=RND(9):IFKT>=7THEN545
334 RETURN
335 CLS
336 PRINT"YOU ENTER AN EAST-WEST CORRIDOR"
337 GOTO332
338 REM TRAP
339 PRINT"YOU ENCOUNTER . . . A TIME TRAP"
340 PRINT". . . . . . . . IN THIS CHAMBER":GT=1:GOSUB134
341 TD=RND(9)
342 IFTD>=7THEN347
343 PRINT
344 PRINT"BUT YOU'RE LUCKY . . . . ."
345 PRINT". . . IT DIDN'T ACTIVATE"
346 RETURN
347 TT=1:PRINT"AND IT ACTIVATED . . . . .":GT=2:GOSUB134
348 FORA=1TO250
349 PRINT"*         %";
350 NEXTA
351 C=RND(8):D=RND(8)
352 PRINT
353 PRINT:G=100
354 PRINT"YOU HAVE BEEN TELEPORTED TO . . . ."
355 PRINT". . . . AN UNKNOWN LOCATION . . . ."
356 PRINT
357 PRINT"AND YOU LOST MOST OF YOUR GOLD"
358 PRINT
359 PRINT"YOU HAVE . . . ";G;" GOLD PIECES LEFT"
```

```
360 GT=6:GOSUB134
361 RETURN
362 PRINT"YOU ARE AT AN EXIT PORTAL"
363 PRINT
364 PRINT"(A KEY IS REQUIRED)"
365 PRINT
366 RETURN
367 H=1:O=9:W=8
368 B=0:E=5:R=14
369 C=0:PR=0
370 GOTO216
371 PRINT:GT=2:GOSUB134
372 PRINT"BUT BEFORE YOU PROCEED . ."
373 PRINT"YOU LOOK TO THE GROUND AND . . ."
374 PRINT" . . . FIND THE CRYSTAL KEY . .":K=1
375 GT=3:GOSUB134
376 GOTO212
377 PRINT"YOU ANSWERED ";CA;" QUESTION(S) CORRECTLY"
378 PRINT" . . . . . IN ";M1;" TURNS,"
379 GOTO409
380 PRINT"THE DOOR CLOSES AND LOCKS BEHIND YOU":GT=1:GOSUB134
381 RETURN
382 REM TIME DISPLAY
383 PRINT@390,"PORTAL YEAR . . . ";Y3
384 PRINT@448,STRING$(64,191)
385 GOSUB134
386 RETURN
387 CLS:REM EXIT PORTAL
388 PRINT"YOU ENTER THE EXIT PORTAL AND"
389 PRINT"INSERT THE CRYSTAL KEY INTO THE SLOT"
390 PRINT:GT=4:GOSUB134
391 PRINT"THE MACHINE BEGINS TO HUM . . . ."
392 PRINT:GT=2:GOSUB134
393 YY=Y2:GOSUB171
394 PRINT
395 PRINT"YOU FOUND YOUR WAY . . . . ."
396 PRINT". . . . BACK TO THE PRESENT"
397 PRINT
398 PRINT"YOU HAVE ACQUIRED ";G;" GOLD PIECES"
399 PRINT
400 GOSUB402
401 GOTO274
402 GG=G+100
403 R=INT((GG*CA-7000+1)/M1)
404 PRINT
405 PRINT"GAME RATING IS ";R
406 PRINT:IFG<=0ORKL=0THEN377
407 PRINT"YOU TOOK ";M1;" TURNS TO FIND THE WAY OUT"
408 PRINT"AND ANSWERED ";CA;" QUESTION(S) CORRECTLY,"
409 PRINT"OUT OF "TR;" QUESTIONS ASKED.":RETURN
410 CLS:Y3=YY
411 GOSUB444
```

```
412 Q3=Q3+1
413 IFQ3>50THENQ3=0:GOTO415
414 GOTO416
415 GOSUB451
416 Q=RND(50)
417 IFB(Q)=1THEN416
418 B(Q)=1
419 PRINT
420 FORAB=1TOQ
421 READ YY,QD$,ID,AD$,I1$,I2$,I3$
422 NEXTAB
423 RESTORE
424 GOSUB171
425 CLS:TR=TR+1
426 PRINT"YOU HAVE ARRIVED AT THE YEAR ";YY
427 PRINT". . . . . . IN ";BZ$:PRINT
428 PRINT"YOU MUST ANSWER THIS QUESTION";
429 PRINT" . . TO CONTINUE YOUR JOURNEY"
430 PRINT"----------------------------------------------------------------"
431 PRINT"THE YEAR IS: ";YY:PRINT:IFID=4THEN164
432 PRINTQD$
433 PRINT"----------------------------------------------------------------"
434 PRINT"QUESTION TYPE: ";
435 ON ID GOSUB 455,456,457,458
436 GOSUB459
437 IFE$=AD$THEN441
438 PRINT"INCORRECT"
439 GOSUB471
440 RETURN
441 PRINT"CORRECT"
442 GOSUB463
443 RETURN
444 PRINT"YOU ENTER INTO A BLUE HAZY . . ."
445 PRINT". . . . . . . TIME PORTAL . . . "
446 PRINT:GT=1:GOSUB134
447 PRINT"A PULSATING GLOW . . . . . . ."
448 PRINT". . . . INDICATES ACTIVATION":PRINT
449 PRINT"PRESENT YEAR . . .  ";Y3:GT=3:GOSUB134
450 RETURN
451 FORI=1TO50
452 B(I)=0
453 NEXTI
454 RETURN
455 PRINT"PEOPLE, PLACES, OR THINGS ?":RETURN
456 PRINT"*** (T)RUE OR (F)ALSE  ?":RETURN
457 PRINT"*** WHO AM I (LAST NAME) ?":RETURN
458 PRINT"*** MULTIPLE CHOICE ?":RETURN
459 PRINT"ENTER CORRECT ANSWER?"
460 INPUTE$
461 G4=RND(500)+125
462 RETURN
463 G=G+G4
```

```
464 PRINT"YOU WIN ";G4;" GOLD PIECES"
465 A(C,D)=RND(2)
466 CA=CA+1:IFK=1THENRETURN
467 IFCA=K4THEN469
468 RETURN
469 GOSUB325
470 RETURN
471 PRINT:G4=RND(400)+25
472 PRINT"THE CORRECT ANSWER IS '";AD$;"'"
473 PRINT:IF(G-G4)<0THENG4=G
474 G=G-G4
475 GT=1:GOSUB134
476 PRINT"YOU LOSE ";G4;" GOLD PIECES"
477 RETURN
478 ZT=5
479 X=RND(8):Y=RND(8)
480 IFA(X,Y)<=2THENA(X,Y)=5:RETURN
481 ZT=ZT-1:IFZT=0THENRETURN
482 GOTO479
483 DATA 1945,FROM 1939 TO 1945 NAZIS MURDERED 6 MILLION JEWS,2,T,0,0,0
484 DATA 1933,HITLER AND HIS .... BECAME GERMANY'S GOVERNMENT,4,NAZIS,NATIONALS,
DEMOCRATICS,COMMUNISTS
485 DATA 1933,HITLER BLAMED THE .... FOR MOST OF GERMANY'S ILLS,4,JEWS,ENGLISH,C
ATHOLICS,PROTESTANTS
486 DATA 1935,THE .... LAWS DEPRIVED ALL JEWS OF CITIZENSHIP,1,NUREMBERG,0,0,0
487 DATA 1934,HITLER'S SECRET POLICE WAS CALLED THE ....,4,GESTAPO,CIA,KBG,SPO
488 DATA 1936,THE SPANISH .... WAR BEGINS,4,CIVIL,COLD,GERMAN,RUSSIAN
489 DATA 1938,HITLER'S TROOPS RODE INTO .... AUSTRIA THIS YEAR,1,VIENNA,0,0,0
490 DATA 1938,GERMANS WORKED ON FORTIFICATIONS CALLED THE .... LINE,4,SIEGFRIED,
MAGINOT,FRONT,WESTERN
491 DATA 1939,AUG 23-RUSSIA SIGNED A .... PACT WITH GERMANY,1,NONAGGRESSION,0,0,
0
492 DATA 1939,SEPT 1-GERMAN FORCES INVADED ....,4,POLAND,FRANCE,RUSSIA,ENGLAND
493 DATA 1939,SEPT 3-GREAT BRITAIN AND .... DELCARED WAR ON GERMANY,1,FRANCE,0,0
,0
494 DATA 1939,GERMAN'S OCCUPYING POLAND KILLED 3 MILLION .... BY 1945,4,JEWS,COM
MUNISTS,SOCIALISTS,TURKS
495 DATA 1945,THE NUREMBERG .... TRIED NAZIS LEADERS FOR WAR CRIMES,1,TRIALS,0,0
,0
496 DATA 1940,MARCH-.... LOST SOME OF HER BEST LAND TO RUSSIA,4,FINLAND,HOLLAND,
FRANCE,ITALY
497 DATA 1939,DEC-BRITISH SHIPS TRAPPED THE GERMAN SHIP .... IN MONTEVIDEO HARBO
R,4,GRAF SPEE,NUREMBERG,SIEGFRIED,LUFTWAFFE
498 DATA 1940,APRIL 9-THE NAZIS INVADED .... & NORWAY,1,DENMARK,0,0,0
499 DATA 1940,APRIL-I WAS A NAZIS SYMPATHIZER IN NORWAY,3,QUISLING,0,0,0
500 DATA 1940,MAY-HITLER BEGAN THE INVASION OF THE NETHERLANDS- LUXEMBERG- & ...
.,4,BELGIUM,NORWAY,DENMARK,FRANCE
501 DATA 1940,BY MAY 10-GERMANS BROKE THRU THE ....-AT SEDAN,1,MAGINOT LINE,0,0,
0
502 DATA 1940,JUNE-GERMAN TROOPS OCCUPIED ....,4,FRANCE,ENGLAND,EGYPT,RUSSIA
503 DATA 1940,JUNE 18-BATTLE OF .... BEGAN AFTER THE FALL OF FRANCE,4,BRITAIN,FR
EEDOM,FRANCE,GERMANY
```

```
504 DATA 1941,HITLER LOST THE BATTLE OF BRITAIN,2,T,0,0,0
505 DATA 1940,THE GERMAN .... (AIR FORCE) GREATLY HURT BRITAIN,1,LUFTWAFFE,0,0,0
506 DATA 1940,OCT-ITALIAN TROOPS INVADED ....,1,GREECE,0,0,0
507 DATA 1941,JUNE 22-HITLER ATTACKED THE SOVIET UNION,2,T,0,0,0
508 DATA 1941,BY 1941-HITLER CONTROLLED THE .... AND WESTERN EUROPE,1,BALKANS,0,
0,0
509 DATA 1941,DEC 7-THE JAPANESE ATTACKED .... HARBOR,1,PEARL,0,0,0
510 DATA 1941,NOV-CONGRESS REPEALED THE .... ACT,1,NEUTRALITY,0,0,0
511 DATA 1942,JAN 1-THE .... NATIONS WAS CREATED DURING WW II,1,UNITED,0,0,0
512 DATA 1942,JUNE-AMERICANS HELD OFF THE JAPANESE AT .... ISLAND,1,MIDWAY,0,0,0
513 DATA 1942,GERMANS FAILED TO TAKE ....-IN RUSSIA,1,STALINGRAD,0,0,0
514 DATA 1943,JAN-ROOSEVELT & CHURCHILL MET IN ....-MOROCCO,1,CASABLANCA,0,0,0
515 DATA 1943,I WAS CALLED THE DESERT FOX (GERMAN),3,ROMMEL,0,0,0
516 DATA 1943,EARLY IN 1943-AMERICANS BEGAN AN OFFENSIVE IN THE ....,1,ALEUTIANS
,0,0,0
517 DATA 1944,JUNE 4-GENERAL CLARK'S AMERICAN TROOPS MARCHED INTO ....,4,ROME,FL
ORENCE,VENICE,NAPLES
518 DATA 1944,GERMANS V-1 ROCKET WAS KNOWN IN BRITAIN AS THE ....,4,BUZZ BOMB,FL
Y BOMB,ROCKET BOMB,DEATH BOMB
519 DATA 1944,SEPT-ALLIES FREED BELGIUM-LUXEMBURG- & MOST OF ....,1,FRANCE,0,0,0
520 DATA 1944,SEPT 12-THE BATTLE OF .... BEGAN,4,GERMANY,FRANCE,OKINAWA,EGYPT
521 DATA 1945,MAY 7-GERMANS SIGNED A SURRENDER AGREEMENT IN ....-CITY,4,REIMS,LO
NDON,PARIS,NICE
522 DATA 1944,JUNE 6-'D-DAY' WAS THE ALLIED INVASION OF ....,4,FRANCE,GERMANY,IT
ALY,SPAIN
523 DATA 1945,THE JAPANESE USED .... OR SUICIDE PLANES,1,KAMIKAZE,0,0,0
524 DATA 1945,JUNE-AMERICANS WON THE JAPANESE ISLAND OF ....,4,OKINAWA,KAMIKAZE,
NAGASAKI,HIROSHIMA
525 DATA 1945,JULY-ALLIES ISSUED THE .... DECLARATION,4,POTSDAM,FREEDOM,FINAL,LA
ST
526 DATA 1945,AUG 6-AN ATOMIC BOMB WAS DROPPED ON ....-CITY,1,HIROSHIMA,0,0,0
527 DATA 1945,AUG 9-AN ATOMIC BOMB WAS DROPPED ON ....-CITY,1,NAGASAKI,0,0,0
528 DATA 1945,AUG 14-JAPAN SURRENDERED AFTER THE ATOMIC DEVASTATION,2,T,0,0,0
529 DATA 1945,SEPT 2-JAPAN FORMALLY SURRENDERED ON THE AMERICAN SHIP ....,4,MISS
OURI,MIDWAY,ENTERPRISE,OHIO
530 DATA 1944,THE INVASION OF FRANCE TOOK PLACE BETWEEN CHERBOURG & ....,4,LE HA
RVE,NICE,CANNES,PARIS
531 DATA 1945,GENOCIDE OF THE JEWS-IN NAZIS CONCENTRATION CAMPS-WAS REVEALED,2,T
,0,0,0
532 DATA 1944,DEC 16-GERMANS COUNTER OFFENSIVE WAS THE 'BATTLE OF THE ....',4,BU
LGE,BOLD,RHINE,SWINE
533 CLS:PRINT"THE TIME DUNGEON * * * MAP"
534 PRINT
535 FORQ=1TO8
536 FORN=1TO8
537 IFC=NANDD=QTHENPRINT"=P= ";:GOTO540
538 S1=A(N,Q)
539 ONS1GOSUB137,137,138,138,139,140,141,139,142
540 NEXTN
541 PRINT
542 NEXTQ
543 GT=RND(8)+RND(CA+5):GOSUB134
```

```
544 CLS:RETURN
545 PRINT:PRINT"ON THE WALL IS A GLOWING SCREEN"
546 PRINT"BELOW THE SCREEN IS A RED BUTTON":PRINT
547 KT=RND(9):KL=RND(15)+2
548 GOSUB565
549 INPUTK$
550 IFK$="Y"THEN552
551 RETURN
552 IFKT>=6THEN533
553 IFKT<=4THEN562
554 PRINT:G4=RND(100)+25:G=G+G4
555 PRINT"YOU RECEIVE ";G4;" GOLD PIECES . . ."
556 PRINT"BUT . . . . . . THE CORRIDOR NARROWS":GT=3:GOSUB134
557 KL=KL-1:IFKL=0THENRETURN
558 GOSUB565
559 INPUTK$
560 IFK$="Y"THEN554
561 RETURN
562 PRINT:PRINT"NOTHING HAPPENS"
563 GT=1:GOSUB134
564 RETURN
565 PRINT:PRINT"DO YOU WISH TO PUSH THE BUTTON?"
566 PRINT"ENTER  (Y)ES  OR  (N)O":RETURN
567 CLS:PRINT"YOU ARE STUCK IN THE NARROW CORRIDOR"
568 PRINT". . . . . . . . . . . AND . . .":PRINT:GT=3:GOSUB134
569 GOTO264
570 PRINT:PRINT"YOU NOTICE A DOOR TO YOUR RIGHT"
571 PRINT
572 KT=RND(9)
573 PRINT"DO YOU WISH TO OPEN THE DOOR?"
574 PRINT"ENTER  (Y)ES  OR  (N)O"
575 INPUTK$
576 IFK$="Y"THEN578
577 RETURN
578 PRINT:PRINT"YOU TRY THE DOOR . . . . .":GT=1:GOSUB134
579 IFKT>=7THEN589
580 IFKT<=4THEN587
581 PRINT:G4=RND(100)+25
582 PRINT"THE DOOR OPENS . . . . . . ."
583 PRINT"REVEALING A CLOSET . . . ."
584 PRINT:G=G+G4
585 PRINT"WHERE YOU FIND ";G4;" GOLD PIECES"
586 PRINT:RETURN
587 PRINT"BUT THE DOOR WON'T OPEN . . . ."
588 PRINT". . . . IT MUST BE LOCKED":RETURN
589 PRINT:PRINT"THE DOOR OPENS . . . AND SUDDENLY"
590 PRINT"THE CHAMBER BEGINS TO . . . SPIN"
591 G7=INT(G/2):G4=RND(G7):MM=RND(20)
592 GT=4:GOSUB134:G=G-G4
593 FORK9=1TO250
594 PRINT"+    =    +";
595 NEXTK9
```

```
596 CLS:PRINT"YOU WERE TELEPORTED INTO . . . ."
597 PRINT". . . . ANOTHER DIMENSION . . . ."
598 PRINT". . AND RETURNED IN AN INSTANT . ."
599 PRINT:PRINT"BUT YOU DROPPED ";G4;" GOLD PIECES"
600 PRINT". . . AND WASTED ";MM;" MOVES . . ."
601 M1=M1+MM
602 GT=4:GOSUB134
603 RETURN
```

Program 1-6. The Time Dungeon: Ancient History, Middle East, 4000 B.C. to 6 B.C., Program Listing

```
100 CLS:CLEAR400:BZ$="ANCIENT HISTORY-MIDDLE EAST":BW$="4000 BC TO 6 BC"
101 PRINT"THE TIME DUNGEON: ";BZ$
102 PRINT"COPYRIGHT (C) 1980 BY HOWARD BERENBON"
103 PRINT"TRS-80 VERSION"
104 PRINT
105 PRINT"AN EDUCATIONAL FANTASY GAME"
106 GT=5:GOSUB134:Q3=0
107 CLS:DIMA(9,9),B(50):GOSUB451
108 PRINT"YOU WILL BE TELEPORTED TO . . ."
109 PRINT
110 PRINT"THE TIME DUNGEON . . . ."
111 PRINT"TO STUDY ";BZ$
112 PRINT
113 RANDOM
114 CA=0:G=1000:M1=1:K=0:KL=1:TT=0:TR=0
115 PRINT"ENTER YOUR CHARACTER'S NAME?"
116 INPUTA$
117 PRINT"ENTER PRESENT YEAR"
118 INPUTY2:YY=Y2:IFY2>2000THEN117
119 PRINT:PRINTA$;" . . . YOU ARE ON YOUR WAY"
120 GT=2:GOSUB134
121 GOSUB143
122 CLS
123 PRINT"YOU HAVE ARRIVED AT . . . ."
124 PRINT
125 PRINT"THE TIME DUNGEON: ";BZ$
126 PRINT"FOR THE YEARS:     ";BW$
127 PRINT
128 PRINT"YOU CARRY 1000 GOLD PIECES":PRINT
129 PRINT"YOU WILL ENCOUNTER . . ."
130 PRINT"TIME PORTALS WHICH TELEPORT"
131 PRINT"YOU TO EVENTS IN ";BZ$
132 GT=8:GOSUB134
133 GOTO199
134 FORZZ=1TO400*GT
135 NEXTZZ
136 RETURN
137 PRINT"O   ";:RETURN
138 PRINT"AP  ";:RETURN
139 PRINT"?   ";:RETURN
140 PRINT"NS  ";:RETURN
141 PRINT"EW  ";:RETURN
142 PRINT"X   ";:RETURN
143 REM SET UP DUNGEON
144 FORX=1TO8
145 FORY=1TO8
146 A(X,Y)=RND(7)
147 NEXTY
148 NEXTX
149 REM TRAPS
150 H=RND(3)+1
```

```
151 FORN=1TOH
152 X=RND(8)
153 Y=RND(8)
154 A(X,Y)=8
155 NEXTN
156 REM EXITS
157 S=RND(4)+1
158 FORN=1TOS
159 X=RND(8)
160 Y=RND(8)
161 A(X,Y)=9
162 NEXTN
163 RETURN
164 R6=RND(4):PRINTQD$;"?:"
165 ONR6GOSUB167,168,169,170
166 GOTO433
167 PRINTAD$,I1$:PRINTI2$,I3$:RETURN
168 PRINTI2$,AD$:PRINTI1$,I3$:RETURN
169 PRINTI1$,I2$:PRINTAD$,I3$:RETURN
170 PRINTI3$,I1$:PRINTI2$,AD$:RETURN
171 CLS
172 PRINTCHR$(23)
173 GT=1
174 GOSUB134
175 FORB=1TO70:B4=RND(1020)
176 PRINT@B4,".";
177 NEXTB
178 GT=.005:Y5=25
179 IFY3=YYTHENPRINT"ALREADY AT . . . .":GOTO196
180 IFY3<YYTHEN188
181 IF(Y3-YY)<=50THEN185
182 Y3=Y3-Y5
183 GOSUB382
184 IFY3=YYTHEN195
185 IF(Y3-YY)<=50THENY5=1
186 IF(Y3-YY)<=5THENGT=.4
187 GOTO182
188 IF(YY-Y3)<=50THEN192
189 Y3=Y3+Y5
190 GOSUB382
191 IFY3=YYTHEN195
192 IF(YY-Y3)<=50THENY5=1
193 IF(YY-Y3)<=5THENGT=.4
194 GOTO189
195 PRINT"ARRIVAL . . . . AT"
196 PRINT"DESTINATION YEAR . . . . ";YY
197 GT=4:GOSUB134
198 CLS:RETURN
199 C=RND(8):D=RND(8):A(C,D)=1
200 K4=RND(4)+3
201 CLS:A=A(C,D):GT=1:GOSUB134
```

```
202 ONAGOSUB292,300,410,410,306,330,335,338,362
203 IFKL=0THEN567
204 PRINT:IFTT=1THENTT=0:GOTO201
205 IFG<=0THEN264
206 PRINTA$;",  WHAT IS YOUR ACTION OR MOVE?"
207 PRINT
208 PRINT"(N)ORTH, (E)AST, (S)OUTH"
209 PRINT"(W)EST, E(X)IT, (G)OLD
210 INPUTM1$
211 M1=M1+1:IFK=0ANDM1>70THEN371
212 IFM1$="N"THEN220
213 IFM1$="E"THEN225
214 IFM1$="S"THEN230
215 IFM1$="W"THEN235
216 IFM1$="X"THEN240
217 IFM1$="G"THEN251
218 PRINT
219 GOTO204
220 REM NORTH
221 IFA=7THEN255
222 IF(D-1)=0THEN281
223 D=D-1
224 GOTO201
225 REM EAST
226 IFA=6THEN260
227 IF(C+1)=9THEN286
228 C=C+1
229 GOTO201
230 REM SOUTH
231 IFA=7THEN255
232 IF(D+1)=9THEN288
233 D=D+1
234 GOTO201
235 REM WEST
236 IFA=6THEN260
237 IF(C-1)=0THEN290
238 C=C-1
239 GOTO201
240 CLS
241 IFA<>9THEN248
242 IFK=1THEN387
243 PRINT"YOU CANNOT EXIT THE TIME DUNGEON"
244 PRINT"YOU DON'T HAVE THE CRYSTAL KEY"
245 GT=2:GOSUB134
246 PRINT
247 GOTO204
248 PRINT"YOU ARE NOT AT AN EXIT PORTAL"
249 GT=2:GOSUB134
250 GOTO204
251 REM GOLD
252 CLS:PRINT"YOU HAVE ";G;" GOLD PIECES WITH YOU"
```

```
253 PRINT
254 GOTO204
255 REM EW
256 CLS:PRINT"YOU ARE IN AN EAST-WEST CORRIDOR"
257 PRINT"YOU CAN ONLY GO EAST OR WEST"
258 PRINT
259 GOTO204
260 REM NS
261 CLS:PRINT"YOU ARE IN A NORTH-SOUTH CORRIDOR"
262 PRINT"YOU CAN ONLY GO NORTH OR SOUTH"
263 GOTO258
264 REM GOLD ZERO
265 GT=2:GOSUB134
266 PRINT
267 PRINT"YOU LOST ALL YOUR GOLD AND YOU WERE"
268 PRINT" . . . UNABLE TO MEET THE DEMANDS OF"
269 PRINT" . . . THE TIME DUNGEON . . . . ."
270 PRINT
271 PRINT
272 GT=3:GOSUB134
273 GOSUB402
274 PRINT
275 PRINT"ANOTHER GAME?"
276 PRINT"ENTER '1'-YES  '0'-NO"
277 INPUTAA
278 IFAA<>1THEN280
279 CLS:GOTO108
280 END
281 CLS:PRINT"YOU ARE AT THE NORTH WALL"
282 PRINT"YOU CANNOT PASS THROUGH"
283 PRINT
284 PRINT"TRY ANOTHER DIRECTION?"
285 GOTO204
286 CLS:PRINT"YOU ARE AT THE EAST WALL"
287 GOTO282
288 CLS:PRINT"YOU ARE AT THE SOUTH WALL"
289 GOTO282
290 CLS:PRINT"YOU ARE AT THE WEST WALL"
291 GOTO282
292 KT=RND(9)
293 PRINT"YOU ARE IN A GLOWING TIME PORTAL"
294 GT=1:GOSUB134
295 PRINT
296 PRINT"THE LIGHT FADES . . . . . ."
297 PRINT"THE PORTAL IS INACTIVE . . . ."
298 IFA=1ANDKT>=8THEN570
299 RETURN
300 PRINT"YOU ARE IN A DUST FILLED PORTAL"
301 GT=1:GOSUB134
302 PRINT
303 PRINT"A BRIGHT LIGHT IS ACTIVATED AND . ."
```

```
304 PRINT
305 GOTO296
306 CLS
307 PRINT"AN ALIEN TRAVELER IS IN THIS CHAMBER"
308 A(C,D)=RND(2):GOSUB478
309 GT=1:GOSUB134
310 TD=RND(10)
311 G4=RND(350)
312 Y=RND(8)
313 IFY<=5THEN320
314 PRINT:IF(G-G4)<0THENG4=G
315 PRINT"HE IS UNFRIENDLY . . . . AND AS HE"
316 PRINT"LEAVES . . . HE TAKES ";G4;" GOLD PIECES"
317 PRINT:G=G-G4
318 IFTD=5ANDK=0THEN325
319 RETURN
320 PRINT
321 PRINT"HE IS FRIENDLY . . . . . AND GIVES YOU"
322 PRINT". . ";G4;" GOLD PIECES, WHICH YOU ACCEPT"
323 PRINT:G=G+G4
324 GOTO318
325 PRINT:GT=2:GOSUB134
326 PRINT"YOU SEARCH THE CHAMBER . . . AND"
327 GT=1:GOSUB134
328 PRINT"FIND . . . . THE CRYSTAL KEY"
329 K=1:RETURN
330 CLS
331 PRINT"YOU ENTER A NORTH-SOUTH CORRIDOR"
332 PRINT"THRU A SECRET DOOR":PRINT:GOSUB380
333 KT=RND(9):IFKT>=7THEN545
334 RETURN
335 CLS
336 PRINT"YOU ENTER AN EAST-WEST CORRIDOR"
337 GOTO332
338 REM TRAP
339 PRINT"YOU ENCOUNTER . . . A TIME TRAP"
340 PRINT". . . . . . . . IN THIS CHAMBER":GT=1:GOSUB134
341 TD=RND(9)
342 IFTD>=7THEN347
343 PRINT
344 PRINT"BUT YOU'RE LUCKY . . . . ."
345 PRINT". . . IT DIDN'T ACTIVATE"
346 RETURN
347 TT=1:PRINT"AND IT ACTIVATED . . . . .":GT=2:GOSUB134
348 FORA=1TO250
349 PRINT"*          %";
350 NEXTA
351 C=RND(8):D=RND(8)
352 PRINT
353 PRINT:G=100
354 PRINT"YOU HAVE BEEN TELEPORTED TO . . . ."
```

```
355 PRINT". . . . AN UNKNOWN LOCATION . . . ."
356 PRINT
357 PRINT"AND YOU LOST MOST OF YOUR GOLD"
358 PRINT
359 PRINT"YOU HAVE . . . ";G;" GOLD PIECES LEFT"
360 GT=6:GOSUB134
361 RETURN
362 PRINT"YOU ARE AT AN EXIT PORTAL"
363 PRINT
364 PRINT"(A KEY IS REQUIRED)"
365 PRINT
366 RETURN
367 H=1:O=9:W=8
368 B=0:E=5:R=14
369 C=0:PR=0
370 GOTO216
371 PRINT:GT=2:GOSUB134
372 PRINT"BUT BEFORE YOU PROCEED . ."
373 PRINT"YOU LOOK TO THE GROUND AND . . ."
374 PRINT" . . . FIND THE CRYSTAL KEY . .":K=1
375 GT=3:GOSUB134
376 GOTO212
377 PRINT"YOU ANSWERED ";CA;" QUESTION(S) CORRECTLY"
378 PRINT" . . . . . IN ";M1;" TURNS,"
379 GOTO409
380 PRINT"THE DOOR CLOSES AND LOCKS BEHIND YOU":GT=1:GOSUB134
381 RETURN
382 REM TIME DISPLAY
383 PRINT@390,"PORTAL YEAR . . . ";Y3;"/"
384 PRINT@448,STRING$(64,191)
385 GOSUB134
386 RETURN
387 CLS:REM EXIT PORTAL
388 PRINT"YOU ENTER THE EXIT PORTAL AND"
389 PRINT"INSERT THE CRYSTAL KEY INTO THE SLOT"
390 PRINT:GT=4:GOSUB134
391 PRINT"THE MACHINE BEGINS TO HUM . . . ."
392 PRINT:GT=2:GOSUB134
393 YY=Y2:GOSUB171
394 PRINT
395 PRINT"YOU FOUND YOUR WAY . . . . ."
396 PRINT". . . . BACK TO THE PRESENT"
397 PRINT
398 PRINT"YOU HAVE ACQUIRED ";G;" GOLD PIECES"
399 PRINT
400 GOSUB402
401 GOTO274
402 GG=G+100
403 R=INT((GG*CA-7000+1)/M1)
404 PRINT
405 PRINT"GAME RATING IS ";R
```

```
406 PRINT:IFG<=0ORKL=0THEN377
407 PRINT"YOU TOOK ";M1;" TURNS TO FIND THE WAY OUT"
408 PRINT"AND ANSWERED ";CA;" QUESTION(S) CORRECTLY,"
409 PRINT"OUT OF ";TR;" QUESTIONS ASKED.":RETURN
410 CLS:Y3=YY
411 GOSUB444
412 Q3=Q3+1
413 IFQ3>50THENQ3=0:GOTO415
414 GOTO416
415 GOSUB451
416 Q=RND(50)
417 IFB(Q)=1THEN416
418 B(Q)=1
419 PRINT
420 FORAB=1TOQ
421 READ YY,QD$,ID,AD$,I1$,I2$,I3$
422 NEXTAB
423 RESTORE
424 GOSUB171
425 CLS:TR=TR+1
426 PRINT"YOU HAVE ARRIVED AT THE YEAR ";YY
427 PRINT". . . . . . IN ";BZ$:PRINT
428 PRINT"YOU MUST ANSWER THIS QUESTION";
429 PRINT" . . TO CONTINUE YOUR JOURNEY"
430 PRINT"---------------------------------------------------------------"
431 PRINT"THE YEAR IS: ";YY:PRINT:IFID=4THEN164
432 PRINTQD$
433 PRINT"---------------------------------------------------------------"
434 PRINT"QUESTION TYPE: ";
435 ON ID GOSUB 455,456,457,458
436 GOSUB459
437 IFE$=AD$THEN441
438 PRINT"INCORRECT"
439 GOSUB471
440 RETURN
441 PRINT"CORRECT"
442 GOSUB463
443 RETURN
444 PRINT"YOU ENTER INTO A BLUE HAZY . . ."
445 PRINT". . . . . . . TIME PORTAL . . . "
446 PRINT:GT=1:GOSUB134
447 PRINT"A PULSATING GLOW . . . . . . ."
448 PRINT". . . . INDICATES ACTIVATION":PRINT
449 PRINT"PRESENT YEAR . . .  ";Y3:GT=3:GOSUB134
450 RETURN
451 FORI=1TO50
452 B(I)=0
453 NEXTI
454 RETURN
455 PRINT"PEOPLE, PLACES, OR THINGS ?":RETURN
456 PRINT"*** (T)RUE OR (F)ALSE  ?":RETURN
```

```
457 PRINT"*** WHO AM I (LAST NAME) ?":RETURN
458 PRINT"*** MULTIPLE CHOICE ?":RETURN
459 PRINT"ENTER CORRECT ANSWER?"
460 INPUTE$
461 G4=RND(500)+125
462 RETURN
463 G=G+G4
464 PRINT"YOU WIN ";G4;" GOLD PIECES"
465 A(C,D)=RND(2)
466 CA=CA+1:IFK=1THENRETURN
467 IFCA=K4THEN469
468 RETURN
469 GOSUB325
470 RETURN
471 PRINT:G4=RND(400)+25
472 PRINT"THE CORRECT ANSWER IS '";AD$;"'"
473 PRINT:IF(G-G4)<0THENG4=G
474 G=G-G4
475 GT=1:GOSUB134
476 PRINT"YOU LOSE ";G4;" GOLD PIECES"
477 RETURN
478 ZT=5
479 X=RND(8):Y=RND(8)
480 IFA(X,Y)<=2THENA(X,Y)=5:RETURN
481 ZT=ZT-1:IFZT=0THENRETURN
482 GOTO479
483 DATA -4000,THE SIGHT OF BABYLON WAS SETTLED BY THE SUMERIANS,2,T,0,0,0
484 DATA -3700,1ST USE OF WRITING WAS IN ....-A SUMERIAN CITY,4,URUK,ERECH,KISH,
AGADE
485 DATA -3500,THE .... SETTLED ALONG THE EUPHRATES,1,SUMERIANS,0,0,0
486 DATA -3000,.... WAS THE LEADING SUMERIAN CITY UNDER KING ETANA,4,KISH,URUK,E
RECH,AGADE
487 DATA -2800,MESKIAGGASHER FOUNDED DYNASTY IN .... -CITY,4,ERECH,URUK,GIZEH,SU
MER
488 DATA -2686,BEGINNING OF THE .... KINGDOM OF EGYPT,4,OLD,2ND,MIDDLE,NEW
489 DATA -2600,THE GREAT .... FOR PHARAOH KHUFU WAS COMPLETED,4,PYRAMID,BATHS,FO
UNTAIN,FORTRESS
490 DATA -2600,GREAT PYRAMID FOR PHARAOH KHUFU WAS BUILT AT GIZEH,2,T,0,0,0
491 DATA -2650,.... REIGNED AS KING OF ERECH-SUMERIAN,1,GILGAMESH,0,0,0
492 DATA -2325,.... THE GREAT RULED OVER MESOPOTAMIA,4,SARGON,URUK,ETANA,KHUFU
493 DATA -2200,GUTIANS CONQUERED SUMERIA AND DESTROYED ....,4,AGADE,GIZEH,URUK,K
ISH
494 DATA -2133,BEGINNING OF THE .... KINGDOM OF EGYPT,4,MIDDLE,2ND,OLD,NEW
495 DATA -2100,UR-NAMMAU FOUNDED THE LAST SUMERIAN DYNASTY,2,T,0,0,0
496 DATA -3200,UPPER AND .... EGYPT UNITED BY PHARAOH MENES,4,LOWER,NEW,MIDDLE,O
LD
497 DATA -3200,.... WAS THE 1ST PHARAOH-BUILT MEMPHIS,4,MENES,SARGON,PILSER,ABRA
HAM
498 DATA -2000,THE .... DESTROYED UR IN MESOPOTAMIA,4,ELAMITES,HITTITES,HEBREWS,
EGYPTIANS
499 DATA -2000,I WAS THE FOUNDER OF JUDAISM,3,ABRAHAM,0,0,0
```

```
500 DATA -2000,THE .... LIVED AS NOMADIC SHEPHERDS IN CANAAN,4,HEBREWS,TURKS,EGY
PTIANS,SUMERIANS
501 DATA -1786,EGYPT RULED BY .... KINGS,4,HYKSOS,HEBREW,ELAMITE,HITTITE
502 DATA -1750,HAMMURABI RULED BABYLONIA-HAD CODE OF LAWS,2,T,0,0,0
503 DATA -1600,BABYLONIAN DYNASTY DESTROYED BY THE ....,4,HITTITES,HEBREWS,SUMER
IANS,EGYPTIANS
504 DATA -1567,BEGINNING OF THE .... KINGDOM IN EGYPT,4,NEW,OLD,MIDDLE,UPPER
505 DATA -1468,EGYPTIANS CONQUERED SYRIA-BATTLE OF ....,1,MEGIDDO,0,0,0
506 DATA -1250,I LED THE HEBREWS OUT OF BONDAGE IN EGYPT,3,MOSES,0,0,0
507 DATA -1250,PHOENICIANS ESTABLISHED THE CITY-STATES OF TYRE & ....,4,SIDON,UR
UK,BABYLON,CANAAN
508 DATA -1250,THE HEBREWS ENTERED ....,4,CANAAN,EGYPT,BABYLON,URUK
509 DATA -1020,.... BECAME KING OF THE HEBREWS,4,SAUL,MOSES,ABRAHAM,DAVID
510 DATA -910,BEGINNING OF THE .... EMPIRE,4,ASSYRIAN,EGYPTIAN,TURKISH,HEBREW
511 DATA -747,TIGLATH-.... III RULED ASSYRIA,1,PILSER,0,0,0
512 DATA -705,SENNACHERIB OF ASSYRIA DESTROYED ....,4,BABYLON,EGYPT,PERSIA,SUMER
IA
513 DATA -705,SENNACHERIB OF ASSYRIA BUILT A PALACE AT ....,1,NINEVEH,0,0,0
514 DATA -705,SARGON II OF ASSYRIA COMPLETED CONQUEST OF ....,4,ISRAEL,EGYPT,TUR
KEY,BABYLON
515 DATA -625,BEGINNING OF THE .... EMPIRE OF MESOPOTAMIA,1,CHALDEAN,0,0,0
516 DATA -606,BATTLE OF .... ENDED THE ASSYRIAN EMPIRE,1,CARCHEMISH,0,0,0
517 DATA -605,BEGINS THE REIGN OF KING NEBUCHADNEZZAR-II OF BABYLONIA,2,T,0,0,0
518 DATA -550,BEGINNING OF THE PERSIAN EMPIRE,2,T,0,0,0
519 DATA -550,PERSIAN EMPIRE FOUNDED BY .... THE GREAT,4,CYRUS,HAMMURABI,PILSER,
DARIUS
520 DATA -538,CYRUS THE GREAT CONQUERED ....,4,BABYLON,EGYPT,TURKEY,ISRAEL
521 DATA -538,PERSIANS CONQUERED BABYLON & RETURNED HEBREWS TO ....,1,JERUSALEM,
0,0,0
522 DATA -525,PERSIANS CONQUERED AND RULED ....,4,EGYPT,IRAN,JORDAN,SYRIA
523 DATA -490,1ST PERSIAN EXPEDITION TO GREECE UNDER DARIUS I,2,T,0,0,0
524 DATA -480,2ND PERSIAN EXPEDITION TO GREECE UNDER ....-I,1,XERXES,0,0,0
525 DATA -334,.... THE GREAT FOUNDED THE CITY ALEXANDRIA,1,ALEXANDER,0,0,0
526 DATA -300,ALEXANDRIA ....-BECAME AN INTELLECTUAL CENTER,4,EGYPT,ISRAEL,TURKE
Y,PERSIA
527 DATA -250,THE .... EMPIRE SUCCEEDED THE PERSIAN EMPIRE,1,PARTHIAN,0,0,0
528 DATA -280,....-II BUILT A LIGHTHOUSE ON PHAROS-ALEXANDRIA,1,PTOLEMY,0,0,0
529 DATA -192,BEGINS .... WAR BETWEEN ROME AND SELEUCIDS,4,SYRIAN,MACCABEES,SELE
UCID,PERSIAN
530 DATA -167,HEBREW .... REVOLTED AGAINST ANTIOCHUS-IV OF SYRIA,1,MACCABEES,0,0
,0
531 DATA -48,AIDED BY CAESAR-I BECAME THE QUEEN OF EGYPT,3,CLEOPATRA,0,0,0
532 DATA -6,.... CHRIST WAS BORN IN BETHLEHEM,1,JESUS,0,0,0
533 CLS:PRINT"THE TIME DUNGEON * * * MAP"
534 PRINT
535 FORQ=1TO8
536 FORN=1TO8
537 IFC=NANDD=QTHENPRINT"=P= ";:GOTO540
538 S1=A(N,Q)
539 ONS1GOSUB137,137,138,138,139,140,141,139,142
540 NEXTN
```

```
541 PRINT
542 NEXTQ
543 GT=RND(8)+RND(CA+5):GOSUB134
544 CLS:RETURN
545 PRINT:PRINT"ON THE WALL IS A GLOWING SCREEN"
546 PRINT"BELOW THE SCREEN IS A RED BUTTON":PRINT
547 KT=RND(9):KL=RND(15)+2
548 GOSUB565
549 INPUTK$
550 IFK$="Y"THEN552
551 RETURN
552 IFKT>=6THEN533
553 IFKT<=4THEN562
554 PRINT:G4=RND(100)+25:G=G+G4
555 PRINT"YOU RECEIVE ";G4;" GOLD PIECES . . ."
556 PRINT"BUT . . . . . . THE CORRIDOR NARROWS":GT=3:GOSUB134
557 KL=KL-1:IFKL=0THENRETURN
558 GOSUB565
559 INPUTK$
560 IFK$="Y"THEN554
561 RETURN
562 PRINT:PRINT"NOTHING HAPPENS"
563 GT=1:GOSUB134
564 RETURN
565 PRINT:PRINT"DO YOU WISH TO PUSH THE BUTTON?"
566 PRINT"ENTER  (Y)ES  OR  (N)O":RETURN
567 CLS:PRINT"YOU ARE STUCK IN THE NARROW CORRIDOR"
568 PRINT". . . . . . . . . . . AND . . .":PRINT:GT=3:GOSUB134
569 GOTO264
570 PRINT:PRINT"YOU NOTICE A DOOR TO YOUR RIGHT"
571 PRINT
572 KT=RND(9)
573 PRINT"DO YOU WISH TO OPEN THE DOOR?"
574 PRINT"ENTER  (Y)ES  OR  (N)O"
575 INPUTK$
576 IFK$="Y"THEN578
577 RETURN
578 PRINT:PRINT"YOU TRY THE DOOR . . . . .":GT=1:GOSUB134
579 IFKT>=7THEN589
580 IFKT<=4THEN587
581 PRINT:G4=RND(100)+25
582 PRINT"THE DOOR OPENS . . . . . . ."
583 PRINT"REVEALING A CLOSET . . . ."
584 PRINT:G=G+G4
585 PRINT"WHERE YOU FIND ";G4;" GOLD PIECES"
586 PRINT:RETURN
587 PRINT"BUT THE DOOR WON'T OPEN . . . ."
588 PRINT". . . . IT MUST BE LOCKED":RETURN
589 PRINT:PRINT"THE DOOR OPENS . . . AND SUDDENLY"
590 PRINT"THE CHAMBER BEGINS TO . . . SPIN"
591 G7=INT(G/2):G4=RND(G7):MM=RND(20)
```

```
592 GT=4:GOSUB134:G=G-G4
593 FORK9=1TO250
594 PRINT"+     =     +";
595 NEXTK9
596 CLS:PRINT"YOU WERE TELEPORTED INTO . . . ."
597 PRINT". . . . ANOTHER DIMENSION . . . ."
598 PRINT". . AND RETURNED IN AN INSTANT . ."
599 PRINT:PRINT"BUT YOU DROPPED ";G4;" GOLD PIECES"
600 PRINT". . . AND WASTED ";MM;" MOVES . . ."
601 M1=M1+MM
602 GT=4:GOSUB134
603 RETURN
```

CHAPTER 2

The Algebra Dungeon

The Algebra Dungeon is an educational fantasy game where the player must solve algebraic equations as he or she wanders through the chambers and corridors of the dungeon. It's a two-level dungeon, based on the fantasy role playing game Dungeons and Dragons.* It's written in BASIC for your microcomputer. See Program 2-1 for the program listing.

THE PROGRAM

You are given 1000 gold pieces and are then teleported to a random location in the lower level of this 128-chamber, two-level dungeon (64 chambers per level). Your goal is to find your way out, with as much gold as possible. Gold pieces are acquired by solving algebraic equations given by monsters that occupy the dungeon. Each time an equation is solved correctly, a random amount of gold is given as a reward. If your answer is incorrect, then a random amount of gold is taken away. The level of math is beginning algebra. See Fig. 2-1 for a sample run.

The Algebra Problems

The problems are generated randomly using program lines 3240 through 3480 and 4360 through 4470. A random number generator subroutine at line 3840 is used to generate the X, Y, P, and Q components of the problems. The following equations are used to generate random problems. In all cases, X must be solved for:

$Y = PX$	$Y = PX - Q$	$Y = PX + Q$
$X = PY$	$X = PY - Q$	$X = PY + Q$

In any case where division is required to solve for X, the division will result in an integer.

In the lower level of the dungeon, level two, the problems are generally less difficult than those at level one. The maximum value generated for X, Y, P, and Q is 50 for level one, and 25 for level two. The values in the random-number generator subroutine may be changed for different difficulty levels.

ACTIONS OR MOVES

In your trip into the dungeon, you will encounter algebra monsters, thieves, empty chambers, trap doors, secret doors leading to north-south or east-west corridors, maps, and enchanted keys.

Enter the letter in parentheses for the following actions or moves in the dungeon:

(N)ORTH movement (up)
(E)AST movement (right)
(S)OUTH movement (down)
(W)EST movement (left)
(U)P movement (when at a stairway, and have the enchanted key)
(M)AP display (if found—when encountering thieves)
(G)OLD pieces left

North Movement

Entering an N allows you to move north through the dungeon. You may not move north under the following conditions:

1. If you reach the North Wall, you cannot pass through it.
2. If you enter an east-west corridor (through a secret door), movement north is not allowed.

* Dungeons and Dragons is a registered trademark of TSR Hobbies, Inc.

```
YOU WILL BE TELEPORTED TO . . .

THE ALGEBRA DUNGEON

ENTER YOUR CHARACTER'S NAME?
? ERIC THE BOLD

YOU CARRY 1000 GOLD PIECES WITH YOU

ERIC THE BOLD . . . YOU ARE ON YOUR WAY


YOU HAVE ARRIVED AT . . . .

THE ALGEBRA DUNGEON . . . LEVEL 2

YOU WILL ENCOUNTER MONSTERS AND
THIEVES, AND GOLD . . . BUT WATCH
YOUR STEP  . . . . . . . . . . .
TRAP DOORS CAN BE COSTLY . . . .



YOU ARE IN A COLD AND DARK
 . . . . . . EMPTY CHAMBER


ERIC THE BOLD,  WHAT IS YOUR ACTION OR MOVE?

(N)ORTH, (E)AST, (S)OUTH, (W)EST
(U)P, (M)AP, (G)OLD
? N


YOU DISTURBED A MONSTER IN THIS CHAMBER
AND HE SPEAKS . . . . . . . . .

HALT . . . I AM THE KEEPER
OF . . . . . . . . ALGEBRA

YOU MAY NOT PASS THRU UNTIL
YOU SOLVE THIS EQUATION FOR X

Y =  19 X

IF Y =  133  THEN SOLVE FOR X

? 7


CORRECT
YOU WIN  59  GOLD PIECES


ERIC THE BOLD,  WHAT IS YOUR ACTION OR MOVE?

(N)ORTH, (E)AST, (S)OUTH, (W)EST
(U)P, (M)AP, (G)OLD
? N


YOU ARE IN A DAMP AND MISTY
 . . . . . . . EMPTY CHAMBER


ERIC THE BOLD,  WHAT IS YOUR ACTION OR MOVE?

(N)ORTH, (E)AST, (S)OUTH, (W)EST
(U)P, (M)AP, (G)OLD
? E

YOU DISTURBED A MONSTER IN THIS CHAMBER
AND HE SPEAKS . . . . . . . . .

HALT . . . I AM THE KEEPER
OF . . . . . . . . ALGEBRA

YOU MAY NOT PASS THRU UNTIL
YOU SOLVE THIS EQUATION FOR X

Y =  13 X -  7

IF Y =  149  THEN SOLVE FOR X

? 12


12
CORRECT
YOU WIN  70  GOLD PIECES

YOU HAVE FOUND THE ENCHANTED KEY . . .


ERIC THE BOLD,  WHAT IS YOUR ACTION OR MOVE?

(N)ORTH, (E)AST, (S)OUTH, (W)EST
(U)P, (M)AP, (G)OLD
? S

YOU DISTURBED A MONSTER IN THIS CHAMBER
AND HE SPEAKS . . . . . . . . .

HALT . . . I AM THE KEEPER
OF . . . . . . . . ALGEBRA

YOU MAY NOT PASS THRU UNTIL
YOU SOLVE THIS EQUATION FOR X

X =  10 Y +  4

IF Y =  16  THEN SOLVE FOR X

? 164


CORRECT
YOU WIN  312  GOLD PIECES


ERIC THE BOLD,  WHAT IS YOUR ACTION OR MOVE?

(N)ORTH, (E)AST, (S)OUTH, (W)EST
(U)P, (M)AP, (G)OLD
? E



YOU ACTIVATED A . . . TRAP DOOR

BUT . . . YOU CAUGHT YOURSELF
FROM FALLING

ERIC THE BOLD,  WHAT IS YOUR ACTION OR MOVE?

(N)ORTH, (E)AST, (S)OUTH, (W)EST
(U)P, (M)AP, (G)OLD
? E



YOU DISTURBED A MONSTER IN THIS CHAMBER
AND HE SPEAKS . . . . . . . . .

HALT . . . I AM THE KEEPER
OF . . . . . . . . ALGEBRA

YOU MAY NOT PASS THRU UNTIL
YOU SOLVE THIS EQUATION FOR X

X =  15 Y

IF Y =  40  THEN SOLVE FOR X

? 600


600
CORRECT
YOU WIN  382  GOLD PIECES


ERIC THE BOLD,  WHAT IS YOUR ACTION OR MOVE?

(N)ORTH, (E)AST, (S)OUTH, (W)EST
(U)P, (M)AP, (G)OLD
? E



YOU ARE AT A STAIRWAY
 . . . . . . GOING UP


ERIC THE BOLD,  WHAT IS YOUR ACTION OR MOVE?

(N)ORTH, (E)AST, (S)OUTH, (W)EST
(U)P, (M)AP, (G)OLD
? U



YOU WALK UP THE STAIRWAY
THE ENCHANTED KEY . . . OPENS THE LOCK
YOU FOUND YOUR WAY . . .
 . . . OUT OF THE ALGEBRA DUNGEON

YOU HAVE ACQUIRED  4289  GOLD PIECES

GAME RATING IS  521

YOU TOOK  155  TURNS TO FIND THE WAY OUT,
AND ANSWERED  20  QUESTIONS CORRECTLY
OUT OF  20  QUESTIONS ASKED.

ANOTHER GAME?
ENTER '1'-YES  '0'-NO
? 1
```

Fig. 2-1. The Algebra Dungeon sample run.

East Movement

Entering an E allows you to move east. You may not move east under the following conditions:

1. If you reach the East Wall, you cannot pass through it.
2. If you enter a north-south corridor (through a secret door), movement east is not allowed.

South Movement

Entering an S allows you to move south. You may not move south under the following conditions:

1. If you reach the South Wall, you cannot pass through it.
2. If you enter an east-west corridor (through a secret door), movement south is not allowed.

West Movement

Entering a W allows you to move west. You may not move west under the following conditions:

1. If you reach the West Wall, you cannot pass through it.
2. If you enter a north-south corridor (through a secret door), movement west is not allowed.

Up Movement

Entering a U, when you are at a stairway and have found the Enchanted Key, allows you to go up to the next level. If you haven't found the key or you are not at a stairway, you cannot go up the stairway. To find the Enchanted Key, you must solve a random number of algebraic equations correctly, for each level. There is a different key for each level.

Map Display

Entering an M when you have found a map will display the map for that level. Each level has a different map, and the maps may be found when you are encountering thieves. The 64-chamber dungeon is displayed using the following symbols:

M = algebra monster
0 = empty chamber
? = unknown contents (either a thief or a trap door)
UP = stairway up
NS = north-south corridor (entered through secret doors)
EW = east-west corridor (entered through secret doors)
P1 = your location in the dungeon

See Fig. 2-2 for a sample map.

A question mark (?) indicates either a thief or a trap door. There is no way of knowing which it is unless you enter the chamber. If you encounter a thief, either you surprise him and he drops some of his gold pieces or he surprises you and steals some of your gold pieces. This is randomly determined, but it's in favor of the thief.

If you activate a trap door, you can either fall through or catch yourself from falling. If you fall through, you will lose most of your gold pieces. There is a 50-percent chance that you will fall through. If you are at level two, you will fall into a deep pit. If you are at level one, you will fall through to level two.

Gold Pieces Left

Entering a G will display the number of gold pieces you have with you. You will start out with 1000 and can gain or lose gold during your trip. But if you lose all your gold pieces, you will lose the game.

GAME RATING

After you complete the game, a game rating is displayed, along with the number of gold pieces acquired, the number of algebraic equations solved correctly out of the number of questions asked, and the number of turns taken. The rating is a number from approximately −600 to +2000, depending on the above statistics. The higher the rating number, the better is the game rating. A negative number indicates a poor rating.

```
THE ALGEBRA DUNGEON  *** MAP LEVEL  1 ***

EW  ?   UP  0   ?   0   NS  0
0   0   EW  M   0   0   EW  0
0   0   0   0   UP  UP  0   EW
EW  M   0   NS  EW  UP  NS  0
?   M   P1  M   M   0   UP  0
0   NS  0   0   M   0   0   0
M   M   M   EW  EW  0   0   0
M   UP  NS  NS  ?   0   NS  NS

ERIC THE BOLD,  WHAT IS YOUR ACTION OR MOVE?

(N)ORTH, (E)AST, (S)OUTH, (W)EST
(U)P, (M)AP, (G)OLD
? E
```

Fig. 2-2. The Algebra Dungeon sample map.

Program 2-1. The Algebra Dungeon Program Listing

```
100 CLS:CLEAR 500
110 PRINT"THE ALGEBRA DUNGEON"
120 PRINT"TRS-80 LEVEL II"
130 PRINT"COPYRIGHT (C) 1980 BY HOWARD BERENBON"
140 PRINT
150 PRINT"AN EDUCATIONAL FANTASY GAME"
160 GOSUB440
170 GOSUB440
180 CLS:DIMA(9,9,2)
190 PRINT"YOU WILL BE TELEPORTED TO . . . "
200 PRINT
210 PRINT"THE ALGEBRA DUNGEON"
220 PRINT
230 RANDOM
240 MA=0:CA=0:G=1000:M1=1:K=0:TR=0
250 PRINT"ENTER YOUR CHARACTER'S NAME?"
260 INPUTA$
270 GOSUB440
280 PRINT:PRINT"YOU CARRY 1000 GOLD PIECES WITH YOU"
290 PRINT:GOSUB440:PRINTA$;" . . . YOU ARE ON YOUR WAY"
300 GOSUB440
310 GOSUB480
320 CLS
330 PRINT"YOU HAVE ARRIVED AT . . . ."
340 PRINT
350 PRINT"THE ALGEBRA DUNGEON . . . LEVEL 2"
360 PRINT
370 PRINT"YOU WILL ENCOUNTER MONSTERS AND"
380 PRINT"THIEVES, AND GOLD . . . BUT WATCH"
390 PRINT"YOUR STEP  . . . . . . . . . . ."
400 PRINT"TRAP DOORS CAN BE COSTLY . . . ."
410 FORAB=1TO2000
420 NEXTAB
430 GOTO1010
440 REM DELAY
450 FOR Z2=1TO400
460 NEXTZ2
470 RETURN
480 REM SET UP 2 LEVEL DUNGEON
490 FORX=1TO8
500 FORY=1TO8
510 FORZ=1TO2
520 A(X,Y,Z)=RND(7)
530 NEXTZ
540 NEXTY
550 NEXTX
560 REM TRAP DOORS #8, MIN-1, MAX-3
570 H=RND(3)
580 FORA=1TO2
590 FORN=1TOH
600 X=RND(8)
610 Y=RND(8)
620 A(X,Y,A)=8
```

```
630 NEXTN
640 NEXTA
650 REM STAIRWAYS #9, MIN-3, MAX-6
660 S=RND(4)+2
670 FORA=1TO2
680 FORN=1TOS
690 X=RND(8)
700 Y=RND(8)
710 A(X,Y,A)=9
720 NEXTN
730 NEXTA
740 RETURN
750 REM STAIRWAY
760 L1=L1-1
770 PRINT"YOU WALK UP THE STAIRWAY"
780 GOSUB440
790 PRINT"THE ENCHANTED KEY . . . OPENS THE LOCK"
800 GOSUB440
810 IFL1=0THEN870
820 MA=0:K=0:K4=RND(4)+4
830 PRINT:CB=CA+K4
840 PRINT"YOU ARE AT . . . . . LEVEL 1"
850 GOSUB440:GOSUB440:GOSUB440:GOSUB440
860 GOTO1070
870 PRINT"YOU FOUND YOUR WAY . . . "
880 PRINT" . . . OUT OF THE ALGEBRA DUNGEON"
890 PRINT
900 PRINT"YOU HAVE ACQUIRED ";G;" GOLD PIECES"
910 GOSUB930
920 GOTO1910
930 GG=G+100:REM RATING
940 R=INT((GG*CA-7000+1)/M1)
950 PRINT
960 PRINT"GAME RATING IS ";R
970 PRINT:IFG<=0THEN4280
980 PRINT"YOU TOOK ";M1;" TURNS TO FIND THE WAY OUT,"
990 PRINT"AND ANSWERED ";CA;" QUESTIONS CORRECTLY"
1000 PRINT"OUT OF ";TR;" QUESTIONS ASKED.":RETURN
1010 REM SET UP 1ST MOVE
1020 C=RND(8)
1030 D=RND(8)
1040 A(C,D,2)=1
1050 L1=2
1060 K4=RND(4)+4
1070 REM PLAYER MOVE ROUTINE
1080 CLS
1090 A=A(C,D,L1)
1100 GOSUB440
1110 ON A GOSUB 2220,2280,2340,2340,2390,2700,2750,2790,3070
1120 PRINT
1130 IFG<=0THEN1820
1140 PRINTA$;", WHAT IS YOUR ACTION OR MOVE?"
1150 PRINT
```

```
1160 PRINT"(N)ORTH, (E)AST, (S)OUTH, (W)EST"
1170 PRINT"(U)P, (M)AP, (G)OLD"
1180 INPUTM1$
1190 M1=M1+1:IFK=0ANDM1>=140/L1THEN4190
1200 IFM1$="N"THEN1290
1210 IFM1$="E"THEN1340
1220 IFM1$="S"THEN1390
1230 IFM1$="W"THEN1440
1240 IFM1$="U"THEN1490
1250 IFM1$="M"THEN1610
1260 IFM1$="G"THEN1670
1270 PRINT
1280 GOTO1120
1290 REM NORTH MOVEMENT
1300 IFA=7THEN1710
1310 IF(D-1)=0THEN1980
1320 D=D-1
1330 GOTO1070
1340 REM EAST MOVEMENT
1350 IFA=6THEN1770
1360 IF(C+1)=9THEN2030
1370 C=C+1
1380 GOTO1070
1390 REM SOUTH MOVEMENT
1400 IFA=7THEN1710
1410 IF(D+1)=9THEN2050
1420 D=D+1
1430 GOTO1070
1440 REM WEST MOVEMENT
1450 IFA=6THEN1770
1460 IF(C-1)=0THEN2070
1470 C=C-1
1480 GOTO1070
1490 CLS:REM STAIRWAY UP
1500 IFA<>9THEN1580
1510 IFK=1THEN750
1520 PRINT
1530 PRINT"YOU CANNOT GO UP THE STAIRWAY"
1540 PRINT"YOU DON'T HAVE THE KEY"
1550 GOSUB440
1560 PRINT
1570 GOTO1120
1580 PRINT"YOU ARE NOT AT A STAIRWAY"
1590 GOSUB440
1600 GOTO 1120
1610 CLS:REM MAP
1620 IF MA=1THEN2090
1630 PRINT"YOU DON'T HAVE THE MAP"
1640 PRINT
1650 GOSUB440
1660 GOTO1120
1670 REM GOLD PIECES
1680 CLS:PRINT"YOU HAVE ";G;" GOLD PIECES WITH YOU"
```

```
1690 PRINT
1700 GOTO 1120
1710 REM EW CORRIDOR
1720 PRINT
1730 CLS:PRINT"YOU ARE IN AN EAST-WEST CORRIDOR"
1740 PRINT"YOU CAN ONLY GO EAST OR WEST"
1750 PRINT
1760 GOTO1120
1770 REM NS CORRIDOR
1780 PRINT
1790 CLS:PRINT"YOU ARE IN A NORTH-SOUTH CORRIDOR"
1800 PRINT"YOU CAN ONLY GO NORTH OR SOUTH"
1810 GOTO1750
1820 REM GOLD ZERO
1830 GOSUB440:GOSUB440
1840 PRINT
1850 PRINT"YOU LOST ALL YOUR GOLD AND YOU WERE"
1860 PRINT" . . . UNABLE TO MEET THE DEMANDS OF"
1870 PRINT" . . . THE ALGEBRA DUNGEON . . ."
1880 PRINT:PRINT
1890 PRINT"BETTER LUCK NEXT TIME"
1900 GOSUB 930
1910 PRINT
1920 PRINT"ANOTHER GAME?"
1930 PRINT"ENTER '1'-YES  '0'-NO"
1940 INPUTAA
1950 IFAA<>1THEN1970
1960 CLS:GOTO210
1970 END
1980 CLS:PRINT"YOU ARE AT THE NORTH WALL"
1990 PRINT"YOU CANNOT PASS THROUGH"
2000 PRINT
2010 PRINT"TRY ANOTHER DIRECTION?"
2020 GOTO 1120
2030 CLS:PRINT"YOU ARE AT THE EAST WALL"
2040 GOTO1990
2050 CLS:PRINT"YOU ARE AT THE SOUTH WALL"
2060 GOTO1990
2070 CLS:PRINT"YOU ARE AT THE WEST WALL"
2080 GOTO1990
2090 REM DISPLAY MAP
2100 CLS
2110 PRINT"THE ALGEBRA DUNGEON  *** MAP LEVEL ";L1;"***"
2120 PRINT
2130 FORQ=1TO8
2140 FORN=1TO8
2150 IFC=N AND D=Q THEN PRINT"P1  ";:GOTO2180
2160 S1=A(N,Q,L1)
2170 ON S1 GOSUB 3110,3110,3130,3130,3150,3170,3190,3210,3220
2180 NEXTN
2190 PRINT
2200 NEXTQ
2210 GOTO1120
```

```
2220 REM EMPTY ROOM
2230 PRINT
2240 PRINT"YOU ARE IN A COLD AND DARK"
2250 PRINT" . . . . . . EMPTY CHAMBER"
2260 PRINT
2270 RETURN
2280 REM EMPTY ROOM 2
2290 PRINT
2300 PRINT"YOU ARE IN A DAMP AND MISTY"
2310 PRINT". . . . . . . EMPTY CHAMBER"
2320 PRINT
2330 RETURN
2340 TR=TR+1:CLS:GOSUB4140
2350 M4=RND(6)
2360 ON M4 GOSUB 3240,3370,3540,3670,4360,4420
2370 PRINT
2380 RETURN
2390 CLS:PRINT"THERE IS A THIEF IN THIS CHAMBER"
2400 A(C,D,L1)=2
2410 GOSUB440
2420 G4=RND(350/L1)
2430 Y=RND(8)
2440 IFY<=3THEN2610
2450 PRINT
2460 PRINT". . . . . . . HE SURPRISES YOU":PRINT
2470 GOSUB440
2480 PRINT"AS HE QUICKLY PASSES BY YOU HE"
2490 PRINT"SNATCHES . . . ";G4;" GOLD PIECES":PRINT
2500 G=G-G4
2510 REM LOOK FOR MAP
2520 IFMA=1THEN RETURN
2530 MA=RND(4):IFMA<=2THENMA=1
2540 IF MA=1THEN2570
2550 RETURN
2560 GOSUB440
2570 PRINT"YOU SEARCH THE CHAMBER AND"
2580 GOSUB440
2590 PRINT"YOU . . . . . FIND A MAP"
2600 RETURN
2610 PRINT"YOU SURPRISED THE THIEF . . . ."
2620 PRINT:GOSUB440
2630 PRINT"AS HE RUNS OUT HE DROPS . . . ."
2640 PRINT" . . . ";G4;" GOLD PIECES."
2650 PRINT"YOU PICK UP THE GOLD PIECES":G=G+G4
2660 PRINT:IFMA=1THENRETURN
2670 MA=RND(4):IFMA<=2THENMA=1
2680 IFMA=1THEN2570
2690 RETURN
2700 CLS:REM NORTH SOUTH CORRIDOR
2710 PRINT
2720 PRINT"YOU ENTER A NORTH-SOUTH CORRIDOR"
2730 PRINT"THRU A SECRET DOOR":PRINT:GOSUB4310
2740 RETURN
```

```
2750 CLS:REM EAST WEST CORRIDOR
2760 PRINT
2770 PRINT"YOU ENTER AN EAST-WEST CORRIDOR"
2780 GOTO2730
2790 REM TRAP DOOR
2800 PRINT"YOU ACTIVATED A . . . TRAP DOOR"
2810 GOSUB440
2820 TD=RND(4)
2830 IFTD>=3THEN2880
2840 PRINT
2850 PRINT"BUT . . . YOU CAUGHT YOURSELF"
2860 PRINT"FROM FALLING"
2870 RETURN
2880 IFL1=2THEN2990
2890 L1=L1+1:PRINT:K=1
2900 PRINT"YOU FELL THRU TO LEVEL 2 . . . AND"
2910 G=100
2920 GOSUB440
2930 PRINT
2940 PRINT"YOU . . . . . . . . LOST"
2950 PRINT"MOST OF YOUR GOLD PIECES":PRINT
2960 PRINT"YOU HAVE . . ";G;" GOLD PIECES LEFT"
2970 PRINT"BUT . . . YOU STILL HAVE YOUR KEY"
2980 RETURN
2990 PRINT"YOU FELL INTO A DEEP . . . PIT"
3000 GOSUB440
3010 PRINT"YOU'RE LUCKY . . . . "
3020 PRINT"YOU DIDN'T GET HURT"
3030 PRINT
3040 GOSUB440
3050 PRINT"BUT IN CLIMBING OUT . . ."
3060 GOTO4230
3070 PRINT"YOU ARE AT A STAIRWAY"
3080 PRINT" . . . . . . GOING UP"
3090 PRINT
3100 RETURN
3110 PRINT"O   ";
3120 RETURN
3130 PRINT"M   ";
3140 RETURN
3150 PRINT"?   ";
3160 RETURN
3170 PRINT"NS  ";
3180 RETURN
3190 PRINT"EW  ";
3200 RETURN
3210 GOTO3150
3220 PRINT"UP  ";
3230 RETURN
3240 REM Y=PX
3250 GOSUB4330
3260 GOSUB 3800
3270 GOSUB3840:Y=P*X
```

```
3280 PRINT"Y = ";P;"X"
3290 PRINT:PRINT"IF Y = ";Y;" THEN SOLVE FOR X"
3300 PRINT:INPUTA1
3310 IFA1=XTHEN3350
3320 REM LOSE GOLD
3330 GOSUB4000
3340 RETURN
3350 GOSUB3900
3360 RETURN
3370 REM Y=PX-Q
3380 GOSUB4330
3390 GOSUB3800
3400 GOSUB3840:Y=P*X
3410 PRINT"Y = ";P;"X - ";Q
3420 PRINT:PRINT"IF Y = ";Y-Q;" THEN SOLVE FOR X"
3430 PRINT:INPUTA1
3440 IFA1=XTHEN3470
3450 GOSUB4000
3460 RETURN
3470 GOSUB3900
3480 RETURN
3490 GOSUB 480
3500 H=1:O=9:W=8
3510 B=0:E=5:R=14
3520 C=0:PR=0
3530 GOTO1010
3540 REM Y=PX+Q
3550 GOSUB4330
3560 GOSUB3800
3570 GOSUB3840:Y=P*X
3580 PRINT"Y = ";P;"X + ";Q
3590 PRINT:PRINT"IF Y = ";Y+Q;" THEN SOLVE FOR X"
3600 PRINT:INPUTA1
3610 IFA1=XTHEN3650
3620 REM LOSE GOLD
3630 GOSUB4000
3640 RETURN
3650 GOSUB3900
3660 RETURN
3670 REM X=PY+Q
3680 GOSUB4330
3690 GOSUB3800
3700 GOSUB3840:X=P*Y+Q
3710 PRINT"X = ";P;"Y + ";Q
3720 PRINT:PRINT"IF Y = ";Y;" THEN SOLVE FOR X"
3730 PRINT:INPUTA1
3740 IFA1=XTHEN3780
3750 REM LOSE GOLD
3760 GOSUB4000
3770 RETURN
3780 GOSUB3900
3790 RETURN
3800 PRINT"YOU MAY NOT PASS THRU UNTIL"
```

```
3810 PRINT"YOU SOLVE THIS EQUATION FOR X"
3820 PRINT
3830 RETURN
3840 REM RANDOM ROUTINE
3850 X=RND(50/L1):P=RND(50/L1)
3860 Y=RND(50/L1):Q=RND(50/L1)
3870 GOSUB 440
3880 GOSUB 440
3890 RETURN
3900 PRINT"CORRECT"
3910 G4=RND(400/L1)+25
3920 G=G+G4
3930 GOSUB 440
3940 PRINT"YOU WIN ";G4;" GOLD PIECES"
3950 A(C,D,L1)=1
3960 CA=CA+1:IFK=1THENRETURN
3970 IFL1=1THEN4210
3980 IFCA=K4THEN4090
3990 RETURN
4000 PRINT
4010 PRINT"INCORRECT"
4020 PRINT"THE CORRECT ANSWER IS ";X
4030 PRINT
4040 G4=RND(350/L1)
4050 G=G-G4
4060 GOSUB440
4070 PRINT"YOU LOSE ";G4;" GOLD PIECES"
4080 RETURN
4090 GOSUB440
4100 K=1
4110 PRINT:PRINT"YOU HAVE FOUND THE ENCHANTED KEY . . ."
4120 GOSUB440
4130 RETURN
4140 PRINT"YOU DISTURBED A MONSTER IN THIS CHAMBER"
4150 GOSUB440
4160 PRINT"AND HE SPEAKS . . . . . . . . .":PRINT
4170 GOSUB440
4180 RETURN
4190 GOSUB4100
4200 GOTO1200
4210 IFCA=CBTHEN4090
4220 RETURN
4230 G=100:GOSUB440:PRINT
4240 PRINT"YOU . . . . . . DROPPED"
4250 PRINT"MOST OF YOUR GOLD PIECES."
4260 PRINT"YOU HAVE . .";G;" GOLD PIECES LEFT"
4270 RETURN
4280 PRINT"YOU ANSWERED ";CA;" QUESTIONS CORRECTLY"
4290 PRINT"OUT OF ";TR;" QUESTIONS ASKED,":PRINT" . . . . . IN ";M1;" TURNS."
4300 RETURN
4310 PRINT"THE DOOR CLOSES AND LOCKS BEHIND YOU":GOSUB440
4320 RETURN
4330 PRINT"HALT . . . I AM THE KEEPER"
```

Program 2-1—cont. The Algebra Dungeon Program Listing

```
4340 PRINT"OF . . . . . . . . . ALGEBRA"
4350 PRINT:RETURN
4360 REM X=PY
4370 GOSUB4330
4380 GOSUB3800
4390 GOSUB3840:X=P*Y
4400 PRINT"X = ";P;"Y"
4410 GOTO3720
4420 REM X=PY-Q
4430 GOSUB4330
4440 GOSUB3800
4450 GOSUB3840:X=P*Y-Q
4460 PRINT"X = ";P;"Y - ";Q
4470 GOTO3720
```

CHAPTER 3

Word Association

The Word Association program is an educational exercise for children. It gives a twenty-question test, with each question displaying four words. The word that is "not like the others" must be chosen. The program is written in BASIC for your microcomputer. See Program 3-1 for the program listing.

THE PROGRAM

The program begins by accepting the student's name, then requesting the entry of a 1 to begin the test. Each question displays four words, three of which are on a related subject, and the fourth is not related. The student must enter the word that is not related to the others. CORRECT is displayed for a correct response, and INCORRECT is displayed for an incorrect entry. This is repeated for all twenty questions, then the student's score is calculated. Finally, the number of correct out of twenty is displayed, along with the percent score. See Fig. 3-1 for a sample run.

THE QUESTIONS

The words are stored in DATA statements beginning at line 690. The first three words in each statement are related, and the fourth is not related. Each time a question is displayed, the unrelated word will appear in one of four positions on the display. The word list may be changed for a different set of questions.

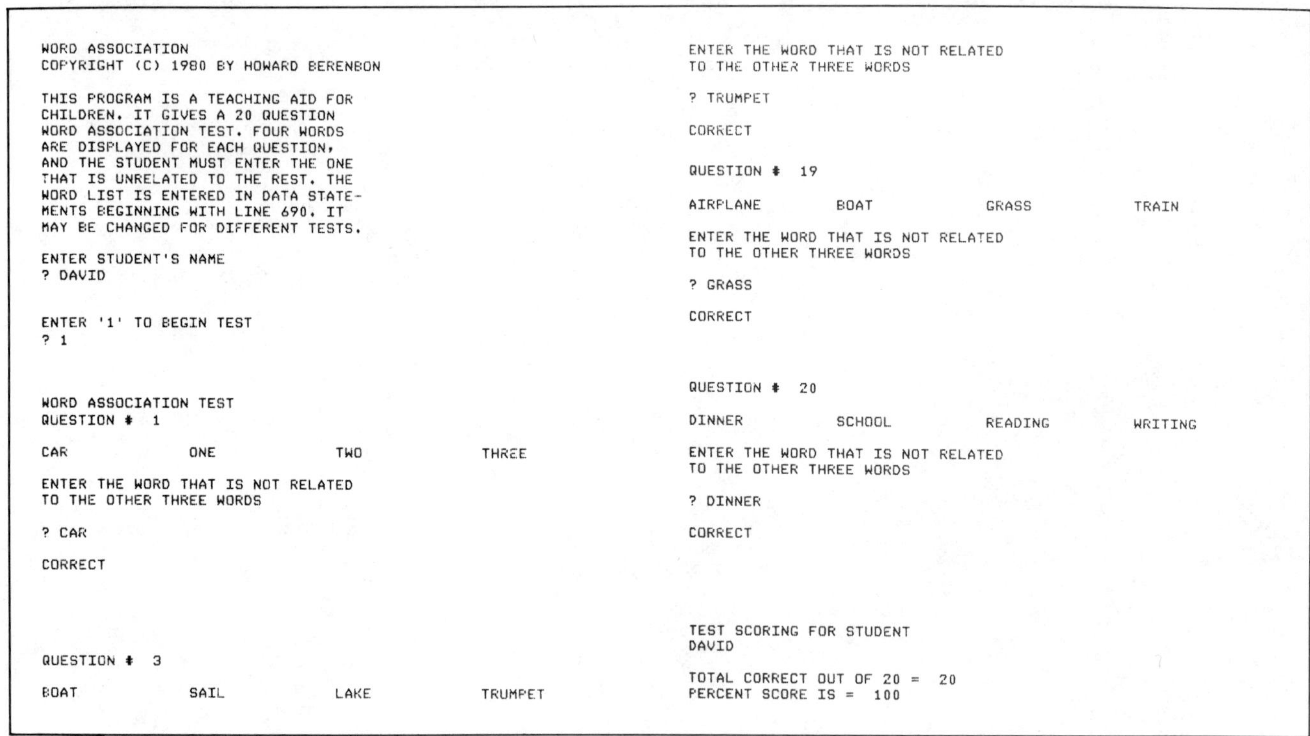

```
WORD ASSOCIATION
COPYRIGHT (C) 1980 BY HOWARD BERENBON

THIS PROGRAM IS A TEACHING AID FOR
CHILDREN. IT GIVES A 20 QUESTION
WORD ASSOCIATION TEST. FOUR WORDS
ARE DISPLAYED FOR EACH QUESTION,
AND THE STUDENT MUST ENTER THE ONE
THAT IS UNRELATED TO THE REST. THE
WORD LIST IS ENTERED IN DATA STATE-
MENTS BEGINNING WITH LINE 690. IT
MAY BE CHANGED FOR DIFFERENT TESTS.

ENTER STUDENT'S NAME
? DAVID


ENTER '1' TO BEGIN TEST
? 1


WORD ASSOCIATION TEST
QUESTION #  1

CAR            ONE            TWO            THREE

ENTER THE WORD THAT IS NOT RELATED
TO THE OTHER THREE WORDS

? CAR

CORRECT



QUESTION #  3

BOAT           SAIL           LAKE           TRUMPET

ENTER THE WORD THAT IS NOT RELATED
TO THE OTHER THREE WORDS

? TRUMPET

CORRECT

QUESTION #  19

AIRPLANE       BOAT           GRASS          TRAIN

ENTER THE WORD THAT IS NOT RELATED
TO THE OTHER THREE WORDS

? GRASS

CORRECT


QUESTION #  20

DINNER         SCHOOL         READING        WRITING

ENTER THE WORD THAT IS NOT RELATED
TO THE OTHER THREE WORDS

? DINNER

CORRECT


TEST SCORING FOR STUDENT
DAVID

TOTAL CORRECT OUT OF 20 =  20
PERCENT SCORE IS =  100
```

Fig. 3-1. Word Association sample run.

Program 3-1. Word Association Program Listing

```
100 CLS:PRINT"WORD ASSOCIATION":CLEAR 500
110 PRINT"COPYRIGHT (C) 1980 BY HOWARD BERENBON"
120 PRINT"TRS-80"
130 PRINT
140 PRINT"THIS PROGRAM IS A TEACHING AID FOR"
150 PRINT"CHILDREN. IT GIVES A 20 QUESTION"
160 PRINT"WORD ASSOCIATION TEST. FOUR WORDS"
170 PRINT"ARE DISPLAYED FOR EACH QUESTION,"
180 PRINT"AND THE STUDENT MUST ENTER THE ONE"
190 PRINT"THAT IS UNRELATED TO THE REST. THE"
200 PRINT"WORD LIST IS ENTERED IN DATA STATE-"
210 PRINT"MENTS BEGINNING WITH LINE 690. IT"
220 PRINT"MAY BE CHANGED FOR DIFFERENT TESTS."
230 PRINT
240 PRINT"ENTER STUDENT'S NAME"
250 INPUTA$:S=0
260 PRINT
270 PRINT"ENTER '1' TO BEGIN TEST"
280 INPUTA:CLS
290 PRINT"WORD ASSOCIATION TEST"
300 FORT=1TO20:PRINT"QUESTION # ";T
310 PRINT:READ B$,C$,D$,E$
320 R=RND(4)
330 ON R GOSUB 450,470,490,510
340 GOSUB420
350 INPUTF$
360 IFF$=E$THEN530
370 PRINT:PRINT"INCORRECT"
380 PRINT
390 PRINT"THE CORRECT WORD IS ";E$
400 GOSUB660:CLS:NEXTT
410 GOTO580
420 PRINT:PRINT"ENTER THE WORD THAT IS NOT RELATED"
430 PRINT"TO THE OTHER THREE WORDS"
440 PRINT:RETURN
450 PRINT B$,C$,D$,E$
460 RETURN
470 PRINT C$,D$,E$,B$
480 RETURN
490 PRINT D$,E$,B$,C$
500 RETURN
510 PRINT E$,B$,C$,D$
520 RETURN
530 S=S+5
540 PRINT
550 PRINT"CORRECT"
560 PRINT
570 GOTO400
580 CLS
590 PRINT"TEST SCORING FOR STUDENT"
600 PRINTA$
610 PRINT
620 PRINT"TOTAL CORRECT OUT OF 20 = ";S/5
```

```
630 PRINT"PERCENT SCORE IS = ";S
640 PRINT
650 END
660 FORA=1TO900
670 NEXTA
680 RETURN
690 DATA ONE,TWO,THREE,CAR
700 DATA TIRE,CAR,FENDER,SAIL
710 DATA BOAT,SAIL,LAKE,TRUMPET
720 DATA GUITAR,TRUMPET,VIOLIN,SISTER
730 DATA BROTHER,SISTER,FATHER,BOOK
740 DATA BINDING,BOOK,PAGES,DRILL
750 DATA SAW,CUT,DRILL,GYM
760 DATA FOOTBALL,BASKETBALL,BASEBALL,TRUCK
770 DATA ARM,HAND,EYES,TIME
780 DATA HOURS,MINUTES,SECONDS,PEOPLE
790 DATA PENCIL,PAPER,PEN,AIRPLANE
800 DATA FLYING,AIRPORT,AIRPLANE,SING
810 DATA TALK,SING,WHISPER,JUMP
820 DATA WALK,STAND,RUN,EAT
830 DATA SALT,PEPPER,GARLIC,GLUE
840 DATA LAKE,RIVER,STREAM,TRAIN
850 DATA COOKIES,CAKE,BROUNIES,STEAM
860 DATA ICE,WATER,STEAM,MOUNTAIN
870 DATA TRAIN,AIRPLANE,BOAT,GRASS
880 DATA SCHOOL,READING,WRITING,DINNER
```

CHAPTER 4

Advanced Math: Algebra

Here's a program that gives a ten-question algebra test. Each question is randomly generated from six different algebra equations. The program is written in BASIC for your microcomputer. See Program 4-1 for the program listing.

THE PROGRAM

After you run the program, enter the difficulty level: 1 for moderate or 2 for difficult. Then the test will begin. An equation will be displayed, where you must solve for the value of X. You have two tries to enter the correct answer. CORRECT will be displayed for a correct response, and the program will go on to the next question; INCORRECT will be displayed for a wrong answer. After two incorrect entries, the correct answer will be displayed, and the program will advance to the next question. After all ten questions are answered, your score will be displayed, with the number correct out of ten and the percent score. Finally, another test may be taken, or you can end the program. See Fig. 4-1 for a sample run.

THE PROBLEMS

The problems are generated randomly using program lines 530 through 1020. A random-number generator subroutine is used to generate the X, Y, P, and Q components of the problems. The following equations are used to generate the problems. In all cases, X must be solved for:

$$Y = PX \qquad Y = PX - Q \qquad Y = PX + Q$$
$$X = PY \qquad X = PY - Q \qquad X = PY + Q$$

In any case where division is required to solve for X, the division will result in an integer.

```
ADVANCED MATH: ALGEBRA
COPYRIGHT (C) 1980 BY HOWARD BERENBON

THIS IS AN ALGEBRA TEST PROGRAM WHICH
RANDOMLY GENERATES A 10-QUESTION TEST.
YOU HAVE 2-TRIES PER QUESTION.

ENTER DIFFICULTY LEVEL

1) MODERATE
2) DIFFICULT
? 1



                    ALGEBRA TEST
PROBLEM  1
TRIAL  1

X =  15 Y +  24

IF Y =  17  THEN SOLVE FOR X

? 279

CORRECT



                    ALGEBRA TEST
PROBLEM  2
TRIAL  1

Y =  4 X +  19

IF Y =  115  THEN SOLVE FOR X

? 24

CORRECT

                    ALGEBRA TEST
PROBLEM  9
TRIAL  1

Y =  6 X -  4

IF Y =  134  THEN SOLVE FOR X

? 23

CORRECT



                    ALGEBRA TEST
PROBLEM  10
TRIAL  1

Y =  19 X -  23

IF Y =  376  THEN SOLVE FOR X

? 21

CORRECT



YOU HAVE  10  CORRECT OUT OF 10
THAT'S A SCORE OF  100  %

ANOTHER TEST? 1-YES  0-NO
? 1
```

Fig. 4-1. Advanced math: Algebra sample run.

Program 4-1. Advanced Math: Algebra Program Listing

```
100 CLS:PRINT"ADVANCED MATH: ALGEBRA"
110 PRINT"TRS-80"
120 PRINT"COPYRIGHT (C) 1980 BY HOWARD BERENBON":PRINT
130 PRINT"THIS IS AN ALGEBRA TEST PROGRAM WHICH"
140 PRINT"RANDOMLY GENERATES A 10-QUESTION TEST."
150 PRINT"YOU HAVE 2-TRIES PER QUESTION."
160 PRINT:GOSUB380
170 S=0
180 FORA=1TO10
190 R=RND(6)
200 T=1
210 GOSUB470
220 CLS:PRINTTAB(18)"ALGEBRA TEST"
230 GOSUB340
240 ON R GOTO 530,610,690,770,950,990
250 NEXTA
260 PRINT
270 PRINT"YOU HAVE ";S;" CORRECT OUT OF 10"
280 PRINT"THAT'S A SCORE OF ";S*10;" %"
290 PRINT
300 PRINT"ANOTHER TEST? 1-YES  0-NO"
310 INPUTZ
320 CLS:IFZ=1THEN160
330 END
340 PRINT"PROBLEM ";A
350 PRINT"TRIAL ";T
360 PRINT
370 RETURN
380 PRINT"ENTER DIFFICULTY LEVEL"
390 PRINT
400 PRINT"1) MODERATE"
410 PRINT"2) DIFFICULT"
420 INPUTE
430 ON E GOTO 450,460
440 GOTO380
450 D=25:RETURN
460 D=50:RETURN
470 X=RND(D):P=RND(D)
480 Y=RND(D):Q=RND(D)
490 RETURN
500 FORZ=1TO600
510 NEXTZ
520 RETURN
530 REM Y=PX
540 Y=P*X
550 PRINT"Y = ";P;"X"
560 PRINT:PRINT"IF Y = ";Y;" THEN SOLVE FOR X"
570 PRINT:INPUTA1
580 IFA1=XTHEN600
590 GOTO880
600 GOTO850
610 REM Y=PX-Q
620 Y=P*X
```

```
630 PRINT"Y = ";P;"X - ";Q
640 PRINT:PRINT"IF Y = ";Y-Q;" THEN SOLVE FOR X"
650 PRINT:INPUTA1
660 IFA1=XTHEN680
670 GOTO880
680 GOTO850
690 REM Y=PX+Q
700 Y=P*X
710 PRINT"Y = ";P;"X + ";Q
720 PRINT:PRINT"IF Y = ";Y+Q;" THEN SOLVE FOR X"
730 PRINT:INPUTA1
740 IFA1=XTHEN760
750 GOTO880
760 GOTO850
770 REM X=PY+Q
780 X=P*Y+Q
790 PRINT"X = ";P;"Y + ";Q
800 PRINT:PRINT"IF Y = ";Y;" THEN SOLVE FOR X"
810 PRINT:INPUTA1
820 IFA1=XTHEN840
830 GOTO880
840 REM CORRECT
850 PRINT"CORRECT":GOSUB500
860 S=S+1
870 GOTO250
880 PRINT
890 PRINT"INCORRECT":GOSUB500
900 T=T+1:IFT=3THEN920
910 GOTO220
920 PRINT"THE CORRECT ANSWER IS ";X
930 GOSUB500
940 GOTO250
950 REM X=PY
960 X=P*Y
970 PRINT"X = ";P;"Y"
980 GOTO800
990 REM X=PY-Q
1000 X=P*Y-Q
1010 PRINT"X = ";P;"Y - ";Q
1020 GOTO800
```

CHAPTER 5

Memory Challenger II: Random Letters

The Memory Challenger II is a game used to test your memory and concentration. It generates and displays random letters (A–Z) of different lengths. You must enter the letters that are flashed on the screen. The program is written in BASIC for your microcomputer. See Program 5-1 for the program listing.

THE PROGRAM

The program begins by accepting entry of the difficulty level. Enter a 1 for easy, 2 for medium difficulty, or 3 for most difficult. Letters will be displayed from slow to fast, depending on the difficulty level; 1 is the slowest and 3 is the quickest.

After entering a 1 to begin, GET READY will be printed at the top center of the display. Then a set of random letters will be displayed at a random location on the screen, for a short period. Enter the letters that were displayed. The correct answer is displayed, and CORRECT or INCORRECT is printed. Then the number of correct answers out of the number of tries is displayed. Finally, TRY AGAIN will be displayed; and you have a choice of playing again at the same difficulty level, playing again at another difficulty level, or ending the test. When you decide to end the test, your final percent score will be displayed. See Fig. 5-1 for a sample run.

```
MEMORY CHALLENGER II: RANDOM LETTERS
COPYRIGHT (C) 1981 BY HOWARD BERENBON

THE PROGRAM GENERATES & DISPLAYS RANDOM
LETTERS OF DIFFERENT LENGTHS. ENTER
THE LETTERS THAT ARE FLASHED AT RANDOM
LOCATIONS ON THE SCREEN.

ENTER DIFFICULTY LEVEL:
1=EASY
2=MEDIUM DIFFICULTY
3=MOST DIFFICULT
? 2


ENTER '1' TO BEGIN
? 1



                         GET READY



                 PFOZ

                    DIFFICULTY LEVEL  2
ENTER LETTERS
? PFOZ
THE ANSWER IS 'PFOZ'


CORRECT
YOU HAVE  1  CORRECT OUT OF  1  TRIES

TRY AGAIN?
1 = YES & SAME DIFFICULTY-**GET READY**
2 = YES & CHANGE DIFFICULTY
0 = NO
? 1


                         GET READY



                                          PCDH

                    DIFFICULTY LEVEL  2
ENTER LETTERS
? PCDH
THE ANSWER IS 'PCDH'

CORRECT
YOU HAVE  2  CORRECT OUT OF  2  TRIES

TRY AGAIN?
1 = YES & SAME DIFFICULTY-**GET READY**
2 = YES & CHANGE DIFFICULTY
0 = NO
? 0

YOUR FINAL SCORE IS  100  PERCENT
```

Fig. 5-1. Memory Challenger II: Random Letters sample run.

Program 5-1. Memory Challenger II: Random Letters Program Listing

```
100 CLS:PRINT"MEMORY CHALLENGER II: RANDOM LETTERS"
110 PRINT"TRS-80 LEV 2":CLEAR 100
120 PRINT"COPYRIGHT (C) 1981 BY HOWARD BERENBON"
130 PRINT:DIMF$(6)
140 PRINT"THE PROGRAM GENERATES & DISPLAYS RANDOM"
150 PRINT"LETTERS OF DIFFERENT LENGTHS. ENTER"
160 PRINT"THE LETTERS THAT ARE FLASHED AT RANDOM"
170 PRINT"LOCATIONS ON THE SCREEN."
180 PRINT:RANDOM
190 Z=0
200 W=0
210 PRINT"ENTER DIFFICULTY LEVEL:"
220 PRINT"1=EASY"
230 PRINT"2=MEDIUM DIFFICULTY"
240 PRINT"3=MOST DIFFICULT"
250 INPUT A
260 CLS
270 IF A=1 THEN 600
280 IF A=2 THEN 640
290 IF A=3 THEN 680
300 GOTO 210
310 CLS
320 IFD=1THEN340
330 PRINT"ENTER '1' TO BEGIN":INPUTB
340 FORT=1TO5
350 F$(T)=""
360 NEXTT
370 CLS
380 PRINT @ 217,"GET READY"
390 FOR D=1 TO 200
400 NEXT D
410 CLS
420 GOSUB870
430 K=RND(900)
440 PRINT@K,G$
450 GOSUB 720
460 CLS
470 PRINT TAB(20)"DIFFICULTY LEVEL ";A
480 PRINT"ENTER LETTERS"
490 Z=Z+1
500 INPUT C$
510 PRINT"THE ANSWER IS '";G$;"'"
520 PRINT
530 IF G$=C$ THEN 570
540 PRINT"INCORRECT"
550 PRINT"YOU HAVE ";W;" CORRECT OUT OF ";Z;" TRIES"
560 GOTO 770
570 PRINT"CORRECT"
580 W=W+1
590 GOTO 550
600 G=35
610 F=2
620 N=RND(200)
```

```
630 GOTO 320
640 N=RND(150)
650 G=45
660 F=4
670 GOTO 320
680 N=RND(100)
690 G=30
700 F=5
710 GOTO 320
720 FOR E=1 TO G+N
730 NEXT E
740 RETURN
750 PRINT"YOUR FINAL SCORE IS ";INT(W/Z*100);" PERCENT"
760 END
770 PRINT
780 PRINT"TRY AGAIN?"
790 PRINT"1 = YES & SAME DIFFICULTY-**GET READY**"
800 PRINT"2 = YES & CHANGE DIFFICULTY"
810 PRINT"0 = NO"
820 INPUT D
830 IF D=1 THEN 260
840 IF D=2 THEN 210
850 IF D=0 THEN 750
860 GOTO 770
870 F$(0)=""
880 FORT=1TOF
890 X=RND(26)
900 FORB=1TOX
910 READ F$(0)
920 NEXTB
930 F$(T)=F$(0)
940 RESTORE
950 NEXTT
960 G$=F$(1)+F$(2)+F$(3)+F$(4)+F$(5)
970 RETURN
980 DATA A,B,C,D,E,F,G,H,I,J,K,L,M
990 DATA N,O,P,Q,R,S,T,U,V,W,X,Y,Z
```

CHAPTER 6

Memory Challenger III: Random Words

The Memory Challenger III is another game used to test your memory and concentration. It's similar to the Memory Challenger II of Chapter 5, except that it displays random words taken from DATA statements beginning at line 1000. You must enter the word that is flashed at a random location on the screen. The program is written in BASIC for your microcomputer. See Program 6-1 for the program listing.

THE PROGRAM

The program begins by accepting entry of the difficulty level. Enter a 1 for easy, 2 for medium difficulty, or 3 for most difficult. Words will be displayed from slow to fast, depending on the difficulty level; 1 is the slowest and 3 is the quickest.

After entering a 1 to begin, GET READY will be printed at the top center of the display. Then a word is displayed at a random location on the screen for a short period. Enter the word that was displayed. The correct answer is displayed, and CORRECT or INCORRECT is printed. Then the number of correct answers out of the number of tries is displayed. Finally, TRY AGAIN will be displayed; and you have a choice of playing again at the same difficulty level, playing again at another difficulty level, or ending the test. When you decide to end the test, your final percent score will be displayed. See Fig. 6-1 for a sample run.

THE WORD LIST

The word list begins at program line 1000. Its content is arbitrary, with no specific purpose in mind. It may be changed, but the choice of words is up to you. They can be just random words with no apparent connection, or they can be words relating to a specific subject.

To enter a new word list, type in a set of 50 words, in DATA statements, beginning at line 1000. Limit the word length to no longer than six characters, otherwise the word may be too difficult to catch when displayed at difficulty levels 2 and 3. Alternately, you may enter longer words, but limit the difficulty level to level 1.

```
MEMORY CHALLENGER III: RANDOM WORDS
COPYRIGHT (C) 1981 BY HOWARD BERENBON

MEMORY CHALLENGER III IS USED TO TEST
YOUR MEMORY. IT DISPLAYS WORDS RANDOMLY
FROM A LIST OF 50 WORDS, LOCATED IN DATA
STATEMENTS BEGINNING AT 1000. EACH WORD
WILL APPEAR AT A RANDOM LOCATION ON THE
SCREEN. ENTER THE WORD THAT WAS FLASHED
ON THE SCREEN.

ENTER DIFFICULTY LEVEL:
1=EASY
2=MEDIUM DIFFICULTY
3=MOST DIFFICULT
? 2


ENTER '1' TO BEGIN
? 1



                        GET READY




      SALUTE





                     DIFFICULTY LEVEL  2
ENTER THE WORD
? SALUTE
THE ANSWER IS 'SALUTE'

CORRECT
YOU HAVE  1  CORRECT OUT OF  1  TRIES
```

```
TRY AGAIN?
1 = YES & SAME DIFFICULTY-**GET READY**
2 = YES & CHANGE DIFFICULTY
0 = NO
? 1



                          GET READY




                                          KIND


                    DIFFICULTY LEVEL  2
ENTER THE WORD
? KIND
THE ANSWER IS 'KIND'

CORRECT
YOU HAVE  2  CORRECT OUT OF  2  TRIES

TRY AGAIN?
1 = YES & SAME DIFFICULTY-**GET READY**
2 = YES & CHANGE DIFFICULTY
0 = NO
? 0


YOUR FINAL SCORE IS  100  PERCENT
```

Fig. 6-1. Memory Challenger III: Random Words sample run.

Program 6-1. Memory Challenger III: Random Words Program Listing

```
100 CLS:PRINT"MEMORY CHALLENGER III: RANDOM WORDS"
105 PRINT"TRS-80 LEV 2"
110 PRINT"COPYRIGHT (C) 1981 BY HOWARD BERENBON"
120 PRINT
125 PRINT"MEMORY CHALLENGER III IS USED TO TEST"
130 PRINT"YOUR MEMORY. IT DISPLAYS WORDS RANDOMLY"
140 PRINT"FROM A LIST OF 50 WORDS, LOCATED IN DATA"
145 PRINT"STATEMENTS BEGINNING AT 1000. EACH WORD"
150 PRINT"WILL APPEAR AT A RANDOM LOCATION ON THE"
155 PRINT"SCREEN. ENTER THE WORD THAT WAS FLASHED"
160 PRINT"ON THE SCREEN."
170 Z=0
180 W=0
190 PRINT"ENTER DIFFICULTY LEVEL:"
200 PRINT"1=EASY"
210 PRINT"2=MEDIUM DIFFICULTY"
220 PRINT"3=MOST DIFFICULT"
230 INPUT A
240 CLS
250 IF A=1 THEN 550
260 IF A=2 THEN 590
270 IF A=3 THEN 630
280 GOTO 190
290 CLS
300 IFD=1THEN330
310 PRINT"ENTER '1' TO BEGIN":INPUTB
330 CLS
340 PRINT @ 217,"GET READY"
350 FOR D=1 TO 200
360 NEXT D
370 GOSUB820
380 CLS
385 R=RND(900)
390 PRINT@R,G$
400 GOSUB 670
410 CLS
420 PRINT TAB(20)"DIFFICULTY LEVEL ";A
430 PRINT"ENTER THE WORD"
440 Z=Z+1
450 INPUT C$
460 PRINT"THE ANSWER IS '";G$;"'"
470 PRINT
480 IF G$=C$ THEN 520
490 PRINT"INCORRECT"
500 PRINT"YOU HAVE ";W;" CORRECT OUT OF ";Z;" TRIES"
510 GOTO 720
520 PRINT"CORRECT"
530 W=W+1
540 GOTO 500
550 REM DIFFICULTY LEVELS
560 G=75
570 N=RND(200)
580 GOTO 300
```

```
590 N=RND(150)
600 G=35
620 GOTO 300
630 N=RND(100)
640 G=30
660 GOTO 300
670 FOR E=1 TO G+N
680 NEXT E
690 RETURN
700 PRINT"YOUR FINAL SCORE IS ";INT(W/Z*100);" PERCENT"
710 END
720 PRINT
730 PRINT"TRY AGAIN?"
740 PRINT"1 = YES & SAME DIFFICULTY-**GET READY**"
750 PRINT"2 = YES & CHANGE DIFFICULTY"
760 PRINT"0 = NO"
770 INPUT D
780 IF D=1 THEN 240
790 IF D=2 THEN 190
800 IF D=0 THEN 700
810 GOTO 720
820 X=RND(50)
830 FORT=1TOX
840 READG$
845 NEXTT
850 RESTORE
860 RETURN
1000 DATA ABOVE,ACID,ADMIT,BARGE,BEAR
1010 DATA CAKE,CAR,COW,DODGE,DUST
1020 DATA EDIT,EGG,EVICT,FIRE,FLASH
1030 DATA GAME,GATE,GOLD,HEAT,HEAVY
1040 DATA INCISE,INFANT,INTO,JUST,JUDGE
1050 DATA KNOW,KIND,LADY,LAUGH,LEAVE
1060 DATA MAGIC,MARK,NICE,NEW,PANE
1070 DATA QUART,QUICK,RAFT,RADIO,SALUTE
1080 DATA TREE,THRUST,ULTRA,UNTIL,VEST
1090 DATA WELL,WHITE,YOUNG,ZOOM,ZINC
```

CHAPTER 7

Perception Testing: Eidetic Imagery

Here's a program that may be used in perception testing. It will test for the ability to form eidetic images. Eidetic imagery is the ability of the mind to form an almost photographic image of an object. A recalled eidetic image is a visual sensation and should be perfect. (A very accurate description is not necessarily eidetic.) The program is written in BASIC for your microcomputer. See Program 7-1 for the program listing.

THE PROGRAM

The program will generate two pictures, each made up of asterisks (*). When one is superimposed on the other, a recognizable pattern will result.

Enter a 1 to display the first picture. Study the picture and try to remember it. When you think you have memorized it, enter a 1 to display the second picture. This will erase the first picture and display the second. Now, try to recall the first picture and superimpose its pattern on the second. If you think you can identify what you have seen, then enter the answer at the keyboard. Otherwise enter NO. See Fig. 7-1 for a sample run.

A person that has the ability to form eidetic images will immediately recognize what he or she sees, and the answer will become apparent.

```
PERCEPTION TESTING
EIDETIC IMAGERY
COPYRIGHT (C) 1980 BY HOWARD BERENBON

THIS PROGRAM WILL TEST YOU FOR
THE ABILITY TO FORM EIDETIC IMAGES.
IT WILL GENERATE TWO PICTURES, WHICH
YOU MUST TRY TO MEMORIZE. IF YOU
CAN IDENTIFY THE IMAGE FORMED BY
SUPERIMPOSING THE 1ST ON THE 2ND
THEN ENTER THE ANSWER.

ENTER '1' TO DISPLAY 1ST
PICTURE
? 1


 ****
*
*
*
*  **
*

*
*    *
 ** *

TRY TO MEMORIZE THIS PICTURE
```

```
ENTER '1' TO DISPLAY 2ND
PICTURE
? 1


*
     *
     *
     *
 **
     *
*    *
     *

*  *

NOW TRY TO RECALL THE 1ST PICTURE AND
SUPERIMPOSE ITS PATTERN ON THE 2ND.

ENTER '1' TO CONTINUE
? 1


IF YOU CAN IDENTIFY WHAT YOU
HAVE SEEN, THEN ENTER YOUR
ANSWER AT THE KEYBOARD.

OTHERWISE ENTER 'NO'.
?
```

Fig. 7-1. Perception Testing: Eidetic Imagery sample run.

Program 7-1. Perception Testing: Eidetic Imagery Program Listing

```
100 CLS:PRINT"PERCEPTION TESTING"
110 PRINT"EIDETIC IMAGERY"
120 PRINT"COPYRIGHT (C) 1980 BY HOWARD BERENBON"
130 PRINT"TRS-80"
140 PRINT
150 PRINT"THIS PROGRAM WILL TEST YOU FOR"
160 PRINT"THE ABILITY TO FORM EIDETIC IMAGES."
170 PRINT"IT WILL GENERATE TWO PICTURES, WHICH"
180 PRINT"YOU MUST TRY TO MEMORIZE. IF YOU"
190 PRINT"CAN IDENTIFY THE IMAGE FORMED BY"
200 PRINT"SUPERIMPOSING THE 1ST ON THE 2ND"
210 PRINT"THEN ENTER THE ANSWER."
220 PRINT
230 PRINT"ENTER '1' TO DISPLAY 1ST"
240 PRINT"PICTURE"
250 INPUTA:CLS
260 GOSUB760
270 PRINT
280 PRINT"TRY TO MEMORIZE THIS PICTURE"
290 PRINT
300 PRINT"ENTER '1' TO DISPLAY 2ND"
310 PRINT"PICTURE"
320 INPUTA:CLS
330 GOSUB870
340 PRINT
350 PRINT"NOW TRY TO RECALL THE 1ST PICTURE AND"
360 PRINT"SUPERIMPOSE ITS PATTERN ON THE 2ND."
370 PRINT
380 PRINT"ENTER '1' TO CONTINUE"
390 INPUTA:CLS
400 PRINT
410 PRINT"IF YOU CAN IDENTIFY WHAT YOU"
420 PRINT"HAVE SEEN, THEN ENTER YOUR"
430 PRINT"ANSWER AT THE KEYBOARD."
440 PRINT
450 PRINT"OTHERWISE ENTER 'NO'."
460 INPUTA$
470 IFA$="B"THEN640
480 IFA$="NO"THEN520
490 PRINT
500 CLS:PRINT"YOUR ENTRY IS INCORRECT . ."
510 PRINT
520 PRINT"FROM THE ABOVE TEST, THERE IS"
530 PRINT"NO INDICATION THAT YOU HAVE THE"
540 PRINT"ABILITY TO FORM EIDETIC IMAGES."
550 GOSUB570
560 GOTO630
570 PRINT
580 PRINT"THE PATTERN SEEN WHEN THE TWO"
590 PRINT"PICTURES ARE SUPERIMPOSED"
600 PRINT"FORMS THE LETTER 'B'."
610 PRINT
620 RETURN
```

```
630 END
640 PRINT
650 CLS:PRINT"CORRECT"
660 GOSUB570
670 PRINT
680 PRINT"THERE IS AN INDICATION"
690 PRINT"THAT YOU HAVE THE ABILITY"
700 PRINT"TO FORM EIDETIC IMAGES."
710 PRINT
720 PRINT"FURTHER TESTING IS RECOMMENDED,"
730 PRINT"TO VERIFY THIS CONCLUSION."
740 PRINT
750 GOTO630
760 PRINT" ****"
770 PRINT"*"
780 PRINT"*"
790 PRINT"*"
800 PRINT"*  **"
810 PRINT"*"
820 PRINT
830 PRINT"*"
840 PRINT"*    *"
850 PRINT" ** *"
860 RETURN
870 PRINT"*"
880 PRINT"     *"
890 PRINT"     *"
900 PRINT"     *"
910 PRINT" **"
920 PRINT"     *"
930 PRINT"*    *"
940 PRINT"     *"
950 PRINT
960 PRINT"*  *"
970 RETURN
```

CHAPTER 8

Presidents of the United States

This program tests your knowledge of the Presidents of the United States. It displays a list of Presidents giving their number, name, party, and first year of term. Then, a ten-question test may be taken. The problems are randomly generated from the list of forty Presidents. The program is written in BASIC for your microcomputer. See Program 8-1 for the program listing.

THE PROGRAM

You may review the list of Presidents by entering a 1. Entering a 2 will generate the ten-question test. Each question will display the President's number, his name, and his political party (abbreviated using initials). It requires entry of the first year of the term of office. CORRECT will be displayed if your entry is correct. If your entry is incorrect, then INCORRECT will be displayed along with the correct answer.

After all ten questions are answered, your final score will be displayed, with the number correct out of ten and your percent score. You may now review the list and take another test, or end the program. Four ten-question tests can be taken before any of the questions will be repeated. See Fig. 8-1 for a sample run.

```
PRESIDENTS OF THE UNITED STATES
COPYRIGHT (C) 1980 BY HOWARD BERENBON

HERE'S AN EDUCATIONAL PROGRAM THAT TESTS
YOUR KNOWLEDGE OF THE PRESIDENTS. IT
DISPLAYS A LIST OF THE PRESIDENTS GIVING
THEIR #, NAME, PARTY, AND FIRST YEAR OF
TERM. THEN, A 10 QUESTION QUIZ  MAY BE
TAKEN. RANDOMLY, A NAME OF A PRESIDENT
IS DISPLAYED. YOU MUST ENTER THE FIRST
YEAR OF THAT TERM.

ENTER A  '1' TO REVIEW THE LIST
ENTER A  '2' TO TAKE THE TEST
? 2


10 QUESTION PRESIDENT QUIZ

ENTER '1' TO BEGIN THE TEST
? 1


QUESTION #  1   PRESIDENTS QUIZ

PRESIDENT OF THE UNITED STATES

PRESIDENT #  31
HERBERT C. HOOVER (R)

1ST YEAR OF TERM?
(ENTER YEAR)
? 1929
CORRECT


QUESTION #  2   PRESIDENTS QUIZ

PRESIDENT OF THE UNITED STATES

PRESIDENT #  32
FRANKLIN D. ROOSEVELT (D)

1ST YEAR OF TERM?
(ENTER YEAR)
? 1933
CORRECT


QUESTION #  3   PRESIDENTS QUIZ

PRESIDENT OF THE UNITED STATES

PRESIDENT #  4
JAMES MADISON (DR)

1ST YEAR OF TERM?
(ENTER YEAR)
? 1809
CORRECT


QUESTION #  10   PRESIDENTS QUIZ

PRESIDENT OF THE UNITED STATES

PRESIDENT #  39
JAMES E. CARTER, JR. (D)

1ST YEAR OF TERM?
(ENTER YEAR)
? 1977
CORRECT


FINAL SCORE
 10  QUESTIONS CORRECT OUT OF 10
THAT'S  100  % CORRECT

ANOTHER QUIZ  AND REVIEW THE LIST?
ENTER  1-YES  2-NO
? 1
```

Fig. 8-1. Presidents of The United States sample run.

Program 8-1. Presidents of the United States Program Listing

```
100 CLS:PRINT"PRESIDENTS OF THE UNITED STATES"
110 PRINT"TRS-80 LEVEL II"
120 PRINT"COPYRIGHT (C) 1980 BY HOWARD BERENBON"
130 PRINT:DIMB(50):GOSUB1150
140 PRINT"HERE'S AN EDUCATIONAL PROGRAM THAT TESTS"
150 PRINT"YOUR KNOWLEDGE OF THE PRESIDENTS. IT"
160 PRINT"DISPLAYS A LIST OF THE PRESIDENTS GIVING"
170 PRINT"THEIR #, NAME, PARTY, AND FIRST YEAR OF"
180 PRINT"TERM. THEN, A 10 QUESTION QUIZ MAY BE"
190 PRINT"TAKEN. RANDOMLY, A NAME OF A PRESIDENT"
200 PRINT"IS DISPLAYED. YOU MUST ENTER THE FIRST"
210 PRINT"YEAR OF THAT TERM."
220 PRINT:Q3=0
230 PRINT"ENTER A  '1' TO REVIEW THE LIST"
240 PRINT"ENTER A  '2' TO TAKE THE TEST"
250 INPUT A
260 IF A=1 THEN 290
270 IF A=2 THEN 410
280 GOTO 230
290 CLS:REM REVIEW THE LIST
300 FOR B=1 TO 40
310 CLS
320 PRINT"PRESIDENT #","NAME AND PARTY      ","1ST YEAR OF TERM"
330 PRINT
340 READ A$,E
350 PRINT B,A$,E
360 GOSUB 920
370 NEXT B
380 RESTORE
390 PRINT
400 GOTO 230
410 CLS:REM 10 QUESTION QUIZ
420 PRINT"10 QUESTION PRESIDENT QUIZ"
430 PRINT
440 PRINT"ENTER '1' TO BEGIN THE TEST"
450 INPUT A
460 CLS
470 IF A=1 THEN 490
480 GOTO 440
490 REM DISPLAY NAME
500 CA=0
510 FOR A=1 TO 10
520 CLS
530 PRINT"QUESTION # ";A,"PRESIDENTS QUIZ"
540 PRINT:GOSUB1190
550 Q=RND(40)
560 IFB(Q)=1THEN550
570 B(Q)=1
580 FORA1=1TOQ
590 READA$,E
600 NEXTA1
610 RESTORE
620 PRINT"PRESIDENT OF THE UNITED STATES"
```

```
630 PRINT
640 PRINT"PRESIDENT # ";Q
650 PRINT A$
660 PRINT
670 PRINT"1ST YEAR OF TERM?"
680 PRINT"(ENTER YEAR)"
690 INPUT F
700 IF F=E THEN 760
710 GOSUB 900
720 PRINT"THE CORRECT YEAR IS ";E
730 GOSUB 920
740 NEXT A
750 GOTO 800
760 PRINT"CORRECT"
770 CA=CA+1
780 GOSUB 920
790 NEXT A
800 CLS
810 PRINT"FINAL SCORE"
820 PRINTCA;" QUESTIONS CORRECT OUT OF 10"
830 PRINT"THAT'S ";10*CA;" % CORRECT"
840 PRINT
850 PRINT"ANOTHER QUIZ AND REVIEW THE LIST?"
860 PRINT"ENTER  1-YES  2-NO"
870 INPUT Y
880 IF Y=1 THEN 230
890 END
900 PRINT"INCORRECT"
910 RETURN
920 FOR T=1 TO 1000
930 NEXT T
940 RETURN
950 DATA "GEORGE WASHINGTON (F)",1789,"JOHN ADAMS (F)     ",1797
960 DATA "THOMAS JEFFERSON (DR)",1801,"JAMES MADISON (DR)",1809
970 DATA "JAMES MONROE (DR)",1817,"JOHN Q. ADAMS (DR)",1825
980 DATA "ANDREW JACKSON (D)",1829,"MARTIN VAN BUREN (D)",1837
990 DATA "WILLIAM H. HARRISON (W)",1841,"JOHN TYLER (W)     ",1841
1000 DATA "JAMES KNOX POLK (D)",1845,"ZACHARY TAYLOR (W)",1849
1010 DATA "MILLARD FILLMORE (W)",1850,"FRANKLIN PIERCE (D)",1853
1020 DATA "JAMES BUCHANAN (D)",1857,"ABRAHAM LINCOLN (R)",1861
1030 DATA "ANDREW JOHNSON (R)",1865,"ULYSSES S. GRANT (R)",1869
1040 DATA "RUTHERFORD B. HAYES (R)",1877,"JAMES A. GARFIELD (R)",1881
1050 DATA "CHESTER A. ARTHUR (R)",1881,"GROVER CLEVELAND (D)",1885
1060 DATA "BENJAMIN HARRISON (R)",1889,"GROVER CLEVELAND (D)",1893
1070 DATA "WILLIAM MCKINLEY (R)",1897,"THEODORE ROOSEVELT (R)",1901
1080 DATA "WILLIAM H. TAFT (R)",1909,"WOODROW WILSON (D)",1913
1090 DATA "WARREN G. HARDING (R)",1921,"CALVIN COOLIDGE (R)",1923
1100 DATA "HERBERT C. HOOVER (R)",1929,"FRANKLIN D. ROOSEVELT (D)",1933
1110 DATA "HARRY S. TRUMAN (D)",1945,"DWIGHT D. EISENHOWER (R)",1953
1120 DATA "JOHN F. KENNEDY (D)",1961,"LYNDON B. JOHNSON (D)",1963
1130 DATA "RICHARD M. NIXON (R)",1969,"GERALD R. FORD (R)",1974
1140 DATA "JAMES E. CARTER, JR. (D)",1977,"RONALD REAGAN (R)",1981
1150 FORI=1TO40
```

```
1160 B(I)=0
1170 NEXTI
1180 RETURN
1190 Q3=Q3+1
1200 IFQ3>40THENQ3=0:GOSUB1150
1210 RETURN
```

CHAPTER 9

State Capitals

This program tests your knowledge of the state capitals of the United States. For a review it displays a list of all fifty states and their capitals. Then a ten-question test may be taken. The program is written in BASIC for your microcomputer. See Program 9-1 for the program listing.

THE PROGRAM

After you run the program, you may enter a 1 to review the state capitals, enter a 2 to take the ten-question test, or enter a 3 to end the program.

After you enter a 2 to take the test, enter a 1 to begin. You are required to enter the name of the state capital for the state that is displayed. CORRECT will be displayed for a correct entry. If your answer is incorrect, then INCORRECT will be displayed, along with the correct answer. When all ten questions are answered, your final score will be displayed, with the number correct out of ten and the percent score. You may now review the states, take another test, or end the program. Five tests may be taken without any of the questions being repeated.

See Fig 9-1 for a sample run.

```
STATE CAPITALS
COPYRIGHT (C) 1980 BY HOWARD BERENBON

THIS PROGRAM TESTS YOUR KNOWLEDGE
OF STATE CAPITALS. IT GIVES A TEN
QUESTION QUIZ , RANDOMLY CHOOSING
THE QUESTIONS. THE LIST OF STATES AND
CAPITALS MAY BE REVIEWED BEFORE TAKING
THE TEST.

ENTER 1-REVIEW STATE CAPITALS
      2-FOR TEST
      3-END PROGRAM
? 2

10 QUESTION STATE CAPITAL TEST

ENTER '1' TO BEGIN
? 1

QUESTION #  1  STATE CAPITALS

THE STATE IS: MASSACHUSETTS

ENTER ITS CAPITAL
? BOSTON

CORRECT

QUESTION #  2  STATE CAPITALS

THE STATE IS: WASHINGTON

ENTER ITS CAPITAL
? OLYMPIA

CORRECT

QUESTION #  3  STATE CAPITALS

THE STATE IS: DELAWARE

ENTER ITS CAPITAL
? DOVER

CORRECT

QUESTION #  10  STATE CAPITALS

THE STATE IS: CONNECTICUT

ENTER ITS CAPITAL
? HARTFORD

CORRECT

FINAL SCORE:
 10  QUESTIONS CORRECT OUT OF 10
THAT'S  100  % CORRECT

ENTER 1-REVIEW STATE CAPITALS
      2-FOR TEST
      3-END PROGRAM
? 1
```

Fig. 9-1. State Capitals sample run.

Program 9-1. State Capitals Program Listing

```
100 CLS:PRINT"STATE CAPITALS"
110 PRINT"COPYRIGHT (C) 1980 BY HOWARD BERENBON"
120 PRINT"TRS-80 LEV 2":Q3=0
130 PRINT:CLEAR60:DIMB(50):GOSUB1100
140 PRINT"THIS PROGRAM TESTS YOUR KNOWLEDGE"
150 PRINT"OF STATE CAPITALS. IT GIVES A TEN"
160 PRINT"QUESTION QUIZE, RANDOMLY CHOOSING"
170 PRINT"THE QUESTIONS. THE LIST OF STATES AND"
180 PRINT"CAPITALS MAY BE REVIEWED BEFORE TAKING"
190 PRINT"THE TEST."
200 PRINT
210 PRINT"ENTER 1-REVIEW STATE CAPITALS"
220 PRINTTAB(6)"2-FOR TEST"
230 PRINTTAB(6)"3-END PROGRAM"
240 INPUTA
250 ONAGOTO270,420,800
260 GOTO200
270 CLS:PRINT"REVIEWING THE STATES"
280 GT=2:GOSUB380
290 FORA=1TO50
300 READ S$,C$
310 PRINT"STATE","CAPITAL"
320 PRINT
330 PRINTS$,C$
340 GT=2:GOSUB380
350 NEXTA
360 RESTORE
370 GOTO200
380 FORT=1TO400*GT
390 NEXTT
400 CLS
410 RETURN
420 CLS:PRINT"10 QUESTION STATE CAPITAL TEST"
430 PRINT
440 PRINT"ENTER '1' TO BEGIN"
450 INPUTD
460 CLS
470 IFD=1THEN490
480 GOTO430
490 CA=0
500 FORQ=1TO10
510 CLS:PRINT"QUESTION # ";Q;" STATE CAPITALS"
520 PRINT:GOSUB810
530 R=RND(50)
540 IFB(R)=1THEN530
550 B(R)=1
560 FORH=1TOR
570 READS$,C$
580 NEXTH
590 RESTORE
600 PRINT"THE STATE IS: ";S$
610 PRINT
620 PRINT"ENTER ITS CAPITAL"
```

```
630 INPUTC1$
640 IFC1$=C$THEN710
650 PRINT
660 PRINT"INCORRECT"
670 PRINT"THE CAPITAL OF ";S$;" IS '";C$;"'"
680 GT=3:GOSUB380
690 NEXTQ
700 GOTO750
710 PRINT
720 PRINT"CORRECT"
730 CA=CA+1
740 GOTO680
750 CLS:PRINT"FINAL SCORE:"
760 PRINTCA;" QUESTIONS CORRECT OUT OF 10"
770 PRINT"THAT'S ";10*CA;" % CORRECT"
780 GT=3:GOSUB380
790 GOTO200
800 END
810 Q3=Q3+1
820 IFQ3>50THENQ3=0:GOTO840
830 RETURN
840 GOSUB1100:RETURN
850 DATA ALABAMA,MONTGOMERY,ALASKA,JUNEAU
860 DATA ARIZONA,PHOENIX,ARKANSAS,LITTLE ROCK
870 DATA CALIFORNIA,SACRAMENTO,COLORADO,DENVER
880 DATA CONNECTICUT,HARTFORD,DELAWARE,DOVER
890 DATA FLORIDA,TALLAHASSEE,GEORGIA,ATLANTA
900 DATA HAWAII,HONOLULU,IDAHO,BOISE
910 DATA ILLINOIS,SPRINGFIELD,INDIANA,INDIANAPOLIS
920 DATA IOWA,DES MOINES,KANSAS,TOPEKA
930 DATA KENTUCKY,FRANKFORT,LOUISIANA,BATON ROUGE
940 DATA MAINE,AUGUSTA,MARYLAND,ANNAPOLIS
950 DATA MASSACHUSETTS,BOSTON,MICHIGAN,LANSING
960 DATA MINNESOTA,ST. PAUL,MISSISSIPPI,JACKSON
970 DATA MISSOURI,JEFFERSON CITY,MONTANA,HELENA
980 DATA NEBRASKA,LINCOLN,NEVADA,CARSON CITY
990 DATA NEW HAMPSHIRE,CONCORD,NEW JERSEY,TRENTON
1000 DATA NEW MEXICO,SANTA FE,NEW YORK,ALBANY
1010 DATA NORTH CAROLINA,RALEIGH,NORTH DAKOTA,BISMARCK
1020 DATA OHIO,COLUMBUS,OKLAHOMA,OKLAHOMA CITY
1030 DATA OREGON,SALEM,PENNSYLVANIA,HARRISBURG
1040 DATA RHODE ISLAND,PROVIDENCE,SOUTH CAROLINA,COLUMBIA
1050 DATA SOUTH DAKOTA,PIERRE,TENNESSEE,NASHVILLE
1060 DATA TEXAS,AUSTIN,UTAH,SALT LAKE CITY
1070 DATA VERMONT,MONTPELIER,VIRGINIA,RICHMOND
1080 DATA WASHINGTON,OLYMPIA,WEST VIRGINIA,CHARLESTON
1090 DATA WISCONSIN,MADISON,WYOMING,CHEYENNE
1100 FORI=1TO50
1110 B(I)=0
1120 NEXTI
1130 RETURN
```

CHAPTER 10

The Student Grader

The Student Grader is a program designed to aid the teacher. It will accept entry of each student's individual grades, and it will display each set of grades with their average. It will also display the class average for any number of students in the list. The program is written in BASIC for your microcomputer. See Program 10-1 for the program listing.

THE PROGRAM

The program accepts entry of the student's grades, in DATA statements, beginning at line 500. Enter each student's name, each grade in percent (separated by commas), and the number 999, which is used to detect the end of each student's grades. After the whole list of students' grades is entered, DATA "END" must be entered as the last DATA statement in the list. The following are examples of DATA statement entries:

```
550 DATA TOM SMITH,86,78,79,88,80,999
560 DATA MIKE ROSS,78,88,90,90,85,83,999
```

Each of the students' grade lists may have a different number of percent scores. The program calculates the average score on the number of grades in each student's DATA statement.

After you run the program, enter a 1 to begin. The program will display each of the student's grades, and the average grade, for all of the students in the list. The program will also display the class average, calculated by adding each average grade of each student and dividing by the total number of students.

See Fig. 10-1 for a sample run.

```
THE STUDENT GRADER
COPYRIGHT (C) 1980 BY HOWARD BERENBON



THIS PROGRAM WILL AID THE TEACHER
IN RECORDING AND GRADING TEST SCORES.

ENTER EACH STUDENT'S NAME AND GRADES
IN DATA STATEMENTS BEGINNING AT LINE
500. ENTER AS FOLLOWS:
DATA NAME,60,70,80,78,79,67,999
999 MUST BE THE LAST NUMBER, WHICH
DETECTS THE END OF THE GRADES. ALSO,
DATA 'END' MUST BE THE LAST DATA
STATEMENT IN THE DATA LIST.

ENTER A '1' TO BEGIN
? 1

THE STUDENT GRADER

NAME      GRADE(%)

RICK  86    78    85    79    88    80    AVE= 83
BRUCE  78    80    78    90    91    78    AVE= 83
DAVE  89    88    87    67    68    90    AVE= 82
MIKE  56    60    67    56    80    70    AVE= 65

CLASS AVERAGE WITH  4  STUDENTS
IS  78  PERCENT
```

Fig. 10-1. The Student Grader sample run.

Program 10-1. The Student Grader Program Listing

```
100 CLS:PRINT"THE STUDENT GRADER"
110 PRINT"COPYRIGHT (C) 1980 BY HOWARD BERENBON"
120 PRINT"TRS-80 LEV 2"
130 PRINT:PRINT:GOSUB480
140 PRINT"THIS PROGRAM WILL AID THE TEACHER"
150 PRINT"IN RECORDING AND GRADING TEST SCORES."
160 PRINT
170 PRINT"ENTER EACH STUDENT'S NAME AND GRADES"
180 PRINT"IN DATA STATEMENTS BEGINNING AT LINE"
190 PRINT"500. ENTER AS FOLLOWS:"
200 PRINT"DATA NAME,60,70,80,78,79,67,999"
210 PRINT"999 MUST BE THE LAST NUMBER, WHICH"
220 PRINT"DETECTS THE END OF THE GRADES. ALSO,"
230 PRINT"DATA 'END' MUST BE THE LAST DATA"
240 PRINT"STATEMENT IN THE DATA LIST."
250 PRINT
260 PRINT"ENTER A '1' TO BEGIN"
270 INPUTS
280 CLS:N=0:C=0
290 N1=0:C1=0
300 PRINT"THE STUDENT GRADER"
310 PRINT
320 PRINT"NAME";TAB(10)"GRADE(%)"
330 PRINT
340 READA$:IFA$="END"THEN440
350 PRINTA$;" ";
360 READB:IFB=999THEN410
370 PRINTB;" ";
380 N=N+1
390 C=B+C
400 GOTO360
410 S1=INT((C/N)+.5):PRINT" AVE=";S1:GOSUB480
420 C1=S1+C1:N=0:C=0:N1=N1+1
430 GOTO340
440 RESTORE:PRINT
450 A1=INT((C1/N1)+.5):PRINT"CLASS AVERAGE WITH ";N1;" STUDENTS"
460 PRINT"IS ";A1;" PERCENT"
470 END
480 FORT=1TO900
490 NEXTT:RETURN
500 DATA "RICK",86,78,85,79,88,80,999
510 DATA "BRUCE",78,80,78,90,91,78,999
520 DATA "DAVE",89,88,87,67,68,90,999
530 DATA "MIKE",56,60,67,56,80,70,999
540 DATA "END"
```

CHAPTER 11

Relativistic Mass Simulation

Here's a scientific program using Einstein's theory of relativity. It takes the formula for the mass of a body in motion as it relates to the speed of light, and allows an interesting simulation. The program will display the change in mass for an object traveling at a given velocity, having a rest mass of m_o. It is written in BASIC for your microcomputer. See Program 11-1 for the program listing.

THE PROGRAM

The program creates the relativistic mass simulation using Einstein's equation:

$$m = \frac{m_o}{\sqrt{1 - v^2/c^2}}$$

where

m is the mass of the moving object,
m_o is the mass of the object at rest,
v is the velocity of the object,
c is the speed of light (2.997925×10^8 meters/second).

It allows the entry of the rest mass, m_o, of a given object, and its velocity, v. Enter the mass of the object in kilograms, and its velocity in meters per second. The program displays the mass of the object at rest, the mass at the velocity entered, the change in mass, and the percent change in mass.

Entering a small velocity will display no apparent change in mass. But as you increase the velocity, the change will become noticeable. When your test velocity approaches the speed of light, the mass change will become more apparent. The program will accept entry of any initial mass value, but it will limit the velocity entry to less than the speed of light, following Einstein's Special Theory of Relativity.

After the simulation is complete, enter a 1 to continue with the same mass and different velocity, enter a 2 to continue the simulation with a different mass, enter a 3 for a new simulation, or enter a 4 to end the program.

See Fig. 11-1 for a sample run.

```
RELATIVISTIC MASS SIMULATION
COPYRIGHT (C) 1980 BY HOWARD BERENBON

THIS PROGRAM  WILL DISPLAY THE
CHANGE IN MASS FOR AN OBJECT
TRAVELING AT A GIVEN VELOCITY,
HAVING A REST MASS OF M0.
IT USES EINSTEIN'S RELATIONSHIP
THAT THE MASS OF AN OBJECT
INCREASES AS ITS VELOCITY INCREASES

ENTER THE NAME OF THE OBJECT
IN THE SIMULATION
? SPACE CAPSULE


ENTER THE MASS AT REST (KG)
FOR THE OBJECT 'SPACE CAPSULE'
? 2724

ENTER SIMULATED VELOCITY (M/S)
FOR THE OBJECT 'SPACE CAPSULE'
? 20000

GIVEN THE OBJECT: SPACE CAPSULE
WITH A REST MASS OF  2724  KG

THE MASS OF THE OBJECT:
SPACE CAPSULE-AT  20000  M/S IS
 2724  KG

THE INCREASE IN MASS IS
 0  KG, OR  0  %

ENTER 1-CONT. SIMULATION-SAME MASS
      2-CONT. SIMULATION-DIFF. MASS
      3-NEW SIMULATION
      4-END PROGRAM
? 1

ENTER THE SIMULATED VELOCITY (M/S)
FOR THE OBJECT 'SPACE CAPSULE'
? 2200000

GIVEN THE OBJECT: SPACE CAPSULE
WITH A REST MASS OF  2724  KG

THE MASS OF THE OBJECT:
SPACE CAPSULE-AT  2.2E+06  M/S IS
 2724.07  KG

THE INCREASE IN MASS IS
 .0732422  KG, OR  2.68877E-03  %

ENTER 1-CONT. SIMULATION-SAME MASS
      2-CONT. SIMULATION-DIFF. MASS
      3-NEW SIMULATION
      4-END PROGRAM
? 1


ENTER THE SIMULATED VELOCITY (M/S)
FOR THE OBJECT 'SPACE CAPSULE'
? 2.24E+08


GIVEN THE OBJECT: SPACE CAPSULE
WITH A REST MASS OF  2724  KG

THE MASS OF THE OBJECT:
SPACE CAPSULE-AT  2.24E+08  M/S IS
 4098.6  KG

THE INCREASE IN MASS IS
 1374.6  KG, OR  50.4624  %

ENTER 1-CONT. SIMULATION-SAME MASS
      2-CONT. SIMULATION-DIFF. MASS
      3-NEW SIMULATION
      4-END PROGRAM
? 4
```

Fig. 11-1. Relativisitc Mass Simulation sample run.

Program 11-1. Relativistic Mass Simulation Program Listing

```
LIST PORTFO (P):LPRINT CHR$(11)
100 CLS:CLEAR 100
110 PRINT"RELATIVISTIC MASS SIMULATION"
120 PRINT"COPYRIGHT (C) 1980 BY HOWARD BERENBON"
130 PRINT"TRS-80 LEV 2"
140 PRINT:C=2.997925E+8
150 PRINT"THIS PROGRAM  WILL DISPLAY THE"
160 PRINT"CHANGE IN MASS FOR AN OBJECT"
170 PRINT"TRAVELING AT A GIVEN VELOCITY,"
180 PRINT"HAVING A REST MASS OF MO."
190 PRINT"IT USES EINSTEIN'S RELATIONSHIP"
200 PRINT"THAT THE MASS OF AN OBJECT"
210 PRINT"INCREASES AS ITS VELOCITY INCREASES"
220 PRINT
230 PRINT"ENTER THE NAME OF THE OBJECT"
240 PRINT"IN THE SIMULATION"
250 INPUTA$
260 PRINT
270 PRINT"ENTER THE MASS AT REST (KG)"
280 PRINT"FOR THE OBJECT '";A$;"'"
290 INPUTM
300 PRINT
310 PRINT"ENTER THE SIMULATED VELOCITY (M/S)"
320 PRINT"FOR THE OBJECT '";A$;"'"
330 INPUTV
340 IFV>=CTHEN570
350 V2=V*V
360 CLS:C2=C*C
370 PRINT"GIVEN THE OBJECT: ";A$
380 PRINT"WITH A REST MASS OF ";M;" KG"
390 Q=SQR(1-(V2/C2))
400 MR=M/Q:T=MR-M
410 PRINT
420 PRINT"THE MASS OF THE OBJECT:"
430 PRINTA$;"-AT ";V;" M/S IS"
440 PRINTMR;" KG"
450 PRINT
460 PRINT"THE INCREASE IN MASS IS"
470 PRINTT;" KG";:GOSUB650
480 PRINT
490 PRINT"ENTER 1-CONT. SIMULATION-SAME MASS"
500 PRINTTAB(6)"2-CONT. SIMULATION-DIFF. MASS"
510 PRINTTAB(6)"3-NEW SIMULATION"
520 PRINTTAB(6)"4-END PROGRAM"
530 INPUTT
540 ONTGOTO300,260,110,560
550 GOTO480
560 END
570 PRINT
580 PRINT"EINSTEIN SAID THAT NO OBJECT CAN"
590 PRINT"TRAVEL EQUAL TO OR GREATER THAN"
600 PRINT"THE SPEED OF LIGHT."
610 PRINT
```

```
620 PRINT"ENTER A VELOCITY LESS THAN THE"
630 PRINT"SPEED OF LIGHT."
640 GOTO300
650 P=(T/M)*100
660 PRINT", OR ";P;" %"
670 RETURN
```

SECTION II

Home Applications

This section describes some useful home application programs including a monthly budget program, a valuables inventory, a telephone number directory, a special date calendar, a weekly calendar, gas and water usage analysis, electrical appliance operating cost analysis, family dental expenses, weekly jogging record, and, finally, a cost of food analysis.

CHAPTER 12

Monthly Budget

Here's a program that will help you budget your household expenses. It accepts entry of your monthly net wage and individual expenses to calculate the amount available to save. The program is written in BASIC for your microcomputer. See Program 12-1 for the program listing.

THE PROGRAM

The program begins by requesting the month number (1–12) for analysis. Then it requests your monthly net wage. Next, you are required to enter all monthly expenses, under the following categories:

1. Rent, or house payment
2. Utility expenses
   a. Telephone bill
   b. Electric bill
   c. Gas or oil costs
   d. Water bill
3. Garbage pickup
4. Monthly food bills
5. Clothing, shoes, linen
6. Drugstore purchases
7. Medical expenses
8. Bank charges
9. House expenses
10. Automobile expenses
11. Entertainment expenses
12. Miscellaneous expenses

The monthly food bill category allows entry of individual food bills, for that month. Entering a 999 allows you to advance to the next category. All other categories accept only one expense entry per month.

After all your monthly expenses are entered, the program calculates the total expense for that month. It then displays the month number, monthly wage (allowed budget amount), and your total monthly expense.

The difference between your total monthly expense and your monthly budget amount is calculated and displayed. If you spent less during the month than your budget allows, then it is recommended that the amount left over be saved. If you are over your monthly budget, then this will be noted.

See Fig. 12-1 for a sample run.

```
MONTHLY BUDGET
COPYRIGHT (C) 1980 BY HOWARD BERENBON

THE MONTHLY BUDGET PROGRAM WILL
HELP YOU BUDGET YOUR HOUSEHOLD
EXPENSES. ENTER YOUR MONTHLY NET
WAGE, OR AMOUNT ALLOWED, AND TOTAL
MONTHLY EXPENSES. THE AMOUNT LEFT
OVER AFTER ALL BILLS ARE PAID WILL
BE THE AMOUNT AVAILABLE TO SAVE.

ENTER MONTH # (1-12)
? 4


ENTER MONTHLY NET WAGE (BUDGET AMT)
? 816


ENTER MONTHLY STATISTICS

RENT OR HOUSE PAYMENT
? 300

UTILITY EXPENSES

TELEPHONE
? 10
ELECTRIC
? 15
GAS OR OIL
? 15
WATER
? 4

GARBAGE PICKUP
? 10


MONTHLY FOOD BILLS
1 BILL PER ENTRY
(ENTER 999 TO STOP)
# 1
? 75
MONTHLY FOOD BILLS
1 BILL PER ENTRY
(ENTER 999 TO STOP)
# 2
? 999



ENTER MONTHLY STATISTICS

CLOTHING, SHOES, LINEN
? 24
DRUG STORE PURCHASES
? 15
MEDICAL EXPENSES
(DOCTOR, DENTIST, ETC.)
? 25
BANK CHARGES
? 0
HOUSE EXPENSES (INSURANCE, REPAIRS, ETC)
? 10

AUTOMOBILE EXPENSES
(REPAIRS, GAS, ETC.)
? 50
ENTERTAINMENT (MOVIES, PLAYS, DINNERS
BOOKS, MAGAZINES, ETC.)
? 85
MISCELLANEOUS EXPENSES
? 25


MONTHLY BUDGET STATISTICS FOR
MONTH # 4

MONTHLY WAGE OR ALLOWED AMT=$ 816

YOUR TOTAL MONTHLY EXPENSE
IS $ 663

YOU SPENT LESS IN MONTH # 4 , AND
HAVE $ 153  LEFT OVER TO SAVE.
```

Fig. 12-1. Monthly Budget sample run.

Program 12-1. Monthly Budget Program Listing

```
100 CLS:PRINT"MONTHLY BUDGET"
110 PRINT"COPYRIGHT (C) 1980 BY HOWARD BERENBON"
120 PRINT"TRS-80"
130 PRINT
140 PRINT"THE MONTHLY BUDGET PROGRAM WILL"
150 PRINT"HELP YOU BUDGET YOUR HOUSEHOLD"
160 PRINT"EXPENSES. ENTER YOUR MONTHLY NET"
170 PRINT"WAGE, OR AMOUNT ALLOWED, AND TOTAL"
180 PRINT"MONTHLY EXPENSES. THE AMOUNT LEFT"
190 PRINT"OVER AFTER ALL BILLS ARE PAID WILL"
200 PRINT"BE THE AMOUNT AVAILABLE TO SAVE."
210 PRINT
220 PRINT"ENTER MONTH # (1-12)"
230 INPUTN:IFN<1ORN>12THEN210
240 PRINT
250 PRINT"ENTER MONTHLY NET WAGE (BUDGET AMT)"
260 INPUTW
270 GOSUB890
280 PRINT"RENT OR HOUSE PAYMENT"
290 INPUTR:PRINT
300 PRINT"UTILITY EXPENSES"
310 PRINT
320 PRINT"TELEPHONE"
330 INPUTT
340 PRINT"ELECTRIC"
350 INPUTE
360 PRINT"GAS OR OIL"
370 INPUTG
380 PRINT"WATER"
390 INPUTWA
400 PRINT"GARBAGE PICKUP"
410 INPUTGA
420 CLS:F=0:FC=1
430 PRINT"MONTHLY FOOD BILLS"
440 PRINT"1 BILL PER ENTRY"
450 PRINT"(ENTER 999 TO STOP)"
460 PRINT"#";FC
470 FC=FC+1
480 INPUTFD:IFFD=999THEN510
490 PRINT:F=FD+F
500 GOTO430
510 GOSUB890
520 PRINT"CLOTHING, SHOES, LINEN"
530 INPUTCL
540 PRINT"DRUG STORE PURCHASES"
550 INPUTDR
560 PRINT"MEDICAL EXPENSES"
570 PRINT"(DOCTOR, DENTIST, ETC.)"
580 INPUTM
590 PRINT"BANK CHARGES"
600 INPUTBC
610 PRINT"HOUSE EXPENSES (INSURANCE, REPAIRS, ETC)"
620 INPUTHR
```

```
630 PRINT"AUTOMOBILE EXPENSES"
640 PRINT"(REPAIRS, GAS, ETC.)"
650 INPUTAU
660 PRINT"ENTERTAINMENT (MOVIES, PLAYS, DINNERS"
670 PRINT"BOOKS, MAGAZINES, ETC.)"
680 INPUTEN
690 PRINT"MISCELLANEOUS EXPENSES"
700 INPUTMS
710 REM CALCULATE EXPENSES
720 TL=R+T+E+G+WA+GA+F+CL+DR+M+BC+HR+AU+EN+MS
730 CLS
740 BU=W-TL
750 PRINT"MONTHLY BUDGET STATISTICS FOR"
760 PRINT"MONTH #";N
770 PRINT
780 PRINT"MONTHLY WAGE OR ALLOWED AMT=$";W
790 PRINT
800 PRINT"YOUR TOTAL MONTHLY EXPENSE"
810 PRINT"IS $";TL
820 PRINT:IFTL>WTHEN860
830 PRINT"YOU SPENT LESS IN MONTH #";N;", AND"
840 PRINT"HAVE $";BU;" LEFT OVER TO SAVE."
850 GOTO880
860 ET=TL-W
870 PRINT"YOU SPENT $";ET;" OVER YOUR BUDGET"
880 END
890 CLS:PRINT"ENTER MONTHLY STATISTICS"
900 PRINT
910 RETURN
```

CHAPTER 13

Valuables Inventory

The Valuables Inventory program keeps a list of your valuables, including the name of each item and its price. It is useful for keeping a record of your valuables for insurance purposes. The program is written in BASIC for your microcomputer. See Program 13-1 for the program listing.

THE PROGRAM

The valuables data must be entered into DATA statements, beginning at line 850. Enter the items in the following format:

DATA CATEGORY #,NAME,PRICE

or

850 DATA 1,BRACELET,225

The category number is a number from 1 to 6. It represents the following types of items:

1—Gold, silver, jewelry
2—Appliances
3—Furniture
4—Clothing
5—Collectables (art, antiques, etc.)
6—Miscellaneous

Each item should have its own data statement with the category number, its name, and its value entered. After all items are entered, then DATA 9999,0,0 must be the last DATA statement in the list.

After running the program, enter a 1 to begin. The program calculates and displays the cumulative total worth of your valuables. Then you have the option of listing the items, prices, and cumulative total for each category separately (1–6), display the total list, or end the program. Enter a 7 to display the total list, or an 8 to end the program. See Fig. 13-1 for a sample run.

IDENTIFICATION NUMBER

Use the DATA statement line number as an identification number (ID) for each item in your valuables list. Engrave the statement number, if possible, to the corresponding item. In case of a fire or theft, you have a record of each item, with its separate ID number. Keep a cassette copy of the program, with the inventory data list, in a safety deposit box for insurance purposes.

```
VALUABLES INVENTORY
COPYRIGHT (C) 1980 BY HOWARD BERENBON

THIS PROGRAM WILL KEEP A LIST
OF YOUR VALUABLES, AND ALLOW YOU
TO DISPLAY A PARTIAL OR FULL LIST
WITH EACH ITEM NAME, VALUE, AND
CUMULATIVE VALUE. ENTER THE ITEMS
IN DATA STATEMENTS BEGINNING AT
LINE 850, IN THE FOLLOWING FORMAT:
DATA CATEGORY,NAME,PRICE
DATA 1,BRACELET,225
DATA 9999,0,0 IS THE LAST STATEMENT
ENTER '1' TO BEGIN
? 1


ENTER CATEGORY #
1-GOLD, SILVER, JEWELRY
2-APPLIANCES
3-FURNITURE
4-CLOTHING
5-COLLECTABLES
6-MISCELLANEOUS
7-TOTAL LIST
8-END PROGRAM

? 5


5
COLLECTABLES

ITEM            PRICE           CUM. TOTAL
OIL PAINTING     1700            1700
WATER COLOR      190             1890



6
MISCELLANEOUS

ITEM            PRICE           CUM. TOTAL
BICYCLE          175             175
CHESS SET        200             375
```

Fig. 13-1. Valuables Inventory sample run.

Program 13-1. Valuables Inventory Program Listing

```
100 CLS:PRINT"VALUABLES INVENTORY"
110 PRINT"COPYRIGHT (C) 1980 BY HOWARD BERENBON"
120 PRINT"TRS-80 LEV 2"
130 PRINT
140 PRINT"THIS PROGRAM WILL KEEP A LIST"
150 PRINT"OF YOUR VALUABLES, AND ALLOW YOU"
160 PRINT"TO DISPLAY A PARTIAL OR FULL LIST"
170 PRINT"WITH EACH ITEM NAME, VALUE, AND"
180 PRINT"CUMULATIVE VALUE. ENTER THE ITEMS"
190 PRINT"IN DATA STATEMENTS BEGINNING AT"
200 PRINT"LINE 850, IN THE FOLLOWING FORMAT:"
210 PRINT"DATA CATEGORY,NAME,PRICE"
220 PRINT"DATA 1,BRACELET,225"
230 PRINT"DATA 9999,0,0 IS THE LAST STATEMENT"
240 PRINT"ENTER '1' TO BEGIN"
250 INPUTA:CLS
260 RESTORE:IFB=7THENA=A+1:PRINT:GOTO400
270 IFT>0THENPRINT"CUM. TOTAL =$";T
280 PRINT:PRINT"ENTER CATEGORY #"
290 T=0:C=0:E=0
300 PRINT"1-GOLD, SILVER, JEWELRY"
310 PRINT"2-APPLIANCES"
320 PRINT"3-FURNITURE"
330 PRINT"4-CLOTHING"
340 PRINT"5-COLLECTABLES"
350 PRINT"6-MISCELLANEOUS"
360 PRINT"7-TOTAL LIST"
370 PRINT"8-END PROGRAM"
380 PRINT
390 INPUTA:IFA=7THENB=7
400 IFB=7THENE=E+1:IFE=7THEN730
410 ONAGOTO460,500,540,580,620,660,700,730
420 GOTO280
430 FORG=1TO900
440 NEXTG
450 RETURN
460 PRINT:PRINT"GOLD, SILVER, JEWELRY"
470 GOSUB750
480 GOSUB780
490 GOTO260
500 PRINT"APPLIANCES"
510 GOSUB750
520 GOSUB780
530 GOTO260
540 PRINT"FURNITURE"
550 GOSUB750
560 GOSUB780
570 GOTO260
580 PRINT"CLOTHING"
590 GOSUB750
600 GOSUB780
610 GOTO260
620 PRINT"COLLECTABLES"
```

```
630 GOSUB750
640 GOSUB780
650 GOTO260
660 PRINT"MISCELLANEOUS"
670 GOSUB750
680 GOSUB780
690 GOTO260
700 PRINT"TOTAL LIST"
710 A=1:E=1
720 GOTO410
730 END
740 REM TABLE
750 PRINT
760 PRINT"ITEM","PRICE","CUM. TOTAL"
770 RETURN
780 READ C,D$,P
790 IFC=9999THENRETURN
800 IFC<>ATHEN780
810 T=P+T
820 PRINT D$,P,T
830 GOSUB430
840 GOTO780
850 DATA 1,"SILVERWARE",1500
860 DATA 1,"GOLD BRACELET",500
870 DATA 5,"OIL PAINTING",1700
880 DATA 4,"MINK COAT",1200
890 DATA 2,"COLOR TV",540
900 DATA 3,"COUCH",1195
910 DATA 3,"CHAIR",875
920 DATA 3,"DINING TABLE",880
930 DATA 2,"STEREO",695
940 DATA 1,"WATCH",295
950 DATA 6,"BICYCLE",175
960 DATA 5,"WATER COLOR",190
970 DATA 2,"COMPUTER",3500
980 DATA 2,"WASHER/DRYER",700
990 DATA 2,"BW TV",95
1000 DATA 6,"CHESS SET",200
1010 DATA 4,"COATS",450
1020 DATA 4,"SHOES",275
1030 DATA 3,"DESK",250
1040 DATA 9999,0,0
```

CHAPTER 14

Telephone Number Directory

The Telephone Number Directory will list names and telephone numbers from your list of names and numbers in DATA statements. The program is written in BASIC for your microcomputer. See Program 14-1 for the program listing.

THE PROGRAM

The program requires that your name and phone number list is stored in DATA statements beginning at line 660. Enter as follows:

DATA NAME,PHONE #

or

660 DATA SMITH,555-1212

The statement DATA END,0 must be the last DATA statement in your list. The size of your phone number list is limited only by your computer's RAM size.

After you run the program, you may display individual numbers by entering an N, display your whole list by entering an L, or end the program by entering an E. If you wish to display individual names and numbers, the computer will request your desired name entry. Enter the name as it appears in the list. The computer will search the list, comparing the name entered with the names in your list. When the name is found, the computer will display that name with its corresponding telephone number. You may now access another number or discontinue this function. If the name entered is not in the list, the computer will display ENTRY NOT FOUND. Entering an N will return the program to the main input routine, allowing access to individual numbers or the whole list. See Fig. 14-1 for a sample run.

```
TELEPHONE NUMBER DIRECTORY
COPYRIGHT (C) 1980 BY HOWARD BERENBON

THIS PROGRAM WILL LIST NAMES &
TELEPHONE NUMBERS FROM YOUR LIST
LOCATED IN DATA STATEMENTS
BEGINNING AT PROGRAM LINE 660.
ENTER THE DATA AS FOLLOWS:
DATA NAME,NUMBER
DATA SMITH,555-1212
THE LAST DATA STATEMENT IN THE
LIST MUST BE: DATA END,0



TELEPHONE # DIRECTORY


ENTER 'N' DISPLAY INDIVIDUAL #'S
      'L' DISPLAY FULL LIST
      'E' END PROGRAM
? N




TELEPHONE # DIRECTORY

ENTER NAME
? DAVE
SEARCHING LIST FOR 'DAVE'

NAME            PHONE NUMBER

DAVE            555-1963

ANOTHER ENTRY?
ENTER 'Y'-YES
      'N'-NO
?
```

Fig. 14-1. Telephone Number Directory sample run.

Program 14-1. Telephone Number Directory Program Listing

```
100 CLS:PRINT"TELEPHONE NUMBER DIRECTORY"
110 PRINT"COPYRIGHT (C) 1980 BY HOWARD BERENBON"
120 PRINT"TRS-80 LEV 2"
130 PRINT
140 PRINT"THIS PROGRAM WILL LIST NAMES &"
150 PRINT"TELEPHONE NUMBERS FROM YOUR LIST"
160 PRINT"LOCATED IN DATA STATEMENTS"
170 PRINT"BEGINNING AT PROGRAM LINE 660."
180 PRINT"ENTER THE DATA AS FOLLOWS:"
190 PRINT"DATA NAME,NUMBER"
200 PRINT"DATA SMITH,555-1212"
210 PRINT"THE LAST DATA STATEMENT IN THE"
220 PRINT"LIST MUST BE: DATA END,0"
230 FORT=1TO4600
240 NEXTT:GOSUB330
250 PRINT:RESTORE
260 PRINT"ENTER 'N' DISPLAY INDIVIDUAL #'S"
270 PRINTTAB(6)"'L' DISPLAY FULL LIST"
280 PRINTTAB(6)"'E' END PROGRAM"
290 INPUTB$
300 IFB$="N"THEN370
310 IFB$="L"THEN570
320 END
330 CLS
340 PRINT"TELEPHONE # DIRECTORY"
350 PRINT
360 RETURN
370 GOSUB330
380 PRINT"ENTER NAME"
390 INPUTA$
400 PRINT"SEARCHING LIST FOR '";A$;"'":PRINT
410 READC$,D$
420 IFC$="END"THEN450
430 IFC$=A$THEN480
440 GOTO410
450 PRINT"ENTRY NOT FOUND"
460 RESTORE
470 GOTO500
480 PRINT"NAME","PHONE NUMBER":PRINT
490 PRINTC$,D$
500 PRINT
510 PRINT"ANOTHER ENTRY?"
520 PRINT"ENTER 'Y'-YES"
530 PRINTTAB(6)"'N'-NO"
540 INPUTB$
550 IFB$="Y"THEN370
560 GOTO250
570 GOSUB330:PRINT"NAME","PHONE NUMBER":PRINT
580 READC$,D$
590 IFC$="END"THEN250
600 PRINTC$,D$
610 GOSUB630
620 GOTO580
```

Program 14-1—cont. Telephone Number Directory Program Listing

```
630 FORT=1TO1000
640 NEXTT
650 RETURN
660 DATA RICK,555-5219
670 DATA BRUCE,555-1694
680 DATA DAVE,555-1963
690 DATA HARRY,555-1282
700 DATA END,0
```

CHAPTER 15

Special Date Calendar

The Special Date Calendar is a program that displays monthly dates and names, which are taken from DATA statements. It's useful in keeping track of your special dates and occasions. The program is written in BASIC for your microcomputer. See Program 15-1 for the program listing.

THE PROGRAM

Enter important dates and their occasion in DATA statements beginning at line 1000. Enter in the following format:

DATA MONTH,DAY,YEAR,OCCASION

or

1000 DATA 1,6,51,RICK'S BIRTHDAY

The statement DATA 999,0,0,0 must be the last DATA statement in the list.

After you run the program, enter the month number (1–12) to be displayed. The program will display each date and occasion in the month entered. After all the data for that month is displayed, you may display another month or end the program. See Fig. 15-1 for a sample run.

```
SPECIAL DATE CALENDAR
COPYRIGHT (C) 1980 BY HOWARD BERENBON

THIS PROGRAM WILL DISPLAY MONTHLY
DATES AND NAMES, SO YOU CAN KEEP
TRACK OF SPECIAL DATES AND OCCASIONS

ENTER IMPORTANT DATES IN DATA
STATEMENTS BEGINNING AT LINE
1000, AS IN THE FOLLOWING FORMAT:
DATA MO,DAY,YR,OCCASION
DATA 1,6,51,RICK'S BIRTHDAY
DATA 999,0,0,0 MUST BE THE LAST
DATA STATEMENT IN YOUR LIST


ENTER MONTH # (1-12)
TO BE DISPLAYED
? 1


SPECIAL DATE CALENDAR: MONTH  1

DATE            OCCASION

 1 / 6 / 51     RICK'S BIRTHDAY
 1 / 11 / 50     HARRY'S BIRTHDAY

ANOTHER MONTH FOR DISPLAY?
1-YES  0-NO
?
```

Fig. 15-1. Special Date Calendar sample run.

Program 15-1. Special Data Calendar Program Listing

```
100 CLS:CLEAR 500
110 PRINT"SPECIAL DATE CALENDAR"
120 PRINT"TRS-80 LEV 2"
130 PRINT"COPYRIGHT (C) 1980 BY HOWARD BERENBON"
140 PRINT
150 PRINT"THIS PROGRAM WILL DISPLAY MONTHLY"
160 PRINT"DATES AND NAMES, SO YOU CAN KEEP"
170 PRINT"TRACK OF SPECIAL DATES AND OCCASIONS"
180 PRINT
190 PRINT"ENTER IMPORTANT DATES IN DATA"
200 PRINT"STATEMENTS BEGINNING AT LINE"
210 PRINT"1000, AS IN THE FOLLOWING FORMAT:"
220 PRINT"DATA MO,DAY,YR,OCCASION"
230 PRINT"DATA 1,6,51,RICK'S BIRTHDAY"
240 PRINT"DATA 999,0,0,0 MUST BE THE LAST"
250 PRINT"DATA STATEMENT IN YOUR LIST"
260 GOSUB520
270 PRINT
280 PRINT"ENTER MONTH # (1-12)"
290 PRINT"TO BE DISPLAYED"
300 INPUTM
310 IFM<1THEN270
320 IFM>12THEN270
330 M=INT(M):CLS
340 PRINT"SPECIAL DATE CALENDAR: MONTH ";M
350 PRINT
360 PRINT"DATE";TAB(16)"OCCASION"
370 PRINT
380 READA,B,C,A$
390 IFA=999THEN450
400 IFA=MTHEN420
410 GOTO380
420 PRINTA;"/";B;"/";C;"   ";A$
430 GOSUB520
440 GOTO380
450 RESTORE:PRINT
460 PRINT"ANOTHER MONTH FOR DISPLAY?"
470 PRINT"1-YES  0-NO"
480 INPUTP
490 IFP=1THEN270
500 END
510 PRINT
520 REM DELAY
530 FORT1=1TO900
540 NEXTT1
550 RETURN
1000 DATA 12,21,52,"BRUCE'S BIRTHDAY"
1010 DATA 8,31,49,"DAVID'S BIRTHDAY"
1020 DATA 1,6,51,"RICK'S BIRTHDAY"
1030 DATA 1,11,50,"HARRY'S BIRTHDAY"
1040 DATA 999,0,0,0
```

CHAPTER 16

Weekly Calendar

The Weekly Calendar program allows you to display a weekly calendar of events. It's useful in keeping track of your daily activities. The program is written in BASIC for your microcomputer. See Program 16-1 for the program listing.

THE PROGRAM

Enter your daily activity data in DATA statements beginning at line 670. Enter in the following format:

DATA DAY #,TIME,ACTIVITY

or

670 1,7-30AM,BREAKFAST

The first element is the day number, where 1 through 7 is Sunday through Saturday. The second element is the time, where a dash (–) is used in place of a colon (:); and the last element is the activity. Enter as many DATA statements, per day, as you have activities, and continue until all your weekly activities are entered. Finally, the statement DATA 99,0,0 must be the last DATA statement in your list.

After you run the program, enter the week date as MM/DD/YY, and the day number to be displayed. The program will display each activity for that day, and the time of the activity. After the data for that day is displayed, you may display another day or end the program. See Fig. 16-1 for a sample run.

```
WEEKLY CALENDAR
COPYRIGHT (C) 1980 BY HOWARD BERENBON

THIS PROGRAM ALLOWS YOU TO
DISPLAY A WEEKLY CALENDAR.
DAILY DATA IS ENTERED INTO DATA
STATEMENTS BEGINNING AT LINE
670. ENTER DAILY ACTIVITIES
AS FOLLOWS:
DATA  DAY #,TIME,ACTIVITY
DATA 1,7-30 AM,BREAKFAST
THE LAST DATA STATEMENT IN
THE LIST MUST BE: DATA 99,0,0


ENTER WEEK DATE
(MM/DD/YY)
? 5/3/81


5/3/81

ENTER DAY # FOR DISPLAY
1-SUN  2-MON  3-TUES  4-WED
5-THUR 6-FRI  7-SAT
? 1




WEEKLY CALENDAR: WEEK DATE 5/3/81

SUNDAY

TIME            ACTIVITY

7-30            BREAKFAST
12              LUNCH
8-00            MOVIE

DISPLAY ANOTHER DAY?
1-YES  0-NO
? 0
```

Fig. 16-1. Weekly Calendar sample run.

Program 16-1. Weekly Calendar Program Listing

```
100 CLS:PRINT"WEEKLY CALENDAR":CLEAR500
110 PRINT"COPYRIGHT (C) 1980 BY HOWARD BERENBON"
120 PRINT"TRS-80 LEV 2"
130 PRINT
140 PRINT"THIS PROGRAM ALLOWS YOU TO"
150 PRINT"DISPLAY A WEEKLY CALENDAR."
160 PRINT"DAILY DATA IS ENTERED INTO DATA"
170 PRINT"STATEMENTS BEGINNING AT LINE"
180 PRINT"670. ENTER DAILY ACTIVITIES"
190 PRINT"AS FOLLOWS:"
200 PRINT"DATA  DAY #,TIME,ACTIVITY"
210 PRINT"DATA 1,7-30 AM,BREAKFAST"
220 PRINT"THE LAST DATA STATEMENT IN"
230 PRINT"THE LIST MUST BE: DATA 99,0,0"
240 PRINT:GOSUB440:GOSUB470
250 PRINT:PRINT"ENTER DAY # FOR DISPLAY"
260 PRINT"1-SUN  2-MON  3-TUES  4-WED"
270 PRINT"5-THUR 6-FRI  7-SAT"
280 INPUTD
290 IFD<1THEN250
300 IFD>7THEN250
310 CLS:PRINT"WEEKLY CALENDAR: WEEK DATE ";W$
320 PRINT
330 READD1,T$,A$
340 IFD1=DTHEN610
350 IFD1=99THEN370
360 GOTO330
370 PRINT:PRINT"NO ACTIVITY DATA FOR DAY ";D;": ";
380 GOSUB510
390 RESTORE:PRINT
400 PRINT"DISPLAY ANOTHER DAY?"
410 PRINT"1-YES  0-NO":INPUTAA
420 IFAA=1THEN250
430 END
440 FORA=1TO900
450 NEXTA
460 RETURN
470 PRINT"ENTER WEEK DATE"
480 PRINT"(MM/DD/YY)"
490 INPUTW$
500 RETURN
510 IFD=1THENPRINT"SUNDAY"
520 IFD=2THENPRINT"MONDAY"
530 IFD=3THENPRINT"TUESDAY"
540 IFD=4THENPRINT"WEDNESDAY"
550 IFD=5THENPRINT"THURSDAY"
560 IFD=6THENPRINT"FRIDAY"
570 IFD=7THENPRINT"SATURDAY"
580 PRINT:RETURN
590 PRINT"TIME","ACTIVITY"
600 RETURN
610 GOSUB510:GOSUB590:PRINT
620 PRINTT$,A$
```

```
630 GOSUB440
640 READD1,T$,A$
650 IFD1=DTHEN620
660 GOTO390
670 DATA 1,7-30,BREAKFAST
680 DATA 1,12,LUNCH
690 DATA 1,8-00,MOVIE
700 DATA 2,7-30,BREAKFAST
710 DATA 2,9-00,BUSINESS MEET
720 DATA 2,12,BUS. LUNCH
730 DATA 2,9-00,DINNER
740 DATA 99,0,0
```

CHAPTER 17

Gas Usage Analysis

Conservation is the key to reducing our energy consumption and costs, with the rising prices and pending shortages of all types of energy. You can help out by using the Gas Usage Analysis program. It will indicate differences in natural gas usage from one year to another, so that you can see possible imbalances in usage and correct them. The program is written in BASIC for your microcomputer. See Program 17-1 for the program listing.

THE PROGRAM

The program requires that your yearly natural gas usage data is stored in DATA statements at program lines 1000 and 1010. The first data element in line 1000 must be the comparison year (base year), followed by twelve months of gas usage units, beginning with January of that year. Program line 1010 holds the data for the "recent" year. Example:

```
1000 DATA 1977,310,268,225,110,76,60,25,28,29,100,
          260,290

1010 DATA 1981,296,282,207,141,58,63,29,27,51,123,
          233,270
```

The "base" year can be any past year, possibly the year that you moved into your house or apartment, or even the previous year. The "recent" year would be a full year's data for a recent energy consumption.

The program prints the "base" year data, including average units used per month, total units used, units used per month, and the percent of total units used per month. Then it prints the "recent" year's data, with a comparison with the "base" year. It gives the difference between the two years, with the monthly increase (+) or decrease (−) from the "base" year. See Fig. 17-1 for a sample run.

ANALYSIS

If there is a significant monthly increase in natural gas usage, pay close attention to those months. You may be using more energy than necessary. Check your insulation for possible air leaks. This leakage can cause your furnace to work overtime and use more gas than necessary. Other increases may be due to natural gas leaks. Have your natural gas appliances periodically checked for leaks; escaping gas can cause explosions and death.

```
GAS USAGE ANALYSIS
COPYRIGHT (C) 1981 BY HOWARD BERENBON

THIS PROGRAM WILL COMPARE AND DISPLAY
A 'BASE' YEAR AND 'RECENT' YEAR GAS
USAGE, IN UNITS.

ENTER THE 'BASE' YEAR DATA AT LINE 1000,
AND THE 'RECENT' YEAR DATA AT LINE 1010.

ENTER A '1' TO DISPLAY
THE 'BASE' YEAR DATA
? 1


BASE YEAR  1977                         AV/MO=  148.417
TOTAL UNITS=  1781
MONTH              UNITS                % TOTAL
 1                  310                  17.4
 2                  268                  15.04
 3                  225                  12.63
 4                  110                  6.17
 5                  76                   4.26
 6                  60                   3.36
 7                  25                   1.4
 8                  28                   1.57
 9                  29                   1.62
 10                 100                  5.61
 11                 260                  14.59
 12                 290                  16.28
ENTER '1' FOR COMPARISON? 1

RECENT YEAR  1981                       AV/MO=  148.333
TOTAL UNITS=  1780     RECENT-BASE= -1
MO.   UNITS    % TOTAL     + OR - FROM BASE
 1     296      16.62       -14
 2     282      15.84        14
 3     207      11.62       -18
 4     141      7.92         31
 5     58       3.25        -18
 6     63       3.53         3
 7     29       1.62         4
 8     27       1.51        -1
 9     51       2.86         22
 10    123      6.91         23
 11    233      13.08       -27
 12    270      15.16       -20
```

Fig. 17-1. Gas Usage Analysis sample run.

Program 17-1. Gas Usage Analysis Program Listing

```
100 CLS:DIM A(50)
110 PRINT"GAS USAGE ANALYSIS: TRS-80"
120 PRINT"COPYRIGHT (C) 1981 BY HOWARD BERENBON"
130 PRINT
140 PRINT"THIS PROGRAM WILL COMPARE AND DISPLAY"
150 PRINT"A 'BASE' YEAR AND 'RECENT' YEAR GAS"
160 PRINT"USAGE, IN UNITS."
170 PRINT
180 PRINT"ENTER THE 'BASE' YEAR DATA AT LINE 1000,"
190 PRINT"AND THE 'RECENT' YEAR DATA AT LINE 1010."
200 PRINT
210 PRINT"ENTER A '1' TO DISPLAY"
220 PRINT"THE 'BASE' YEAR DATA"
230 INPUT A
240 B=0:R=0
250 READ P
260 FOR E=1TO12
270 READ C
280 A(E)=C
290 B=A(E)+B
300 NEXT E
310 READ T
320 FOR E=13TO24
330 READ C
340 A(E)=C
350 R=A(E)+R
360 NEXT E
370 PRINT"BASE YEAR ";P,"AV/MO= ";B/12
380 PRINT"TOTAL UNITS= ";B
390 PRINT"MONTH","UNITS","% TOTAL"
400 FOR A=1TO12
410 PRINT A,A(A),INT(A(A)/B*10000)/100
420 NEXT A
430 PRINT"ENTER '1' FOR COMPARISON";
440 INPUT A
450 PRINT
460 PRINT
470 PRINT"RECENT YEAR ";T,"AV/MO= ";R/12
480 PRINT"TOTAL UNITS= ";R;"   RECENT-BASE= ";R-B
490 PRINT"MO.   UNITS    % TOTAL    + OR - FROM BASE"
500 FOR A=13TO24
510 PRINT A-12;TAB(6);A(A);TAB(15);INT(A(A)/R*10000)/100;TAB(26);A(A)-A(A-12)
520 NEXT A
530 GOTO 530
980 REM ENTER 'BASE' YEAR GAS DATA IN LINE 1000
990 REM ENTER 'RECENT' YEAR GAS DATA IN LINE 1010
1000 DATA 1977,310,268,225,110,76,60,25,28,29,100,260,290
1010 DATA 1981,296,282,207,141,58,63,29,27,51,123,233,270
```

CHAPTER 18

Water Usage Analysis

Here is a program that can help you reduce your water usage. (It's similar to the Gas Usage Analysis program in Chapter 17.) It will indicate differences in water usage from one year to another, so that you can see possible imbalances in usage and correct them. The program is written in BASIC for your microcomputer. See Program 18-1 for the program listing.

THE PROGRAM

The program requires that your yearly water usage data is stored in DATA statements at program lines 1000 and 1010. The first data element in line 1000 must be the comparison year (base year), followed by the four quarters of water usage units, beginning with January or February of that year. Program line 1010 holds the data for the "recent" year. Example:

```
1000 DATA 1977,15,19,19,18

1010 DATA 1981,14,17,14,17
```

The "base" year can be any past year, possibly the year that you moved into your house, or even the previous year. The "recent" year would be a full year's data for a recent water consumption.

The program prints the "base" year data, including average units used per quarter, total units used, units used per quarter, and the percent of total units used per quarter. Then it prints the "recent" year's data, with a comparison with the "base" year. It gives the difference between the two years, with the quarterly increase (+) or decrease (−) from the "base" year. See Fig. 18-1 for a sample run.

ANALYSIS

If there is a significant quarterly increase in water usage, pay close attention to those quarters. You may be using more water than necessary. Check your faucets and pipes for leaks. Replace worn washers or faucets and pipes if necessary.

```
WATER USAGE ANALYSIS
COPYRIGHT (C) 1981 BY HOWARD BERENBON

THIS PROGRAM WILL COMPARE AND DISPLAY
A 'BASE' YEAR AND 'RECENT' YEAR WATER
USAGE, IN UNITS.

ENTER THE 'BASE' YEAR DATA AT LINE 1000,
AND THE 'RECENT' YEAR DATA AT LINE 1010.

ENTER A '1' TO DISPLAY
THE 'BASE' YEAR DATA
? 1


BASE YEAR  1977                       AV/QU=  17.75
TOTAL UNITS=  71
QUART              UNITS              % TOTAL
 1                  15                 21.12
 2                  19                 26.76
 3                  19                 26.76
 4                  18                 25.35
ENTER '1' FOR COMPARISON? 1




RECENT YEAR  1981                     AV/QU=  15.5
TOTAL UNITS=  62     RECENT-BASE= -9
QU.    UNITS     % TOTAL     + OR - FROM BASE
 1      14        22.58       -1
 2      17        27.41       -2
 3      14        22.58       -5
 4      17        27.41       -1
```

Fig. 18-1. Water Usage Analysis sample run.

Program 18-1. Water Usage Analysis Program Listing

```
100 CLS:DIM A(10)
110 PRINT"WATER USAGE ANALYSIS: TRS-80"
120 PRINT"COPYRIGHT (C) 1981 BY HOWARD BERENBON"
130 PRINT
140 PRINT"THIS PROGRAM WILL COMPARE AND DISPLAY"
150 PRINT"A 'BASE' YEAR AND 'RECENT' YEAR WATER"
160 PRINT"USAGE, IN UNITS."
170 PRINT
180 PRINT"ENTER THE 'BASE' YEAR DATA AT LINE 1000,"
190 PRINT"AND THE 'RECENT' YEAR DATA AT LINE 1010."
200 PRINT
210 PRINT"ENTER A '1' TO DISPLAY"
220 PRINT"THE 'BASE' YEAR DATA"
230 INPUT A:CLS
240 B=0:R=0
250 READ P
260 FOR E=1TO4
270 READ C
280 A(E)=C
290 B=A(E)+B
300 NEXT E
310 READ T
320 FOR E=5TO8
330 READ C
340 A(E)=C
350 R=A(E)+R
360 NEXT E
370 PRINT"BASE YEAR ";P,"AV/QU= ";B/4
380 PRINT"TOTAL UNITS= ";B
390 PRINT"QUART","UNITS","% TOTAL"
400 FOR A=1TO4
410 PRINT A,A(A),INT(A(A)/B*10000)/100
420 NEXT A
430 PRINT"ENTER '1' FOR COMPARISON";
440 INPUT A
450 PRINT
460 PRINT
470 PRINT"RECENT YEAR ";T,"AV/QU= ";R/4
480 PRINT"TOTAL UNITS= ";R;"   RECENT-BASE= ";R-B
490 PRINT"QU.   UNITS   % TOTAL    + OR - FROM BASE"
500 FOR A=5TO8
510 PRINT A-4;TAB(6);A(A);TAB(15);INT(A(A)/R*10000)/100;TAB(26);A(A)-A(A-4)
520 NEXT A
530 GOTO 530
980 REM ENTER 'BASE' YEAR WATER USAGE DATA IN LINE 1000
990 REM ENTER 'RECENT' YEAR WATER USAGE DATA IN LINE 1010
1000 DATA 1977,15,19,19,18
1010 DATA 1981,14,17,14,17
```

CHAPTER 19

Appliance Operating Cost Analysis

An interesting and useful application program for the home computer is the Appliance Operating Cost Analysis program. It's written in BASIC for your microcomputer. See Program 19-1 for the program listing.

THE PROGRAM

The program will calculate the cost of operating electrical appliances, given the number of watts they consume, the average number of hours of daily use, and the cost per kilowatt hour, for each appliance under analysis.

After you run the program, enter the number of appliances for analysis. Then enter the cost of electrical use per kilowatt-hour, in dollars. (Example: typically $0.065. Call your local power company for the exact amount. This will vary for different areas of the country.) The program will print APPLIANCE #1 and request the name of the first appliance (limit entry to eight characters). Enter the power consumed in watts and the average number of hours (or minutes) in daily use. The program is set to accept hours, but will accept minutes if 9999 is entered first. Then it will advance to accept data on the next appliance. After the last appliance data is entered, the analysis will begin.

The program then displays a table with the appliance name, watts consumed, operating cost per day, estimated cost per month, and the estimated kilowatt-hour use per month. This is repeated for each appliance. Finally, the program displays the total kilowatt-hours used and the total monthly cost for all appliances.

See Fig. 19-1 for a sample run.

ANALYSIS

The program will show you what operating each appliance costs. It may help you decide to use less of one or more appliances that require a lot of power to run, to save on energy costs.

Probably the most expensive electrical appliance to operate is the air conditioner. Proper home insulation will allow it to operate more efficiently. Also, raising the thermostat will reduce the amount of energy required to cool your home, thus reducing electricity costs.

The proper use of lighting can greatly reduce your electric bills. Make sure that all unnecessary lights are turned off. Also, the wattage of some of the light bulbs you use could be higher than necessary. Changing these bulbs to a lower wattage will reduce energy costs.

```
APPLIANCE OPERATING COST ANALYSIS
COPYRIGHT (C) 1980 BY HOWARD BERENBON

THIS PROGRAM WILL CALCULATE
THE COST OF OPERATING ELECTRICAL
APPLIANCES, GIVEN THE NUMBER OF
WATTS THEY CONSUME, THE AVERAGE
NUMBER OF HOURS OF DAILY USE,
AND THE COST PER KILOWATT HOUR
FOR EACH APPLIANCE UNDER ANALYSIS

ENTER THE # OF APPLIANCES
UNDER ANALYSIS
? 3


ENTER THE COST PER KILOWATT HOUR
(TYPICAL - $.065)
? .07←


APPLIANCE # 1
ENTER TYPE (NAME)
LIMIT TO 8 CHARACTERS
? COLOR TV

ENTER POWER CONSUMED IN WATTS
? 110

ENTER AVERAGE # OF HOURS IN
DAILY USE (MAY ENTER FRACTIONS).
IF YOU DESIRE TO ENTER MINUTES
THEN ENTER 9999
? 5


APPLIANCE # 2
ENTER TYPE (NAME)
LIMIT TO 8 CHARACTERS
? STEREO

ENTER POWER CONSUMED IN WATTS
? 200

ENTER AVERAGE # OF HOURS IN
DAILY USE (MAY ENTER FRACTIONS).
IF YOU DESIRE TO ENTER MINUTES
THEN ENTER 9999
? 3

APPLIANCE # 3
ENTER TYPE (NAME)
LIMIT TO 8 CHARACTERS
? LIGHTS

ENTER POWER CONSUMED IN WATTS
? 500

ENTER AVERAGE # OF HOURS IN
DAILY USE (MAY ENTER FRACTIONS).
IF YOU DESIRE TO ENTER MINUTES
THEN ENTER 9999
? 8


APPLIANCE OPERATING COST ANALYSIS

APPL.       WATTS     COST/DAY     COST/MO     KWHS/MO
COLOR TV     110       .0385        1.155       16.5
STEREO       200       .042         1.26        18
LIGHTS       500       .28          8.4         120

TOTAL KILOWATT HOURS USED PER MONTH
FOR  3  APPLIANCES IS  154.5  KWHOURS

TOTAL MONTHLY COST FOR  3
APPLIANCE(S) IS $ 10.82
```

Fig. 19-1. Appliance Operating Cost Analysis sample run.

Program 19-1. Appliance Operating Cost Analysis Program Listing

```
100 CLS:CLEAR 200
110 PRINT"APPLIANCE OPERATING COST ANALYSIS"
120 PRINT"TRS-80 LEVEL II"
130 PRINT"COPYRIGHT (C) 1980 BY HOWARD BERENBON"
140 PRINT
150 PRINT"THIS PROGRAM WILL CALCULATE"
160 PRINT"THE COST OF OPERATING ELECTRICAL"
170 PRINT"APPLIANCES, GIVEN THE NUMBER OF"
180 PRINT"WATTS THEY CONSUME, THE AVERAGE"
190 PRINT"NUMBER OF HOURS OF DAILY USE,"
200 PRINT"AND THE COST PER KILOWATT HOUR"
210 PRINT"FOR EACH APPLIANCE UNDER ANALYSIS"
220 PRINT
230 PRINT"ENTER THE # OF APPLIANCES"
240 PRINT"UNDER ANALYSIS"
250 INPUTI
260 DIMB$(I),W(I),U(I),R(I),S(I)
270 PRINT
280 PRINT"ENTER THE COST PER KILOWATT HOUR"
290 PRINT"(TYPICAL - $.065)
300 INPUTK
310 FORQ=1TOI
320 CLS
330 PRINT"APPLIANCE #";Q
340 PRINT"ENTER TYPE (NAME)"
350 PRINT"LIMIT TO 8 CHARACTERS"
360 INPUTA$:B$(Q)=A$
370 PRINT
380 PRINT"ENTER POWER CONSUMED IN WATTS"
390 INPUTW:W(Q)=W
400 PRINT
410 PRINT"ENTER AVERAGE # OF HOURS IN"
420 PRINT"DAILY USE (MAY ENTER FRACTIONS)."
430 PRINT"IF YOU DESIRE TO ENTER MINUTES"
440 PRINT"THEN ENTER 9999"
450 INPUTH
460 IFH=9999THEN700
470 C=(W/1000)*H
480 U(Q)=C*K
490 R(Q)=U(Q)*30
500 S(Q)=C*30
510 NEXTQ
520 CLS:S=0:V=0
530 PRINT"APPLIANCE OPERATING COST ANALYSIS"
540 PRINT
550 PRINT"APPL.      WATTS    COST/DAY    COST/MO    KWHS/MO"
560 FORQ=1TOI
570 PRINTB$(Q);TAB(12);W(Q);TAB(21);U(Q);TAB(33);R(Q);TAB(44);S(Q)
580 S=S+R(Q)
590 V=V+S(Q)
600 FORA=1TO660
610 NEXTA
620 NEXTQ
```

```
630 PRINT
640 PRINT"TOTAL KILOWATT HOURS USED PER MONTH"
650 PRINT"FOR ";I;" APPLIANCES IS ";V;" KWHOURS"
660 PRINT:S=INT(100*S+.5)/100
670 PRINT"TOTAL MONTHLY COST FOR ";I
680 PRINT"APPLIANCE(S) IS $";S
690 END
700 PRINT"ENTER AVERAGE # OF MINUTES"
710 PRINT"IN DAILY USE"
720 INPUTM
730 H=M/60
740 GOTO470
```

CHAPTER 20

Family Dental Expenses

A useful way to keep track of your dental expenses is with the Family Dental Expense program. It's written in BASIC for your microcomputer. See Program 20-1 for the program listing.

THE PROGRAM

The program requires that you enter dental expenses in DATA statements beginning with program line 500. Limit the type of expense to a 14-character description. Enter each dental expense as follows:

DATA DATE,TYPE OF EXPENSE,COST

or

DATA 1/17/80,CLEANING,25

DATA END,0,0 must be the last DATA statement in the list.

After you run the program, enter the year of the report. Then enter a 1 to begin. The program will display each dental expense with the date, the type (description), the cost, and the cumulative total. After all the data is displayed, then the total yearly expense is given. See Fig. 20-1 for a sample run.

```
FAMILY DENTAL EXPENSES
COPYRIGHT (C) 1980 BY HOWARD BERENBON

THIS PROGRAM WILL KEEP TRACK OF
YOUR FAMILY DENTAL EXPENSES.
ENTER EACH DENTAL EXPENSE RECEIPT
IN DATA STATEMENTS BEGINNING AT
LINE 500, AS FOLLOWS:
DATA DATE,TYPE,COST
DATA 1/17/80,CLEANING,25-LIMIT TYPE
TO A 14 CHARACTER DESCRIPTION.
DATA END,0,0 MUST BE THE LAST
STATEMENT IN YOUR LIST.

ENTER THE YEAR OF THE REPORT
? 1980


ENTER '1' TO BEGIN
? 1


FAMILY DENTAL EXPENSE REPORT
FOR THE YEAR:  1980

DATE            TYPE            COST            CUM. TOT.

1/17/80         CLEANING        25              25
1/25/80         FILLING         35              60
2/20/80         FILLING         30              90
2/27/80         CROWN WORK      75              165
3/10/80         CROWN WORK      100             265
3/17/80         CROWN WORK      15              280
3/25/80         CROWN DONE      100             380
6/14/80         CLEAN-XRAY      35              415


FAMILY DENTAL EXPENSE REPORT
FOR THE YEAR:  1980

THE TOTAL YEARLY EXPENSE =$ 415
```

Fig. 20-1. Family Dental Expenses sample run.

Program 20-1. Family Dental Expenses Program Listing

```
100 CLS:PRINT"FAMILY DENTAL EXPENSES"
110 PRINT"COPYRIGHT (C) 1980 BY HOWARD BERENBON"
120 PRINT"TRS-80 VERSION"
130 GOSUB470:GOSUB470
140 CLS:PRINT:C=0
150 PRINT"THIS PROGRAM WILL KEEP TRACK OF"
160 PRINT"YOUR FAMILY DENTAL EXPENSES."
170 PRINT"ENTER EACH DENTAL EXPENSE RECEIPT"
180 PRINT"IN DATA STATEMENTS BEGINNING AT"
190 PRINT"LINE 500, AS FOLLOWS:"
200 PRINT"DATA DATE,TYPE,COST"
210 PRINT"DATA 1/17/80,CLEANING,25-LIMIT TYPE"
220 PRINT"TO A 14 CHARACTER DESCRIPTION."
230 PRINT"DATA END,0,0 MUST BE THE LAST"
240 PRINT"STATEMENT IN YOUR LIST."
250 PRINT
260 PRINT"ENTER THE YEAR OF THE REPORT"
270 INPUTY
280 PRINT
290 PRINT"ENTER '1' TO BEGIN"
300 INPUTA
310 CLS:PRINT"FAMILY DENTAL EXPENSE REPORT"
320 PRINT"FOR THE YEAR: ";Y
330 PRINT
340 PRINT"DATE","TYPE","COST","CUM. TOT."
350 PRINT
360 READA$,B$,B
370 IFA$="END"THEN420
380 C=C+B
390 PRINTA$,B$,B,C
400 GOSUB470
410 GOTO360
420 PRINT:PRINT"FAMILY DENTAL EXPENSE REPORT"
430 PRINT"FOR THE YEAR: ";Y
440 PRINT
450 PRINT"THE TOTAL YEARLY EXPENSE =$";C
460 END
470 FORA=1TO1000
480 NEXTA
490 RETURN
500 DATA 1/17/80,CLEANING,25
510 DATA 1/25/80,FILLING,35
520 DATA 2/20/80,FILLING,30
530 DATA 2/27/80,CROWN WORK,75
540 DATA 3/10/80,CROWN WORK,100
550 DATA 3/17/80,CROWN WORK,15
560 DATA 3/25/80,CROWN DONE,100
570 DATA 6/14/80,CLEAN-XRAY,35
580 DATA END,0,0
```

CHAPTER 21

Weekly Jogging Record

Jogging has been a popular pastime for many people. It's a good form of exercise that requires very little cost to do. If you're a jogger, then this program can help you. It keeps a record of your weekly jogging data and displays a graph of your performance. It's written in BASIC for your microcomputer. See Program 21-1 for the program listing.

THE PROGRAM

The program requires that you enter your weekly jogging distance data in DATA statements beginning at line 960. Enter the maximum distance you ran (in miles or fraction of miles) for each day of week 1 through week W. Only enter the data for the days that you ran. If you ran three days out of seven, only enter three numbers, or all seven if you ran every day of that week. Also, 99 must be the last number in each DATA statement, and DATA 555 must be the last DATA statement in your list. Enter the data as in the following example:

```
Week 1    960   DATA 2,2,4,1,3,99
Week 2    970   DATA 2,2,2,3,4,2,99
Week 3    980   DATA 3,3,4,4,5,4,5,99
Week 4    990   DATA 4,3,4,5,99
          1000  DATA 555
```

After you run the program, it calculates the number of weeks in your data list. It then calculates the number of miles you ran for each week and the average daily miles per week. Then a table is displayed with the week number, the average miles per day, the total miles per week, and the approximate calories expended per week.

ANALYSIS

The data is analyzed using your first week of data as the "base" week. The average jog during a "base" week day is displayed. Then the average jog during the last week day is displayed. Next, the (+) increase or (−) decrease in the average daily jogging distance, from a "base" week to the last (final) week W, is displayed. Finally, you can have a plot of your weekly progress. Enter a 1 for yes or 0 for no. The plot will display the average daily miles per week, for each week in your data list. It is a horizontal plot, using the TAB function to display a plus (+) sign on the horizontal line, for the average daily miles per week. The maximum distance that can be plotted is 40 miles per week.

See Fig. 21-1 for a sample run.

```
WEEKLY JOGGING RECORD
COPYRIGHT (C) 1980 BY HOWARD BERENBON

HERE'S A PROGRAM THAT KEEPS A RECORD
OF YOUR WEEKLY JOGGING DATA, AND
GIVES A PLOT OF YOUR PERFORMANCE.
ENTER THE MAXIMUM DISTANCE YOU RAN
(IN MILES OR FRACTIONS) FOR EACH DAY
OF WEEK 1 THRU WEEK W, IN DATA STATE-
MENTS BEGINNING AT LINE 960. ENTER
ONLY THE DATA FOR DAYS THAT YOU RAN.
IF YOU RAN 3 DAYS OUT OF 7, THEN ONLY
ENTER 3 NUMBERS; OR ALL 7 IF YOU RAN
EACH DAY. ENTER AS FOLLOWS:
ENTER '1' TO CONTINUE? 1


DATA DAY1,DAY2,DAY3,DAY4,DAY5,DAY6,DAY7,99
DATA 2.5,2,3.5,5,4.5,4,5,99-99 MUST BE
LAST ENTRY IN EACH DATA STATEMENT; DATA 555
MUST BE THE LAST STATEMENT IN THE LIST.
ENTER '1' TO CONTINUE? 1


WEEK#           AV-MIL/D        MILES/WK        CALORIES/WK

 1               2.375           9.5             902.5
 2               2.7             13.5            1282.5
 3               3.2             16              1520
 4               2.7             13.5            1282.5
 5               3.75            15              1425
 6               4               16              1520

AVERAGE JOGG DURING A BASE WEEK (#1)
DAY =  2.38  MILES

AVERAGE JOGG DURING A LAST (FINAL)
WEEK DAY =  4  MILES

ENTER '1' TO CONTINUE? 1
```

Fig. 21-1. Weekly Jogging Record sample run.

Program 21-1. Weekly Jogging Record Program Listing

```
100 CLS:PRINT"WEEKLY JOGGING RECORD"
110 PRINT"COPYRIGHT (C) 1980 BY HOWARD BERENBON"
120 PRINT"TRS-80 VERSION"
130 GOSUB900
140 PRINT"HERE'S A PROGRAM THAT KEEPS A RECORD"
150 PRINT"OF YOUR WEEKLY JOGGING DATA, AND"
160 PRINT"GIVES A PLOT OF YOUR PERFORMANCE."
170 PRINT"ENTER THE MAXIMUM DISTANCE YOU RAN"
180 PRINT"(IN MILES OR FRACTIONS) FOR EACH DAY"
190 PRINT"OF WEEK 1 THRU WEEK W, IN DATA STATE-"
200 PRINT"MENTS BEGINNING AT LINE 960. ENTER"
210 PRINT"ONLY THE DATA FOR DAYS THAT YOU RAN."
220 PRINT"IF YOU RAN 3 DAYS OUT OF 7, THEN ONLY"
230 PRINT"ENTER 3 NUMBERS; OR ALL 7 IF YOU RAN"
240 PRINT"EACH DAY. ENTER AS FOLLOWS:":GOSUB930
250 PRINT"DATA DAY1,DAY2,DAY3,DAY4,DAY5,DAY6,DAY7,99"
260 PRINT"DATA 2.5,2,3.5,5,4.5,4,5,99-99 MUST BE"
270 PRINT"LAST ENTRY IN EACH DATA STATEMENT; DATA 555"
280 PRINT"MUST BE THE LAST STATEMENT IN THE LIST."
290 GOSUB930
300 CLS:W=0:R1=0:Q=0
310 READR
320 IFR=99THENW=W+1
330 IFR=555THEN350
340 GOTO310
350 RESTORE
360 READR
370 IFR=99THEN400
380 Q=Q+1:R1=R+R1
390 GOTO360
400 R1=R1/Q:RESTORE
410 DIMA(W+1),B(W+1)
420 FORG=1TOW
430 Q=0:S=0
440 READR
450 IFR=99THEN480
460 Q=Q+1:S=R+S:GOTO440
470 NEXTG:GOTO500
480 S1=S/Q:A(G)=S1
490 B(G)=S:GOTO470
500 R1=INT(R1*100+.5)/100
510 S1=INT(S1*100+.5)/100
520 CLS
530 PRINT"WEEK#","AV-MIL/D","MILES/WK","CALORIES/WK"
540 PRINT
550 FORG=1TOW
560 PRINTG,A(G),B(G),95*B(G)
570 GOSUB900
580 NEXTG
590 PRINT
600 PRINT"AVERAGE JOG DURING A BASE WEEK (#1)"
610 PRINT"DAY = ";R1;" MILES"
620 PRINT
```

```
630 PRINT"AVERAGE JOG DURING A LAST (FINAL)"
640 PRINT"WEEK DAY = ";S1;" MILES"
650 PRINT
660 GOSUB930:GOSUB820
670 PRINT
680 PRINT"DO YOU WISH A PLOT?"
690 PRINT"1-YES  0-NO"
700 INPUTA
710 IFA=1THEN730
720 END
730 CLS:PRINT"PLOT OF WEEKLY PROGRESS"
740 PRINT
750 PRINT"AVERAGE MILES/DAY (TOTAL DAYS)"
760 PRINT"0+++++++++5+++++++++10++++++++15++++++++20"
770 FORG=1TOW:Z=INT(A(G)+.5)
780 PRINTTAB(Z*2)"+   WEEK #";G
790 GOSUB900
800 NEXTG
810 GOTO720
820 PRINT"THE (+) INCREASE OR (-) DECREASE IN THE"
830 PRINT"AVERAGE DAILY JOGGING DISTANCE, FROM THE"
840 PRINT"BASE (1ST) WEEK TO THE LAST (FINAL) WEEK ";W;","
850 D=S1-R1:PC=(D/R1)*100
860 PRINT"IS ";D;" MILES"
870 PRINT:PC=INT(PC*100)/100
880 PRINT"THAT'S A ";PC;" PERCENT CHANGE"
890 RETURN
900 FORA=1TO1000
910 NEXTA
920 RETURN
930 PRINT"ENTER '1' TO CONTINUE";
940 INPUTA:PRINT
950 RETURN
960 DATA 2,2.5,2,3,99
970 DATA 2.5,2.5,3,3.5,2,99
980 DATA 3,3,3.5,3,3.5,99
990 DATA 2.5,2,2.5,3,3.5,99
1000 DATA 3,4,4,4,99
1010 DATA 4,4,4.5,3.5,99
1020 DATA 555
```

CHAPTER 22

Cost of Food Analysis

The cost of living has been on a constant increase over the years. Due to inflation, each year it takes more and more money to buy the same goods, compared with previous years' prices. This program is used to calculate the change in cost of food, by comparing the weekly price of six "basic" foods to previous weeks' price data. It will indicate the weekly changes in these prices, to help you budget your allotted food money more efficiently. The program is written in BASIC for your microcomputer. See Program 22-1 for the program listing.

THE PROGRAM

Enter the week's food price data in DATA statements beginning at line 850, as follows:

```
DATA P1,P2,P3,P4,P5,P6
```

where P1 through P6 are the prices of one gallon of milk, one pound of butter, one dozen eggs, one pound of hamburger, one loaf of bread (20 oz), and five pounds of sugar, respectively.

Enter any number of weeks of data, beginning with a "base" week's pricing. The "base" week's data should be taken from some weeks past. The final week in your data list should be the most recent week's food costs. The last DATA statement in your list must be DATA 0,0,0,0,0,0.

Example of Data List

```
BASE WEEK   DATA 1.95,.75,.85,1.79,.61,1.59
            DATA 2.00,.85,.95,1.85,.72,1.78
            DATA 2.09,.89,.95,1.85,.75,1.75
FINAL WEEK  DATA 2.05,.79,.87,2.20,.65,1.79
            DATA 0,0,0,0,0,0
```

After you run the program, it will display the "base" week's total "basic" food cost. Then for each week, it prints the total "basic" food cost and the difference between the previous week's (N−1) total "basic" food cost and the current week's (N) total, and the percent change. Also displayed is the total change/increase from week No. 1 (the "base" week) to the previous week (N−1), and the percent change. Finally, a cost of food plot may be displayed, by entering a 1 for yes. The plot will display the total "basic" food cost for each week in your data list. It is a horizontal plot, using the TAB function to display a plus (+) sign on the horizontal line, for the weekly food costs. Then the program will display the total change/increase from week No. 1 (the "base" week) to the final (most recent) week in your data list, along with the percent change.

See Fig. 22-1 for a sample run.

```
COST OF FOOD ANALYSIS
COPYRIGHT (C) 1980 BY HOWARD BERENBON

THIS PROGRAM IS USED TO CALCULATE THE
CHANGE IN COST OF FOOD, BY COMPARING
THE WEEKLY PRICE OF MILK, BUTTER, EGGS,
HAMBURGER, BREAD, AND SUGAR TO PREVIOUS
WEEKS DATA. IT ALSO PLOTS THE COMBINED
PRICE OF THESE ITEMS FROM WEEK TO WEEK,
TO SHOW THE RISE OR FALL OF PRICES FOR
A GIVEN NUMBER OF WEEKS.

ENTER A '1' TO CONTINUE
? 1


ENTER THE WEEKS FOOD PRICE DATA IN
DATA STATEMENTS BEGINNING AT LINE 850,
AS FOLLOWS:
DATA P1,P2,P3,P4,P5,P6   WHERE
P1 THRU P6 ARE THE PRICES OF 1 GALLON
OF MILK, 1 LB OF BUTTER, 1 DOZ EGGS,
1 LB HAMBURGER, 1 LOAF OF BREAD, AND
5 LBS OF SUGAR, RESPECTIVELY.
ENTER ANY # OF WEEKS OF DATA BEGINNING
WITH A BASE WEEK PRICING, TAKEN SOME
WEEKS PAST. THE LAST DATA STATEMENT IN
THE LIST MUST BE: DATA 0,0,0,0,0,0

ENTER A '1' TO CONTINUE
? 1

BASE WEEK  1  : FOOD PRICE=$ 7.54
WEEK #  2  : FOOD PRICE=$ 8.15

DIFFERENCE FROM WEEK #  1 TO
 2  IS $ .61
A CHANGE OF  7.48466  PERCENT

ENTER A '1' TO CONTINUE
? 1

WEEK #  3  : FOOD PRICE=$ 8.28

DIFFERENCE FROM WEEK #  2 TO
 3  IS $ .13
A CHANGE OF  1.57005  PERCENT

ENTER A '1' TO CONTINUE
? 1


WEEK #  4  : FOOD PRICE=$ 8.35

DIFFERENCE FROM WEEK #  3 TO
 4  IS $ .0700007
A CHANGE OF  .838331  PERCENT

ENTER A '1' TO CONTINUE
? 1

TOTAL CHANGE/INCREASE FROM WEEK
1 TO  4  IS $ .810001
A CHANGE OF  10.7427  PERCENT

DO YOU WISH A PLOT?
1-YES  0-NO
? 1


COST OF FOOD PLOT

FOOD COST
0.........5.........10........15........20
WEEK #  1      +
WEEK #  2       +
WEEK #  3       +
WEEK #  4       +

TOTAL CHANGE/INCREASE FROM WEEK
1 TO  4  IS $ .810001
A CHANGE OF  10.7427  PERCENT
```

Fig. 22-1. Cost of Food Analysis sample run.

Program 22-1. Cost of Food Analysis Program Listing

```
100 CLS:PRINT"COST OF FOOD ANALYSIS"
110 PRINT"COPYRIGHT (C) 1980 BY HOWARD BERENBON"
120 PRINT"TRS-80"
130 PRINT:Z=0
140 PRINT"THIS PROGRAM IS USED TO CALCULATE THE"
150 PRINT"CHANGE IN COST OF FOOD, BY COMPARING"
160 PRINT"THE WEEKLY PRICE OF MILK, BUTTER, EGGS,"
170 PRINT"HAMBURGER, BREAD, AND SUGAR TO PREVIOUS"
180 PRINT"WEEKS DATA. IT ALSO PLOTS THE COMBINED"
190 PRINT"PRICE OF THESE ITEMS FROM WEEK TO WEEK,"
200 PRINT"TO SHOW THE RISE OR FALL OF PRICES FOR"
210 PRINT"A GIVEN NUMBER OF WEEKS."
220 PRINT
230 GOSUB780
240 PRINT"ENTER THE WEEKS FOOD PRICE DATA IN"
250 PRINT"DATA STATEMENTS BEGINNING AT LINE 850,"
260 PRINT"AS FOLLOWS:"
270 PRINT"DATA P1,P2,P3,P4,P5,P6   WHERE"
280 PRINT"P1 THRU P6 ARE THE PRICES OF 1 GALLON"
290 PRINT"OF MILK, 1 LB OF BUTTER, 1 DOZ EGGS,"
300 PRINT"1 LB HAMBURGER, 1 LOAF OF BREAD, AND"
310 PRINT"5 LBS OF SUGAR, RESPECTIVELY."
320 PRINT"ENTER ANY # OF WEEKS OF DATA BEGINNING"
330 PRINT"WITH A BASE WEEK PRICING, TAKEN SOME"
340 PRINT"WEEKS PAST. THE LAST DATA STATEMENT IN"
350 PRINT"THE LIST MUST BE: DATA 0,0,0,0,0,0"
360 PRINT:N=1
370 GOSUB780
380 GOSUB710:FA=BA
390 PRINT"BASE WEEK ";N;" : FOOD PRICE=$";BA
400 N=N+1:GOSUB710:IFB=0THEN440
410 PRINT"WEEK # ";N;" : FOOD PRICE=$";BA
420 GOSUB660
430 GOSUB780:GOTO400
440 PRINT:GOSUB580
450 PRINT"DO YOU WISH A PLOT?"
460 PRINT"1-YES  0-NO"
470 INPUTA
480 IFA=1THEN500
490 END
500 CLS:PRINT"COST OF FOOD PLOT":PRINT
510 PRINT"FOOD COST"
520 PRINT"0.........5.........10........15........20"
530 N=1:RESTORE
540 GOSUB710
550 IFB=0THEN640
560 PRINT"WEEK # ";N;TAB(Z*2)"+"
570 N=N+1:GOSUB820:GOTO540
580 PRINT:HA=Z-FA
590 PRINT"TOTAL CHANGE/INCREASE FROM WEEK"
600 PRINT"1 TO ";N-1;" IS $";HA
610 PRINT"A CHANGE OF ";HA/FA*100;" PERCENT"
620 PRINT
```

```
630 RETURN
640 GOSUB580
650 GOTO490
660 PRINT
670 PRINT"DIFFERENCE FROM WEEK # ";N-1;"TO"
680 PRINTN;" IS $";GA
690 PRINT"A CHANGE OF ";GA/Z*100;" PERCENT"
700 PRINT:RETURN
710 READ B,C,D,E,F,G
720 H=B+C+D+E+F+G
730 AV=H
740 BA=INT(AV*100+.5)/100
750 GA=BA-Z:IFB=0THEN770
760 Z=BA
770 RETURN
780 PRINT"ENTER A '1' TO CONTINUE"
790 INPUTA
800 CLS
810 RETURN
820 FORA=1TO900
830 NEXTA
840 RETURN
850 DATA 1.95,.75,.85,1.79,.61,1.59
860 DATA 2.00,.85,.95,1.85,.72,1.78
870 DATA 2.09,.89,.95,1.85,.75,1.75
880 DATA 2.05,.79,.87,2.20,.65,1.79
890 DATA 0,0,0,0,0,0
```

SECTION III

Money and Investment

This section describes some useful application programs dealing with money and investment, including a checkbook balancing program, a monthly savings plan, compound interest program, money market interest, a stock buying guide, a stock record keeper, and, finally, a stock plotter.

CHAPTER 23

Double Check

Double Check is a program that will help you keep a record of your personal checks and keep your checking account in balance. It's written in BASIC for your microcomputer. See Program 23-1 for the program listing.

THE PROGRAM

The program accepts your check and deposit data in DATA statements beginning at line 570. Enter each check, bank charge, and deposit in the following format:

DATA CHECK #,DATE (MM/DD/YY),NAME PAYABLE TO,AMOUNT

or

DATA 702,12/10/80,EDISON,14.75

DATA CHARGE CODE,DATE (MM/DD/YY),CHARGE, AMOUNT

or

DATA C,12/19/80,BANK CHARGE,4.00

DATA DEPOSIT CODE,DATE (MM/DD/YY),DEPOSIT, AMOUNT

or

DATA D,12/22/80,DEPOSIT,350

The first entry into your data list must be a past balance or a deposit. Then enter the checks, bank charges, and deposits, as they appear in your checking account deposit record.

Enter the check number, the date (as MM/DD/YY—do not use commas), the name payable to, and the amount for each check written. Enter your bank charges with a C for the charge code, the date, the words BANK CHARGE, and the charge amount. Enter the deposit with a D for the deposit code, the date, the word DEPOSIT, and the deposit amount. Finally, the last statement in your data list must be DATA END,0,0,0.

After you run the program, it will list each check, bank charge, and deposit, as entered in the data list, plus the balance after each transaction. Then it will display the total number of transactions and the balance in your account. See Fig. 23-1 for a sample run.

SAVING THE PROGRAM AND DATA LIST

Each time there is a transaction in your checking account, enter it into the data list in the program. Then save the program on cassette or disk, to keep an ongoing record of your transactions.

```
DOUBLE CHECK
COPYRIGHT (C) 1980 BY HOWARD BERENBON

THIS PROGRAM WILL HELP YOU KEEP A
RECORD OF YOUR PERSONAL CHECKS, &
KEEP YOUR ACCOUNT IN BALANCE. IT'S
USED TO DOUBLE CHECK YOUR PERSONAL
CHECKING ACCOUNT RECORDS.
ENTER THE DATA IN DATA STATEMENTS
BEGINNING AT LINE 570, AS FOLLOWS:
DATA CHECK#,DATE,NAME PAYABLE TO,AMT.
YOUR DEPOST OR LAST BALANCE MUST BE
THE FIRST ENTRY IN YOUR DATA LIST.
THE LAST STATEMENT IN THE DATA LIST
MUST BE: DATA END,0,0,0


          DOUBLE CHECK

#    DATE     NAME         AMT       BAL

D    12/19/80 BALANCE      545.15    545.15
702  12/19/80 ELECTRIC     14.75     530.4
703  12/20/80 TELEPHONE    10.55     519.85
704  12/22/80 VISA         145.12    374.73
705  12/23/80 DR. SIMONS   5         369.73
706  12/23/80 RADIO SHACK  70        299.73
707  12/28/80 BOOK CLUB    9.95      289.78
D    12/28/80 DEPOSIT      200.35    490.13


THE TOTAL # OF TRANSACTIONS
IS  8 . YOUR BALANCE IS $ 490.13 .

CHECK THIS BALANCE WITH THE BALANCE
IN YOUR CHECKING ACCOUNT DEPOSIT
RECORD, AND COMPARE WITH YOUR BANK
STATEMENT FOR ACCURACY.
```

Fig. 23-1. Double Check sample run.

Program 23-1. Double Check Program Listing

```
100 CLS:PRINT"DOUBLE CHECK"
110 PRINT"COPYRIGHT (C) 1980 BY HOWARD BERENBON"
120 PRINT"TRS-80 LEV 2"
130 GT=2:GOSUB540:CLS
140 B=0:N=0
150 PRINT"THIS PROGRAM WILL HELP YOU KEEP A"
160 PRINT"RECORD OF YOUR PERSONAL CHECKS, &"
170 PRINT"KEEP YOUR ACCOUNT IN BALANCE. IT'S"
180 PRINT"USED TO DOUBLE CHECK YOUR PERSONAL"
190 PRINT"CHECKING ACCOUNT RECORDS."
200 PRINT"ENTER THE DATA IN DATA STATEMENTS"
210 PRINT"BEGINNING AT LINE 570, AS FOLLOWS:"
220 PRINT"DATA CHECK#,DATE,NAME PAYABLE TO,AMT."
230 PRINT"YOUR DEPOSIT OR LAST BALANCE MUST BE"
240 PRINT"THE FIRST ENTRY IN YOUR DATA LIST."
250 PRINT"THE LAST STATEMENT IN THE DATA LIST"
260 PRINT"MUST BE: DATA END,0,0,0"
270 GT=12:GOSUB540
280 CLS
290 PRINTTAB(10)"DOUBLE CHECK"
300 PRINT
310 READN$,D$,NA$,AM
320 IFN$="END"THEN350
330 N=N+1
340 GOTO310
350 RESTORE
360 PRINT"#    DATE     NAME          AMT        BAL"
370 PRINT
380 READN$,D$,NA$,AM
390 IFN$="END"THEN450
400 IFN$="D"THENB=B+AM:GOTO420
410 B=B-AM
420 PRINTN$;TAB(5);D$;TAB(14);NA$;TAB(26);AM;TAB(36);B
430 GT=2:GOSUB540
440 GOTO380
450 GT=2:GOSUB540:PRINT
460 PRINT"THE TOTAL # OF TRANSACTIONS"
470 PRINT"IS ";N;". YOUR BALANCE IS $";B;"."
480 PRINT
490 PRINT"CHECK THIS BALANCE WITH THE BALANCE"
500 PRINT"IN YOUR CHECKING ACCOUNT DEPOSIT"
510 PRINT"RECORD, AND COMPARE WITH YOUR BANK"
520 PRINT"STATEMENT FOR ACCURACY."
530 END
540 FORA=1TO400*GT
550 NEXTA
560 RETURN
570 DATA D,12/19/80,BALANCE,545.15
580 DATA 702,12/19/80,ELECTRIC,14.75
590 DATA 703,12/20/80,TELEPHONE,10.55
600 DATA 704,12/22/80,VISA,145.12
610 DATA 705,12/23/80,DR. SIMONS,5.00
620 DATA 706,12/23/80,RADIO SHACK,70.00
```

Program 23-1—cont. Double Check Program Listing

```
630 DATA 707,12/28/80,BOOK CLUB,9.95
640 DATA D,12/28/80,DEPOSIT,200.35
650 DATA END,0,0,0
```

CHAPTER 24

Monthly Savings Plan

A savings plan is a good way to force yourself to save money for some future purchase. Here is a program that will calculate and display a monthly savings plan, given the initial amount, the monthly savings amount, the yearly interest rate, and the number of months to be displayed. The interest is calculated on a monthly basis. The program is written in BASIC for your microcomputer. See Program 24-1 for the program listing.

THE PROGRAM

After you run the program, enter the initial amount of your savings plan, the monthly savings amount, the yearly interest rate (in percent), and the number of months to be displayed. The program will display the initial amount, the interest rate, and the starting amount (initial amount plus monthly savings amount). Then it will display a table including the month number, the balance, the interest, and the cumulative interest for each month in your savings plan. Finally, it will display the balance in your savings account and the total cumulative interest for the number of months in your plan.

You can use this program to project the number of months to a savings goal. By adjusting the amount entered into your account each month, or the number of months in your plan, you can reach your savings goal in a specific period.

See Fig. 24-1 for a sample run.

```
MONTHLY SAVINGS PLAN
COPYRIGHT (C) 1980 BY HOWARD BERENBON

THIS PROGRAM CALCULATES AND DISPLAYS
A MONTHLY SAVINGS PLAN, GIVEN THE
INITIAL AMOUNT, MONTHLY SAVINGS
AMOUNT, THE YEARLY INTEREST RATE,
AND THE # OF MONTHS TO BE DISPLAYED.

ENTER THE INITIAL AMOUNT OF THE PLAN
? 200

ENTER THE MONTHLY SAVINGS AMOUNT
? 100

ENTER THE YEARLY INTEREST RATE (%)
? 5.25

ENTER THE # OF MONTHS TO BE DISPLAYED
? 12


MONTHLY SAVINGS PLAN
INITIAL AMOUNT = $ 200           INTEREST RATE =  5.25
MONTHLY SAVINGS AMT = $ 100      STARTING AMT = $ 300
MONTH           BALANCE          INTEREST         CUM. INT.
 1               301.31           1.31             1.31
 2               403.07           1.76             3.07
 3               505.27           2.2              5.27
 4               607.92           2.65             7.92
 5               711.02           3.1              11.02
 6               814.57           3.55             14.57
 7               918.57           4                18.57
 8               1023.03          4.46             23.03
 9               1127.94          4.91             27.94
 10              1233.31          5.37             33.31
 11              1339.14          5.83             39.14
 12              1445.44          6.3              45.44


BALANCE AFTER  12  MONTHS = $ 1445.44
TOTAL CUMULATIVE INTEREST = $ 45.44
ANOTHER DISPLAY?
1 = YES    0 = NO
? 0
```

Fig. 24-1. Monthly Savings Plan sample run.

Program 24-1. Monthly Savings Plan Program Listing

```
100 PRINT"MONTHLY SAVINGS PLAN"
110 PRINT"TRS-80":DEFDBL B,J,K,P
120 PRINT"COPYRIGHT (C) 1980 BY HOWARD BERENBON"
130 PRINT:CI=0
140 PRINT"THIS PROGRAM CALCULATES AND DISPLAYS"
150 PRINT"A MONTHLY SAVINGS PLAN, GIVEN THE"
160 PRINT"INITIAL AMOUNT, MONTHLY SAVINGS"
170 PRINT"AMOUNT, THE YEARLY INTEREST RATE,"
180 PRINT"AND THE # OF MONTHS TO BE DISPLAYED."
190 PRINT
200 PRINT"ENTER THE INITIAL AMOUNT OF THE PLAN"
210 INPUT J
220 PRINT
230 PRINT"ENTER THE MONTHLY SAVINGS AMOUNT"
240 INPUT P
250 K=P
260 B=J
270 PRINT
280 PRINT"ENTER THE YEARLY INTEREST RATE (%)"
290 INPUT I
300 PRINT
310 PRINT"ENTER THE # OF MONTHS TO BE DISPLAYED"
320 INPUT M
330 MI=(I/12)/100
340 CLS
350 PRINT"MONTHLY SAVINGS PLAN"
360 PRINT"INITIAL AMOUNT = $";J,"INTEREST RATE = ";I
370 PRINT"MONTHLY SAVINGS AMT = $";K,"STARTING AMT = $";J+K
380 PRINT"MONTH","BALANCE","INTEREST","CUM. INT."
390 FOR A=1 TO M
400 GOSUB 520
410 PRINTA,B,IN,CI
420 FOR T=1 TO 400
430 NEXTT
440 NEXTA
450 PRINT"BALANCE AFTER ";M;" MONTHS = $";B
460 PRINT"TOTAL CUMULATIVE INTEREST = $";CI
470 PRINT"ANOTHER DISPLAY?"
480 PRINT"1 = YES   0 = NO"
490 INPUT A
500 IF A=1 THEN 100
510 END
520 REM CALCULATE MONTHLY DATA
530 B=B+P
540 IN=B*MI
550 IN=INT(IN*100+.5)/100
560 B=B+IN
570 B=INT(B*100+.5)
580 B=B/100
590 CI=CI+IN
600 RETURN
```

CHAPTER 25

Compound Interest Table

This program calculates and displays the compound interest for a savings account, given the type of compounding, the principal, and the yearly interest rate. It's written in BASIC for your microcomputer. See Program 25-1 for the program listing.

THE PROGRAM

After you run the program, it requests your entry of the type of compounding. Enter 1 for daily, 2 for monthly, or 3 for quarterly interest compounding. Then it requests entry of the principal amount of your account and the yearly interest rate of your savings and loan or bank. Now enter the number of days, months, or quarters to be displayed. A table will be printed for the type of compounding requested. It displays the principal, the yearly interest rate, the day, month, or quarter number, the balance, the interest, and the cumulative interest for the desired number of days, months, or quarters. Finally, the balance is displayed with the total cumulative interest. You may now enter a 1 for another display, or a 0 to end the program. See Fig. 25-1 for a sample run.

```
COMPOUND INTEREST TABLE
COPYRIGHT (C) 1980 BY HOWARD BERENBON

THIS PROGRAM CALCULATES AND DISPLAYS
THE COMPOUND INTEREST FOR A SAVINGS
ACCOUNT, GIVEN THE TYPE OF COMPOUNDING,
THE PRINCIPAL, & YEARLY INTEREST RATE.

ENTER THE TYPE OF COMPOUNDING:
1 = DAILY
2 = MONTHLY
3 = QUARTERLY
? 1

ENTER THE PRINCIPAL AMOUNT
? 2500

ENTER THE YEARLY INTEREST RATE (%)
? 5.25

DAILY INTEREST TABLE

ENTER THE # OF DAYS TO BE DISPLAYED
? 12

DAILY COMPOUND INTEREST TABLE
PRINCIPAL = $ 2500            INTEREST RATE =   5.25
DAY           BALANCE         INTEREST          CUM. INT.
 1            2500.36          .36               .36
 2            2500.72          .36               .72
 3            2501.08          .36              1.08
 4            2501.44          .36              1.44
 5            2501.8           .36              1.8
 6            2502.16          .36              2.16
 7            2502.52          .36              2.52
 8            2502.88          .36              2.88
 9            2503.25          .37              3.25
 10           2503.62          .37              3.62
 11           2503.99          .37              3.99
 12           2504.36          .37              4.36

BALANCE AFTER  12  DAYS = $ 2504.36
TOTAL CUM. INTEREST = $ 4.36
ANOTHER DISPLAY?
1 = YES    0 = NO
? 1

ENTER THE TYPE OF COMPOUNDING:
1 = DAILY
2 = MONTHLY
3 = QUARTERLY
? 2

ENTER THE PRINCIPAL AMOUNT
? 2500

ENTER THE YEARLY INTEREST RATE (%)
? 5.25

MONTHLY INTEREST TABLE

ENTER THE # OF MONTHS TO BE DISPLAYED
? 12

MONTHLY COMPOUND INTEREST TABLE
PRINCIPAL = $ 2500            INTEREST RATE =   5.25
MONTH         BALANCE         INTEREST          CUM. INT.
 1            2510.94         10.94             10.94
 2            2521.93         10.99             21.93
 3            2532.96         11.03             32.96
 4            2544.04         11.08             44.04
 5            2555.17         11.13             55.17
 6            2566.35         11.18             66.35
 7            2577.58         11.23             77.58
 8            2588.86         11.28             88.86
 9            2600.19         11.33             100.19
 10           2611.57         11.38             111.57
 11           2623            11.43             123
 12           2634.48         11.48             134.48

BALANCE AFTER 12 MONTHS = $ 2634.48
TOTAL CUM. INTEREST = $ 134.48
ANOTHER DISPLAY?
1 = YES    0 = NO
? 0
```

Fig. 25-1. Compound Interest Table sample run.

Program 25-1. Compound Interest Table Program Listing

```
100 PRINT"COMPOUND INTEREST TABLE"
110 PRINT"TRS-80":DEFDBL B,P
120 PRINT"COPYRIGHT (C) 1980 BY HOWARD BERENBON"
130 PRINT:CI=0
140 PRINT"THIS PROGRAM CALCULATES AND DISPLAYS"
150 PRINT"THE COMPOUND INTEREST FOR A SAVINGS"
160 PRINT"ACCOUNT, GIVEN THE TYPE OF COMPOUNDING,"
170 PRINT"THE PRINCIPAL, AND THE YEARLY INTEREST RATE."
180 PRINT
190 PRINT"ENTER THE TYPE OF COMPOUNDING:"
200 PRINT"1 = DAILY"
210 PRINT"2 = MONTHLY"
220 PRINT"3 = QUARTERLY"
230 INPUT CP
240 IF CP=1 THEN CM=360
250 IF CP=2 THEN CM=12
260 IF CP=3 THEN CM=4
270 IF CP<1 OR CP>3 THEN 190
280 PRINT
290 PRINT"ENTER THE PRINCIPAL AMOUNT"
300 INPUT P
310 PRINT
320 PRINT"ENTER THE YEARLY INTEREST RATE (%)"
330 INPUT I
340 PRINT
350 ON CP GOTO 390,620,800
360 FOR T=1 TO 400
370 NEXT T
380 RETURN
390 REM DAILY INTEREST
400 CLS
410 PRINT"DAILY INTEREST TABLE"
420 PRINT
430 PRINT"ENTER THE # OF DAYS TO BE DISPLAYED"
440 INPUT D
450 DI=(I/CM)/100
460 CLS
470 PRINT"DAILY COMPOUND INTEREST TABLE"
480 PRINT"PRINCIPAL = $";P,"INTEREST RATE = ";I
490 PRINT"DAY","BALANCE","INTEREST","CUM. INT."
500 FOR A=1 TO D
510 GOSUB 980
520 PRINTA,B,IN,CI
530 GOSUB 360
540 NEXTA
550 PRINT"BALANCE AFTER ";D;" DAYS = $";B
560 PRINT"TOTAL CUM. INTEREST = $";CI
570 PRINT"ANOTHER DISPLAY?"
580 PRINT"1 = YES   0 = NO"
590 INPUTG
600 IF G=1 THEN 100
610 END
620 REM MONTHLY INTEREST
```

```
690 CLS
700 PRINT"MONTHLY COMPOUND INTEREST TABLE"
710 PRINT"PRINCIPAL = $";P,"INTEREST RATE = ";I
720 PRINT"MONTH","BALANCE","INTEREST","CUM. INT."
730 FOR A=1TOM
740 GOSUB 1060
750 PRINTA,B,IN,CI
760 GOSUB 360
770 NEXTA
780 PRINT"BALANCE AFTER ";M;" MONTHS = $";B
790 GOTO 560
800 REM QUARTERLY INTEREST
810 CLS
820 PRINT"QUARTERLY INTEREST TABLE"
830 PRINT
840 PRINT"ENTER THE # OF QUARTERS TO BE DISPLAYED"
850 INPUT Q
860 QI=(I/CM)/100
870 CLS
880 PRINT"QUARTERLY COMPOUND INTEREST TABLE"
890 PRINT"PRINCIPAL = $";P,"INTEREST RATE = ";I
900 PRINT"QUARTER","BALANCE","INTEREST","CUM. INT."
910 FOR A=1TOQ
920 GOSUB 1140
930 PRINTA,B,IN,CI
940 GOSUB 360
950 NEXTA
960 PRINT"BALANCE AFTER ";Q;" QUARTERS = $";B
970 GOTO 560
980 REM CALCULATE DAILY DATA
990 B=P
1000 IN=P*DI
1010 IN=INT(IN*100+.5)/100
1020 B=P+IN:B=INT(B*100+.5)
1030 B=B/100:P=B
1040 CI=CI+IN
1050 RETURN
1060 REM CALCULATE MONTHLY DATA
1070 B=P
1080 IN=P*MI
1090 IN=INT(IN*100+.5)/100
1100 B=P+IN:B=INT(B*100+.5)
1110 B=B/100:P=B
1120 CI=CI+IN
1130 RETURN
1140 REM CALCULATE QUARTERLY DATA
1150 B=P
1160 IN=P*QI
1170 IN=INT(IN*100+.5)/100
1180 B=P+IN:B=INT(B*100+.5)
1190 B=B/100:P=B
1200 CI=CI+IN
1210 RETURN
```

```
630 CLS
640 PRINT"MONTHLY INTEREST TABLE"
650 PRINT
660 PRINT"ENTER THE # OF MONTHS TO BE DISPLAYED"
670 INPUT M
680 MI=(I/CM)/100
```

CHAPTER 26

Money Market Interest Table

Here's another program for calculating interest on your savings. It's a Money Market interest calculator that calculates the simple interest for Money Market type accounts. The program is written in BASIC for your microcomputer. See Program 26-1 for the program listing.

THE PROGRAM

The program will display a table, given the type of interest calculation (daily, monthly, or quarterly), the principal, the yearly interest rate, and the number of days, months, or quarters for display.

After you run the program, enter the type of interest calculation desired. Enter a 1 for daily, 2 for monthly, or 3 for quarterly interest. Then the program requests entry of the principal amount of your Money Market Certificate and the yearly interest rate. Now enter the number of days, months, or quarters to be displayed. A table will be printed for the type of interest calculation requested. It displays the yearly interest rate, the day, month, or quarter number, the principal, the interest, and the cumulative interest for the desired number of days, months, or quarters. Finally, the total cumulative interest is displayed for the requested number of days, months, or quarters. You may now enter a 1 for another display, or a 0 to end the program. See Fig. 26-1 for a sample run.

```
MONEY MARKET INTEREST TABLE
COPYRIGHT (C) 1980 BY HOWARD BERENBON

THIS PROGRAM CALCULATES AND DISPLAYS
THE SIMPLE INTEREST FOR A MONEY MARKET
CERTIFICATE, GIVEN THE TYPE OF INTEREST
CALCULATION, THE PRINCIPAL, AND YEARLY
INTEREST RATE.

ENTER THE TYPE OF INTEREST
CALCULATION:
1 = DAILY
2 = MONTHLY
3 = QUARTERLY
? 1


ENTER THE PRINCIPAL AMOUNT
? 10000

ENTER THE YEARLY INTEREST RATE (%)
? 15.43


DAILY INTEREST TABLE

ENTER THE # OF DAYS TO BE DISPLAYED
? 12



DAILY INTEREST TABLE
INTEREST RATE =  15.43
DAY           PRINCIPAL       INTEREST        CUM. INT.
 1             10000          4.29            4.29
 2             10000          4.29            8.58
 3             10000          4.29            12.87
 4             10000          4.29            17.16
 5             10000          4.29            21.45
 6             10000          4.29            25.74
 7             10000          4.29            30.03
 8             10000          4.29            34.32
 9             10000          4.29            38.61
 10            10000          4.29            42.9
 11            10000          4.29            47.19
 12            10000          4.29            51.48
```

```
TOTAL CUM. INT. AFTER  12  DAYS
. . . IS $ 51.48
ANOTHER DISPLAY?
1 = YES    0 = NO
? 1


ENTER THE TYPE OF INTEREST
CALCULATION:
1 = DAILY
2 = MONTHLY
3 = QUARTERLY
? 2

ENTER THE PRINCIPAL AMOUNT
? 10000

ENTER THE YEARLY INTEREST RATE (%)
? 15.43


MONTHLY INTEREST TABLE

ENTER THE # OF MONTHS TO BE DISPLAYED
? 12



MONTHLY INTEREST TABLE
INTEREST RATE =  15.43
MONTH         PRINCIPAL       INTEREST        CUM. INT.
 1             10000          128.58          128.58
 2             10000          128.58          257.16
 3             10000          128.58          385.74
 4             10000          128.58          514.32
 5             10000          128.58          642.9
 6             10000          128.58          771.48
 7             10000          128.58          900.06
 8             10000          128.58          1028.64
 9             10000          128.58          1157.22
 10            10000          128.58          1285.8
 11            10000          128.58          1414.38
 12            10000          128.58          1542.96


TOTAL CUM. INT. AFTER  12  MONTHS
. . . IS $ 1542.96
ANOTHER DISPLAY?
1 = YES    0 = NO
? 0
```

Fig. 26-1. Money Market Interest Table sample run.

Program 26-1. Money Market Interest Table Program Listing

```
100 PRINT"MONEY MARKET INTEREST TABLE"
110 PRINT"TRS-80":DEFDBL B,P
120 PRINT"COPYRIGHT (C) 1980 BY HOWARD BERENBON"
130 PRINT:CI=0
140 PRINT"THIS PROGRAM CALCULATES AND DISPLAYS"
150 PRINT"THE SIMPLE INTEREST FOR A MONEY MARKET"
160 PRINT"CERTIFICATE, GIVEN THE TYPE OF INTEREST"
170 PRINT"CALCULATION, THE PRINCIPAL, AND YEARLY"
180 PRINT"INTEREST RATE."
190 PRINT
200 PRINT"ENTER THE TYPE OF INTEREST"
210 PRINT"CALCULATION:"
220 PRINT"1 = DAILY"
230 PRINT"2 = MONTHLY"
240 PRINT"3 = QUARTERLY"
250 INPUT CP
260 IF CP=1 THEN CM=360
270 IF CP=2 THEN CM=12
280 IF CP=3 THEN CM=4
290 IF CP<1 OR CP>3 THEN 200
300 PRINT
310 PRINT"ENTER THE PRINCIPAL AMOUNT"
320 INPUT P
330 PRINT
340 PRINT"ENTER THE YEARLY INTEREST RATE (%)"
350 INPUT I
360 PRINT
370 ON CP GOTO 410,640,820
380 FOR T=1 TO 400
390 NEXT T
400 RETURN
410 REM DAILY INTEREST
420 CLS
430 PRINT"DAILY INTEREST TABLE"
440 PRINT
450 PRINT"ENTER THE # OF DAYS TO BE DISPLAYED"
460 INPUT D
470 DI=(I/CM)/100
480 CLS
490 PRINT"DAILY INTEREST TABLE"
500 PRINT"PRINCIPAL = $";P,"INTEREST RATE = ";I
510 PRINT"DAY","PRINCIPAL","INTEREST","CUM. INT."
520 FOR A=1 TO D
530 GOSUB 1000
540 PRINTA,P,IN,CI
550 GOSUB 380
560 NEXTA
570 PRINT"TOTAL CUM. INT. AFTER ";D;" DAYS"
580 PRINT". . . IS $";CI
590 PRINT"ANOTHER DISPLAY?"
600 PRINT"1 = YES   0 = NO"
610 INPUTG
620 IF G=1 THEN 100
```

```
630 END
640 REM MONTHLY INTEREST
650 CLS
660 PRINT"MONTHLY INTEREST TABLE"
670 PRINT
680 PRINT"ENTER THE # OF MONTHS TO BE DISPLAYED"
690 INPUT M
700 MI=(I/CM)/100
710 CLS
720 PRINT"MONTHLY INTEREST TABLE"
730 PRINT"PRINCIPAL = $";P,"INTEREST RATE = ";I
740 PRINT"MONTH","PRINCIPAL","INTEREST","CUM. INT."
750 FOR A=1TOM
760 GOSUB 1060
770 PRINTA,P,IN,CI
780 GOSUB 380
790 NEXTA
800 PRINT"TOTAL CUM. INT. AFTER ";M;" MONTHS"
810 GOTO 580
820 REM QUARTERLY INTEREST
830 CLS
840 PRINT"QUARTERLY INTEREST TABLE"
850 PRINT
860 PRINT"ENTER THE # OF QUARTERS TO BE DISPLAYED"
870 INPUT Q
880 QI=(I/CM)/100
890 CLS
900 PRINT"QUARTERLY INTEREST TABLE"
910 PRINT"PRINCIPAL = $";P,"INTEREST RATE = ";I
920 PRINT"QUARTER","PRINCIPAL","INTEREST","CUM. INT."
930 FOR A=1TOQ
940 GOSUB 1110
950 PRINTA,P,IN,CI
960 GOSUB 380
970 NEXTA
980 PRINT"TOTAL CUM. INT. AFTER ";Q;" QUARTERS"
990 GOTO 580
1000 REM CALCULATE DAILY DATA
1010 B=P
1020 IN=P*DI
1030 IN=INT(IN*100+.5)/100
1040 CI=CI+IN
1050 RETURN
1060 REM CALCULATE MONTHLY DATA
1070 IN=P*MI
1080 IN=INT(IN*100+.5)/100
1090 CI=CI+IN
1100 RETURN
1110 REM CALCULATE QUARTERLY DATA
1120 IN=P*QI
1130 IN=INT(IN*100+.5)/100
1140 CI=CI+IN
1150 RETURN
```

CHAPTER 27

Stock Buying Guide

Here's an investment program for the small investor. It's a stock market buying guide questionnaire to help you determine if a particular stock is a right choice for investment. The program is written in BASIC for your microcomputer. See Program 27-1 for the program listing.

THE PROGRAM

The program consists of a fifteen-question questionnaire, requiring entry of different point values per question. A total score of 27 or better is a recommendation to invest in the stock. A preliminary question must be answered with a "no" response, to allow entry into the questionnaire.

After you run the program, the following preliminary question will be displayed:

IS THE COMPANY IN A DEFICIT?
1—Yes 0—No

The entry of a 1 indicates a "yes" and 0 indicates a "no." If the answer is "yes" (the company is in a deficit), then the program will display:

THE STOCK IS NOT ACCEPTABLE
IT IS NOT RECOMMENDED FOR PURCHASE

You will not be allowed entry into the questionnaire, since the stock is a bad risk.

Answering the question with a "no" (0 entry) allows entry into the questionnaire, and question No. 1 will be displayed. Enter the number of points that is indicated for your stock. If zero is indicated, then enter 0. The program will print the "point value so far" and advance to the next question. After all fifteen questions are answered, it displays the final point score and whether the stock is acceptable, and recommended, or not acceptable, and not recommended for purchase. See Fig. 27-1 for a sample run.

ANALYSIS

A total score of 27 or greater is an indication that your stock choice will be a safe investment. But before investing, since the market is so unpredictable, consult your stockbroker for recent information on the company, and use this program along with your judgment, as a guide for investing.

```
STOCK BUYING GUIDE
COPYRIGHT (C) 1980 BY HOWARD BERENBON


USE THE FOLLOWING QUESTIONNAIRE TO
HELP DETERMINE IF A PARTICULAR STOCK
WILL BE A GOOD INVESTMENT. THERE ARE
15 QUESTIONS WITH DIFFERENT POINT
VALUES FOR EACH ANSWER. A TOTAL SCORE
OF 27 OR BETTER IS A RECOMMENDATION
TO INVEST IN THE STOCK. THE PRELIMINARY
QUESTION MUST BE ANSWERED WITH A 'NO'
TO ALLOW ENTRY INTO THE QUESTIONNAIRE.

PRELIMINARY QUESTION

IS THE COMPANY IN A DEFICIT?
1-YES  0-NO
? 0

STOCK BUYING GUIDE

#1-STOCK PRICE

$6 TO $30 = 4 POINTS
GREATER THAN $30 = 2 POINTS
LESS THAN $6 = 0

ENTER POINT VALUE
? 2


POINTS SO FAR =  2

#2-PRICE FLUCTUATION
(LAST 6 MONTHS)

UP=2 POINTS
DOWN = 0
NO CHANGE = 1

ENTER POINT VALUE
? 2


POINTS SO FAR =  4

#3-PE RATIO

4/1 TO 8/1 = 4 POINTS
9/1 TO 13/1 = 3
```

Fig. 27-1. Stock Buying Guide sample run.

```
14/1 TO 17/1 = 2
18/1 TO 24/1 = 1
25/1 AND ABOVE = 0

ENTER POINT VALUE
? 1


POINTS SO FAR =  5

#4-VOLUME SOLD, LAST (HUNDREDS)

0 TO 300 = 0 POINTS
301 TO 600 = 1
601 TO 1000 = 2
1001 AND GREATER = 3

ENTER POINT VALUE
? 3


POINTS SO FAR =  8

#5-DIVIDENDS

NONE = 0 POINTS
1 TO 2% = 1
2.1 TO 3% = 2
3.1 TO 6% = 3
6.1 TO 12% = 4
12.1% AND ABOVE =2

ENTER POINT VALUE
? 0


POINTS SO FAR =  8

#6-EARNINGS

UP = 2 POINTS
DOWN = 0
NO CHANGE = 1

ENTER POINT VALUE
? 2


POINTS SO FAR =  10

#7-RECENT NEWS ABOUT COMPANY

NO NEWS = 1
GOOD NEWS = 2
BAD NEWS = 0

ENTER POINT VALUE
? 2


POINTS SO FAR =  12

#8-INVESTMENT TYPE

SHORT TERM INVESTMENT = 2
LONG TERM INVESTMENT = 1

ENTER POINT VALUE
? 2


POINTS SO FAR =  14

#9-RECENT SPLITS

YES = 4
NO = 0

ENTER POINT VALUE
? 4


POINTS SO FAR =  18

#10-BROKER COMMISSION

3% OR LESS = 2 POINTS
3.1 TO 4% = 1
4.1% OR GREATER = 0

ENTER POINT VALUE
? 2


POINTS SO FAR =  20

#11-EXCHANGE TRADED ON

NEW YORK = 4 POINTS
AMERICAN = 2
OTHERS = 0

ENTER POINT VALUE
? 4


POINTS SO FAR =  24

#12-NUMBER OF YEARS IN BUSINESS

0 TO 6 = 0
7 TO 20 = 1
21 TO 30 = 2
31 TO 40 = 3
41 AND ABOVE = 4

ENTER POINT VALUE
? 2


POINTS SO FAR =  26

#13-SIZE OF BUSINESS

LARGE CORPORATION OR COMPANY = 4
MEDIUM SIZE = 2
SMALL = 0

ENTER POINT VALUE
? 4


POINTS SO FAR =  30

#14-EARNINGS AND DIVIDEND RANKING

A+ = 4 POINTS
A  = 3
A- = 3
B+ = 2
B  = 2
B- = 1
C  = 0
D  = 0


ENTER POINT VALUE
? 2


POINTS SO FAR =  32

#15-STOCK MARKET CONDITIONS

UP = 2 POINTS
DOWN OR NO CHANGE = 0

ENTER POINT VALUE
? 2


POINTS SO FAR =  34


FINAL POINT SCORE IS  34

THE STOCK IS ACCEPTABLE

IT IS RECOMMENDED FOR PURCHASE
```

Fig. 27-1—cont. Stock Buying Guide sample run.

Program 27-1. Stock Buying Guide Program Listing

```
100 CLS:PRINT"STOCK BUYING GUIDE"
110 PRINT"COPYRIGHT (C) 1980 BY HOWARD BERENBON"
120 PRINT"TRS-80"
130 GOSUB1710:CLS
140 PRINT"USE THE FOLLOWING QUESTIONNAIRE TO"
150 PRINT"HELP DETERMINE IF A PARTICULAR STOCK"
160 PRINT"WILL BE A GOOD INVESTMENT. THERE ARE"
170 PRINT"15 QUESTIONS WITH DIFFERENT POINT"
180 PRINT"VALUES FOR EACH ANSWER. A TOTAL SCORE"
190 PRINT"OF 27 OR BETTER IS A RECOMMENDATION"
200 PRINT"TO INVEST IN THE STOCK. THE PRELIMINARY"
210 PRINT"QUESTION MUST BE ANSWERED WITH A 'NO'"
220 PRINT"TO ALLOW ENTRY INTO THE QUESTIONNAIRE."
230 PRINT
240 PRINT"PRELIMINARY QUESTION"
250 PRINT
260 PRINT"IS THE COMPANY IN A DEFICIT?"
270 PRINT"1-YES  0-NO"
280 INPUTA
290 IFA=1THEN1740
300 IFA=0THEN320
310 GOTO230
320 CLS
330 PRINT"STOCK BUYING GUIDE"
340 PRINT
350 S1=0
360 PRINT"#1-STOCK PRICE"
370 PRINT
380 PRINT"$6 TO $30 = 4 POINTS"
390 PRINT"GREATER THAN $30 = 2 POINTS"
400 PRINT"LESS THAN $6 = 0"
410 GOSUB1610
420 GOSUB1660
430 PRINT"#2-PRICE FLUCTUATION"
440 PRINT"(LAST 6 MONTHS)"
450 PRINT
460 PRINT"UP=2 POINTS"
470 PRINT"DOWN = 0"
480 PRINT"NO CHANGE = 1"
490 GOSUB1610
500 GOSUB1660
510 PRINT"#3-PE RATIO"
520 PRINT
530 PRINT"4/1 TO 8/1 = 4 POINTS"
540 PRINT"9/1 TO 13/1 = 3"
550 PRINT"14/1 TO 17/1 = 2"
560 PRINT"18/1 TO 24/1 = 1"
570 PRINT"25/1 AND ABOVE = 0"
580 GOSUB1610
590 GOSUB1660
600 PRINT"#4-VOLUME SOLD, LAST (HUNDREDS)"
610 PRINT
620 PRINT"0 TO 300 = 0 POINTS"
```

```
630 PRINT"301 TO 600 = 1"
640 PRINT"601 TO 1000 = 2"
650 PRINT"1001 AND GREATER = 3"
660 GOSUB1610
670 GOSUB1660
680 PRINT"#5-DIVIDENDS"
690 PRINT
700 PRINT"NONE = 0 POINTS"
710 PRINT"1 TO 2% = 1"
720 PRINT"2.1 TO 3% = 2"
730 PRINT"3.1 TO 6% = 3"
740 PRINT"6.1 TO 12% = 4"
750 PRINT"12.1% AND ABOVE =2"
760 GOSUB1610
770 GOSUB1660
780 PRINT"#6-EARNINGS"
790 PRINT
800 PRINT"UP = 2 POINTS"
810 PRINT"DOWN = 0"
820 PRINT"NO CHANGE = 1"
830 GOSUB1610
840 GOSUB1660
850 PRINT"#7-RECENT NEWS ABOUT COMPANY"
860 PRINT
870 PRINT"NO NEWS = 1"
880 PRINT"GOOD NEWS = 2"
890 PRINT"BAD NEWS = 0"
900 GOSUB1610
910 GOSUB1660
920 PRINT"#8-INVESTMENT TYPE"
930 PRINT
940 PRINT"SHORT TERM INVESTMENT = 2"
950 PRINT"LONG TERM INVESTMENT = 1"
960 GOSUB1610
970 GOSUB1660
980 PRINT"#9-RECENT SPLITS"
990 PRINT
1000 PRINT"YES = 4"
1010 PRINT"NO = 0"
1020 GOSUB1610
1030 GOSUB1660
1040 PRINT"#10-BROKER COMMISSION"
1050 PRINT
1060 PRINT"3% OR LESS = 2 POINTS"
1070 PRINT"3.1 TO 4% = 1"
1080 PRINT"4.1% OR GREATER = 0"
1090 GOSUB1610
1100 GOSUB1660
1110 PRINT"#11-EXCHANGE TRADED ON"
1120 PRINT
1130 PRINT"NEW YORK = 4 POINTS"
1140 PRINT"AMERICAN = 2"
1150 PRINT"OTHERS = 0"
```

```
1160 GOSUB1610
1170 GOSUB1660
1180 PRINT"#12-NUMBER OF YEARS IN BUSINESS"
1190 PRINT
1200 PRINT"0 TO 6 = 0"
1210 PRINT"7 TO 20 = 1"
1220 PRINT"21 TO 30 = 2"
1230 PRINT"31 TO 40 = 3"
1240 PRINT"41 AND ABOVE = 4"
1250 GOSUB1610
1260 GOSUB1660
1270 PRINT"#13-SIZE OF BUSINESS"
1280 PRINT
1290 PRINT"LARGE CORPORATION OR COMPANY = 4"
1300 PRINT"MEDIUM SIZE = 2"
1310 PRINT"SMALL = 0"
1320 GOSUB1610
1330 GOSUB1660
1340 PRINT"#14-EARNINGS AND DIVIDEND RANKING"
1350 PRINT
1360 PRINT"A+ = 4 POINTS"
1370 PRINT"A  = 3"
1380 PRINT"A- = 3"
1390 PRINT"B+ = 2"
1400 PRINT"B  = 2"
1410 PRINT"B- = 1"
1420 PRINT"C  = 0"
1430 PRINT"D  = 0"
1440 GOSUB1610
1450 GOSUB1660
1460 PRINT"#15-STOCK MARKET CONDITIONS"
1470 PRINT
1480 PRINT"UP = 2 POINTS"
1490 PRINT"DOWN OR NO CHANGE = 0"
1500 GOSUB1610
1510 GOSUB1660
1520 PRINT
1530 PRINT"FINAL POINT SCORE IS ";S1
1540 PRINT
1550 IFS1<27THEN1740
1560 PRINT
1570 PRINT"THE STOCK IS ACCEPTABLE"
1580 PRINT
1590 PRINT"IT IS RECOMMENDED FOR PURCHASE"
1600 END
1610 PRINT
1620 PRINT"ENTER POINT VALUE"
1630 INPUTS
1640 S1=S+S1:CLS
1650 RETURN
1660 PRINT
1670 PRINT"POINTS SO FAR = ";S1
1680 PRINT
```

```
1690 PRINT
1700 RETURN
1710 FORA=1TO900
1720 NEXTA
1730 RETURN
1740 PRINT
1750 PRINT"THE STOCK IS NOT ACCEPTABLE"
1760 PRINT
1770 PRINT"IT IS NOT RECOMMENDED FOR PURCHASE"
1780 GOTO1600
```

CHAPTER 28

Stock Record Keeper

If you're an investor in the stock market then the Stock Record Keeper can help you. The program allows you to keep a record of each of the stocks in your portfolio, and it gives gain or loss information on your stocks. It's written in BASIC for your microcomputer. See Program 28-1 for the program listing.

THE PROGRAM

The program requires that you enter your stock data in DATA statements beginning at line 1000. Enter the data in the following format:

```
DATA COMPANY NAME,# OF SHARES,DATE OF
PURCHASE,PURCHASE PRICE,RECENT PRICE
```

or

```
DATA GM,100,2/1/80,54,55.5
```

The last DATA statement in your list must be DATA END,0,0,0,0.

The program allows you to list data on one or all of the stocks, including the company name, the number of shares held, the date of purchase (entered MM/DD/YY), the purchase price, and the recent price. It also displays the net worth, gain or loss, and the percent (%) gain or loss for your stocks. Finally, you can display the total gain or loss in your portfolio.

After you run the program, you have the following four options:

1. Enter a 1 to list one stock.
2. Enter a 2 to list all stocks.
3. Enter a 3 to list total gain or loss.
4. Enter a 4 to end the program.

List One Stock

Entering a 1 allows you to list the data on a single stock. The program requests entry of the stock name, and it searches the list for that name. If the name is found, the stock data is displayed. If the name is not found, the computer will display ENTRY NOT FOUND and then allow you to enter into one of the four previously listed options.

List All Stocks

Entering a 2 allows you to list the data on all the stocks in your portfolio. The program will list one stock at a time. After the data for a stock is displayed, enter a 1 to continue to the next stock in your list. When all the stock data has been displayed, the program will allow you to enter into one of the four options listed.

List Total Gain or Loss

Entering a 3 allows you to list the total gain or loss for the stocks in your portfolio. The program lists the total stock costs and their total worth. Then it displays the total (+) gain or (−) loss and the percent (+) gain or (−) loss, and then it allows you to enter into one of the four options listed.

See Fig. 28-1 for a sample run.

ONE LAST NOTE

This program does not take into account the brokerage fees associated with the buying and selling of your stocks. But these fees must be included when calculating your gains or losses for income tax purposes.

```
STOCK RECORD KEEPER
COPYRIGHT (C) 1980 BY HOWARD BERENBON

THIS PROGRAM ALLOWS YOU TO KEEP
A RECORD OF YOUR STOCK PORTFOLIO.
YOU CAN LIST ONE OR ALL OF YOUR
STOCKS INCLUDING THE NAME, # OF
SHARES, THE DATE OF PURCHASE,
PURCHASE PRICE, AND RECENT PRICE.
IT ALSO DISPLAYS THE NET WORTH, GAIN
OR LOSS, % GAIN OR LOSS, AND THE
TOTAL GAIN OR LOSS IN YOUR PORTFOLIO.

ENTER '1' TO CONTINUE
? 1

ENTER YOUR STOCK DATA IN DATA
STATEMENTS BEGINNING AT LINE 1000,
IN THE FOLLOWING FORMAT:
DATA NAME,# SHARES,PUR DATE,PUR PRICE,REC PRICE
DATA GM,100,2/1/80,54,55.5
THE LAST STATEMENT IN THE LIST MUST BE:
DATA END,0,0,0,0

ENTER '1' TO CONTINUE
? 1



ENTER CHOICE

1-LIST ONE STOCK
2-LIST ALL STOCKS
3-GIVE TOTAL GAIN OR LOSS
4-END PROGRAM
? 1


LIST ONE STOCK

ENTER STOCK NAME
? AMPEX

STOCK DATA

STOCK NAME: AMPEX

# OF SHARES =  100    DATE OF PURCHASE IS 7/18/80
PURCHASE PRICE = $ 14.5    TOTAL COST = $ 1450

RECENT PRICE = $ 19.25    NET WORTH = $ 1925

(+) GAIN OR (-) LOSS IF SOLD = $ 475
PERCENT (+) GAIN OR (-) LOSS =  32.75


ENTER '1' TO CONTINUE
? 1

ENTER CHOICE

1-LIST ONE STOCK
2-LIST ALL STOCKS
3-GIVE TOTAL GAIN OR LOSS
4-END PROGRAM
? 3



TOTAL COST = $ 23125    NET WORTH =$ 25600

TOTAL (+) GAIN OR (-) LOSS FOR
ALL STOCKS IS $ 2475   OR  10.7  PERCENT

ENTER '1' TO CONTINUE
? 1
ENTER CHOICE

1-LIST ONE STOCK
2-LIST ALL STOCKS
3-GIVE TOTAL GAIN OR LOSS
4-END PROGRAM
? 4
```

Fig. 28-1. Stock Record Keeper sample run.

Program 28-1. Stock Record Keeper Program Listing

```
100 CLS:PRINT"STOCK RECORD KEEPER":CLEAR500
110 PRINT"COPYRIGHT (C) 1980 BY HOWARD BERENBON"
120 PRINT"TRS-80 LEV 2"
130 PRINT
140 PRINT"THIS PROGRAM ALLOWS YOU TO KEEP"
150 PRINT"A RECORD OF YOUR STOCK PORTFOLIO."
160 PRINT"YOU CAN LIST ONE OR ALL OF YOUR"
170 PRINT"STOCKS INCLUDING THE NAME, # OF"
180 PRINT"SHARES, THE DATE OF PURCHASE,"
190 PRINT"PURCHASE PRICE, AND RECENT PRICE."
200 PRINT"IT ALSO DISPLAYS THE NET WORTH, GAIN"
210 PRINT"OR LOSS, % GAIN OR LOSS, AND THE"
220 PRINT"TOTAL GAIN OR LOSS IN YOUR PORTFOLIO."
230 GOSUB710
240 CLS
250 PRINT"ENTER YOUR STOCK DATA IN DATA"
260 PRINT"STATEMENTS BEGINNING AT LINE 1000,"
270 PRINT"IN THE FOLLOWING FORMAT:"
280 PRINT"DATA NAME,# SHARES,PUR DATE,PUR PRICE,REC PRICE"
290 PRINT"DATA GM,100,2/1/80,54,55.5
300 PRINT"THE LAST STATEMENT IN THE LIST MUST BE:"
310 PRINT"DATA END,0,0,0,0"
320 GOSUB710
330 PRINT"ENTER CHOICE":RESTORE
340 PRINT:P=0:Q=0
350 PRINT"1-LIST ONE STOCK"
360 PRINT"2-LIST ALL STOCKS"
370 PRINT"3-GIVE TOTAL GAIN OR LOSS"
380 PRINT"4-END PROGRAM"
390 INPUTB:CLS
400 ONBGOTO420,530,600,890
410 GOTO320
420 PRINT"LIST ONE STOCK"
430 PRINT
440 PRINT"ENTER STOCK NAME"
450 INPUTA$
460 READB$,C,C2$,D,E
470 IFB$="END"THEN690
480 IFB$=A$THEN500
490 GOTO460
500 GOSUB740
510 PRINT
520 GOTO320
530 PRINT"LIST ALL STOCKS"
540 PRINT
550 READB$,C,C2$,D,E
560 IFB$="END"THEN330
570 GOSUB750
580 GOSUB710
590 GOTO540
600 PRINT:T2=0:T5=0
610 GOSUB900
620 Q=INT((P*100+.5))/100
```

Program 28-1—cont. Stock Record Keeper Program Listing

```
630 R=(Q/T2)*100:R=INT(R*100)/100
640 PRINT"TOTAL COST = $";T2;"   NET WORTH =$";T5
650 PRINT
660 PRINT"TOTAL (+) GAIN OR (-) LOSS FOR"
670 PRINT"ALL STOCKS IS $";Q;" OR ";R;" PERCENT"
680 GOTO320
690 PRINT"STOCK '";A$;"' NOT FOUND"
700 GOTO320
710 PRINT:PRINT"ENTER '1' TO CONTINUE"
720 INPUTA
730 RETURN
740 CLS:PRINT"STOCK DATA"
750 PRINT
760 PRINT"STOCK NAME: ";B$
770 PRINT
780 PRINT"# OF SHARES = ";C;"   DATE OF PURCHASE IS ";C2$
790 PRINT"PURCHASE PRICE = $";D;"   TOTAL COST = $";C*D
800 PRINT
810 PRINT"RECENT PRICE = $";E;"   NET WORTH = $";C*E
820 PRINT:GOSUB960
830 PRINT"(+) GAIN OR (-) LOSS IF SOLD = $";T1
840 C2=C*D
850 R=(T1/C2)*100:R=INT(R*100)/100
860 PRINT"PERCENT (+) GAIN OR (-) LOSS = ";R
870 PRINT
880 RETURN
890 END
900 READB$,C,C2$,D,E
910 IFB$="END"THEN950
920 GOSUB960
930 P=P+T1
940 GOTO900
950 RETURN
960 N=C*E:M=C*D
970 T1=N-M:T2=T2+M:T5=T5+N
980 RETURN
1000 DATA GM,200,5/11/80,54,55.5
1010 DATA FORD,200,5/23/80,26.5,26
1020 DATA NVF,300,5/23/80,4.75,4.75
1030 DATA CHRYSLER,100,6/20/80,10.75,6.25
1040 DATA SONY,300,6/27/80,10.25,17.75
1050 DATA AMPEX,100,7/18/80,14.5,19.25
1060 DATA END,0,0,0,0
```

CHAPTER 29

Stock Plotter

A third program for the stock investor is the Stock Plotter. It will display a plot, using the TAB function, for any stock with a high price of up to $200, given a series of prices. These prices may be made of daily, weekly, or monthly data on a particular stock. The program is written in BASIC for your microcomputer. See Program 29-1 for the program listing.

THE PROGRAM

The stock price data must be entered into DATA statements beginning at line 810. Enter the data in the following format:

DATA PRICE1,PRICE2,PRICE3,PRICE4, . . . PRICEN

or

DATA 14.5,13.75,14.25,13.75

The last DATA statement in the list must be DATA 9999; this is used to test for the end of the data.

After you run the program, it requests your entry of the type of data plot. Enter a 1 for daily, 2 for weekly, or 3 for monthly. Then it requests an entry of the company name and the starting date of the plot (MM/DD/YY). Finally, enter a 1 to start the plot.

Now the program will find the highest price of the stock. Then it uses this price for scaling the output of the plot. The program will then print the company name, the date of the plot, and whether the plot is for daily, weekly, or monthly data. It then prints a horizontal scale from 0, at the left end, up to 200, at the right end. This scaling is dependent on the high price of the stock. Finally, the program plots each stock price using a plus sign (+) for each point. After all the data points are plotted, the program will display the average price of the stock over the given number of days, weeks, or months, and print the high price for that period.

See Fig. 29-1 for a sample run.

```
STOCK PLOTTER
COPYRIGHT (C) 1980 BY HOWARD BERENBON


THIS PROGRAM WILL PLOT ANY STOCK,
GIVEN A SERIES OF PRICES FOR
DAILY, WEEKLY, OR MONTHLY DATA.

DATA IS STORED IN DATA STATEMENTS,
BEGINNING AT LINE 810. ENTER IN
THE FOLLOWING FORMAT:
DATA 14.5,13.75,14.25,13.75
THE LAST DATA STATEMENT SHOULD BE
DATA 9999. THIS IS USED TO TEST
FOR THE END OF THE DATA.

ENTER TYPE OF DATA?
1=DAILY  2=WEEKLY  3=MONTHLY
? 3


3

ENTER NAME OF THE COMPANY
? ABC

ENTER THE STARTING DATE OF PLOT
(MM/DD/YY)
? 06/15/80

ENTER A '1' FOR PLOT
? 1




COMPANY=ABC  DATE=06/15/80
MONTH              PRICE
0            12.5        25          37.5        50
+++++++++++++++++++++++++++++++++++++++++++++++++++
 1          +
 2            +
 3          +
 4           +
 5             +
 6             +
 7             +
 8                +
 9             +
 10                 +
 11                +
 12                      +



 AVERAGE PRICE OF THE STOCK
 ABC, OVER A PERIOD OF  12  MONTHS
 IS $ 16.1
 HIGH PRICE FOR THAT PERIOD IS $ 25.25
```

Fig. 29-1. Stock Plotter sample run.

Program 29-1. Stock Plotter Program Listing

```
100 CLS:CLEAR 500
110 PRINT"STOCK PLOTTER"
120 PRINT"TRS-80 LEVEL II"
130 PRINT"COPYRIGHT (C) 1980 BY HOWARD BERENBON"
140 GOSUB690:CLS
150 PRINT"THIS PROGRAM WILL PLOT ANY STOCK,"
160 PRINT"GIVEN A SERIES OF PRICES FOR"
170 PRINT"DAILY, WEEKLY, OR MONTHLY DATA."
180 PRINT
190 PRINT"DATA IS STORED IN DATA STATEMENTS,"
200 PRINT"BEGINNING AT LINE 810. ENTER IN"
210 PRINT"THE FOLLOWING FORMAT:"
220 PRINT"DATA 14.5,13.75,14.25,13.75"
230 PRINT"THE LAST DATA STATEMENT SHOULD BE"
240 PRINT"DATA 9999. THIS IS USED TO TEST"
250 PRINT"FOR THE END OF THE DATA."
260 PRINT
270 REM BEGIN PLOT
280 PRINT"ENTER TYPE OF DATA?"
290 PRINT"1=DAILY  2=WEEKLY  3=MONTHLY"
300 INPUTT
310 PRINT
320 PRINT"ENTER NAME OF THE COMPANY"
330 INPUTA$
340 PRINT
350 PRINT"ENTER THE STARTING DATE OF PLOT"
360 PRINT"(MM/DD/YY)"
370 INPUTD$:S=0
380 GOSUB620
390 GOSUB410
400 GOTO450
410 IFS<=10THENP=10:A=5:RETURN
420 IFS<=50THENP=50:A=1:RETURN
430 IFS<=100THENP=100:A=.5:RETURN
440 IFS<=200THENP=200:A=.25:RETURN
450 PRINT:PRINT"ENTER A '1' FOR PLOT"
460 INPUTJ
470 CLS:C=1
480 PRINT"COMPANY=";A$;"  DATE=";D$
490 IFT=1THENP$="DAY"
500 IFT=2THENP$="WEEK"
510 IFT=3THENP$="MONTH"
520 PRINTP$;TAB(20)"PRICE"
530 PRINT"0";TAB(12);P/4;TAB(24);P/2;TAB(36);INT((P/1.3333)*100)/100;TAB(49);P:R
=0
540 PRINT"+++++++++++++++++++++++++++++++++++++++++++++++++++++++++++++++"
550 READD:U=INT(D*A+.5)
560 IFD=9999THEN720
570 R=R+D
580 PRINTC;TAB(U)"+":C=C+1
590 FORB=1TO660
600 NEXTB
610 GOTO550
```

Program 29-1—cont. Stock Plotter Program Listing

```
620 REM FIND HIGH PRICE
630 S=A
640 READA:IFA=9999THEN670
650 IFS>ATHEN640
660 GOTO630
670 RESTORE
680 RETURN
690 FORG=1TO1400
700 NEXTG
710 RETURN
720 GOSUB690
730 C=C-1:U=R/C
740 U=INT(100*U)/100
750 PRINT
760 PRINT"AVERAGE PRICE OF THE STOCK"
770 PRINTA$;", OVER A PERIOD OF ";C;" ";P$;"S"
780 PRINT"IS $";U
790 PRINT"HIGH PRICE FOR THAT PERIOD IS $";S
800 END
810 DATA 12.25,13.75,12,13,15.25,14.75
820 DATA 15.25,17.5,15.25,19.75,19.25,25.25
830 DATA 9999
```

SECTION IV

ESP Testing

This section is directed to the study of extrasensory perception, also known as ESP or psi. It consists of two programs that test for ESP. The first program tests the subject for clairvoyance, and the second program tests for precognition.

CHAPTER 30

Parapsychology Test 1: Clairvoyance

Clairvoyance is defined as the ability to perceive things that are not in sight or that cannot be seen. This program tests for clairvoyance using five each of the symbols *, +, −, =, and 0 stored in the computer. The subject will try to guess the symbol card, from the shuffled deck of 25. After the test is completed, a score is given. A score of 6 or more, after at least five consecutive tests, may be an indication of clairvoyance. The program is written in BASIC for your microcomputer. See Program 30-1 for the program listing.

THE PROGRAM

After you run the program, enter your name, or the subject's name, and the date (MM/DD/YY). Then enter a 1 to shuffle the deck. The computer will randomly mix the symbols and store them in array C$(M). After the shuffling is done, the computer will print SHUFFLING COMPLETED. Then the clairvoyance test number is displayed along with the date, the subject's name, and CARD# 1. You are then requested to enter the symbol guess.

Before entering your guess of the symbol, try to imagine yourself looking into the computer's memory and seeing the first symbol which appears in the shuffled deck. This first symbol will be stored in array C$(1), the second will be in C$(2), and so on through the twenty-fifth card. Enter the first symbol that appears in your mind. The program will advance to card No. 2. Continue entering the symbols in this manner until all 25 guesses are entered. You may now take another test by entering a Y, or end the testing with an N.

Entering an N will cause the computer to display your test data, including your score out of 25, for each test, the average score out of G tests taken, and the percent score. Then an analysis is given. If your average score is 6 or above, the program will indicate that there is a possibility that you are clairvoyant. If your average score is 5 or less, the program will indicate that you have an average score and there is no indication of clairvoyance.

It is recommended that at least five tests be taken to ensure an accurate analysis of your test data. The program allows a maximum of 25 consecutive tests.

PLOT

After your test scoring is complete, you may see a plot of the test data. The total score for each test is plotted horizontally, using the TAB function. A period (.) is displayed, along with the test number, at TAB(GG) on the horizontal line, where GG is the test score for each test as taken from the array T(A).

See Fig. 30-1 for a sample run.

```
PARAPSYCHOLOGY TEST 1
CLAIRVOYANCE
COPYRIGHT (C) 1980 BY HOWARD BERENBON

THIS IS A TEST FOR CLAIRVOYANCE. USING
FIVE EACH OF THE SYMBOLS *, +, -, =,
AND 0, THE SUBJECT WILL TRY TO GUESS THE
SYMBOL CARD, FROM THE SHUFFLED DECK,
IN ORDER FROM 1 TO 25. AFTER THE TEST IS
COMPLETED, A SCORE IS GIVEN. A SCORE OF
5 OR LESS IS AVERAGE. A SCORE OF 6 OR
MORE, AFTER AT LEAST 5 TESTS, MAY BE AN
INDICATION OF CLAIRVOYANCE.

ENTER SUBJECT'S NAME
? BRUCE

BRUCE

ENTER DATE (MM/DD/YY)
? 05/07/80


ENTER A '1' TO SHUFFLE THE CARDS
? 1
NOW SHUFFLING


SHUFFLING COMPLETED


CLAIRVOYANCE TEST  1

DATE :  05/07/80
SUBJECT: BRUCE

CARD#  1          TEST  1

ENTER SYMBOL GUESS
(* + - = 0)
? +


CARD#  2          TEST  1

ENTER SYMBOL GUESS
(* + - = 0)
? 0


CARD#  3          TEST  1

ENTER SYMBOL GUESS
(* + - = 0)
? 0



CARD#  4          TEST  1

ENTER SYMBOL GUESS
(* + - = 0)
? 0

CARD#  5          TEST  1

ENTER SYMBOL GUESS
(* + - = 0)
? +



CARD#  24         TEST  1

ENTER SYMBOL GUESS
(* + - = 0)
? =


CARD#  25         TEST  1

ENTER SYMBOL GUESS
(* + - = 0)
? +


ANOTHER TEST?
Y=YES  N=NO
? N


CLAIRVOYANCE TEST SCORING
DATE:  05/07/80
SUBJECT:  BRUCE

CORRECT SCORE OUT OF 25
TEST #  1
 5
AVERAGE SCORE OUT OF  1
TEST(S) IS  5

THAT'S  20  PERCENT CORRECT



YOU HAVE AN AVERAGE SCORE.
AT THIS TIME, THERE IS NO
INDICATION OF CLAIRVOYANCE.
WOULD YOU LIKE A PLOT
OF THE TEST SCORES
Y=YES  N=NO
? Y


PLOT OF CLAIRVOYANCE TEST DATA
SUBJECT:  BRUCE    DATE: 05/07/80

0    5    10   15        25
+++++++++++++++++++++++++
     .   TEST #  1
```

Fig. 30-1. Parapsychology Test 1: Clairvoyance sample run.

Program 30-1. Parapsychology Test 1: Clairvoyance Program Listing

```
100 CLS:PRINT"PARAPSYCHOLOGY TEST 1"
110 PRINT"CLAIRVOYANCE"
120 PRINT"TRS-80 LEVEL II"
130 PRINT"COPYRIGHT (C) 1980 BY HOWARD BERENBON"
140 PRINT
150 CLEAR 500
160 DIM A(25),C$(25),T(25)
170 PRINT"THIS IS A TEST FOR CLAIRVOYANCE. USING"
180 PRINT"FIVE EACH OF THE SYMBOLS *, +, -, =,"
190 PRINT"AND 0, THE SUBJECT WILL TRY TO GUESS THE"
200 PRINT"SYMBOL CARD, FROM THE SHUFFLED DECK,"
210 PRINT"IN ORDER FROM 1 TO 25. AFTER THE TEST IS"
220 PRINT"COMPLETED, A SCORE IS GIVEN. A SCORE OF"
230 PRINT"5 OR LESS IS AVERAGE. A SCORE OF 6 OR"
240 PRINT"MORE, AFTER AT LEAST 5 TESTS, MAY BE AN"
250 PRINT"INDICATION OF CLAIRVOYANCE."
260 GOSUB1260
270 GOSUB1260
280 PRINT
290 PRINT"ENTER SUBJECT'S NAME"
300 INPUT N$:PRINT
310 PRINT"ENTER DATE (MM/DD/YY)"
320 INPUT D$
330 PRINT
340 CLS:G=0:T=0
350 PRINT"ENTER A '1' TO SHUFFLE THE CARDS"
360 INPUTA
370 IFA<>1THEN340
380 PRINT"NOW SHUFFLING":GOSUB840
390 PRINT:G=G+1:T=T+1
400 PRINT"SHUFFLING COMPLETED"
410 GOSUB1260
420 GOSUB1260
430 CLS
440 PRINT"CLAIRVOYANCE TEST ";T
450 PRINT:PRINT"DATE :  ";D$
460 PRINT"SUBJECT: ";N$
470 PRINT
480 FORA=1TO25
490 PRINT"CARD# ";A,"TEST ";T
500 PRINT
510 PRINT"ENTER SYMBOL GUESS"
520 PRINT"(* + - = 0)"
530 INPUT C$:CLS
540 IFC$=C$(A) THEN T(G)=T(G)+1
550 NEXTA
560 PRINT
570 PRINT"ANOTHER TEST?"
580 PRINT"Y=YES  N=NO"
590 INPUT A$
600 IF A$="Y" THEN 350
610 CLS
620 PRINT"CLAIRVOYANCE TEST SCORING"
```

```
630 PRINT"DATE:  ";D$
640 PRINT"SUBJECT:  ";N$
650 PRINT
660 PRINT"CORRECT SCORE OUT OF 25"
670 J=0
680 FORA=1TOG
690 PRINT"TEST # ";A
700 PRINT T(A):J=T(A)+J
710 NEXTA
720 GOSUB1260
730 PRINT"AVERAGE SCORE OUT OF ";G
740 PRINT"TEST(S) IS ";J/G
750 PRINT
760 PRINT"THAT'S ";J/G*4;" PERCENT CORRECT"
770 GOSUB1260:GOSUB1260:GOSUB1140
780 PRINT"WOULD YOU LIKE A PLOT"
790 PRINT"OF THE TEST SCORES"
800 PRINT"Y=YES  N=NO"
810 INPUT A$
820 IFA$="Y" THEN 980
830 END
840 FORN=1TO25
850 A(N)=0
860 NEXTN
870 FORN=1TO25
880 M=RND(25)
890 FORA=1TOM
900 READ B$
910 NEXTA
920 RESTORE
930 IF A(M)=1THEN880
940 A(M)=1
950 C$(M)=B$
960 NEXTN
970 RETURN
980 PRINT"PLOT OF CLAIRVOYANCE TEST DATA"
990 PRINT"SUBJECT:  ";N$;"   DATE: ";D$
1000 PRINT
1010 PRINT"0    5    10   15        25"
1020 PRINT"+++++++++++++++++++++++++"
1030 FORA=1TOG
1040 GG=T(A)
1050 PRINT TAB(GG)".   TEST # ";A
1060 GOSUB1260
1070 NEXTA
1080 END
1090 DATA"*","*","*","*","*"
1100 DATA"+","+","+","+","+"
1110 DATA"-","-","-","-","-"
1120 DATA"=","=","=","=","="
1130 DATA"0","0","0","0","0"
1140 PRINT
1150 IF J/G>=6THEN 1210
```

```
1160 PRINT
1170 PRINT"YOU HAVE AN AVERAGE SCORE."
1180 PRINT"AT THIS TIME, THERE IS NO"
1190 PRINT"INDICATION OF CLAIRVOYANCE."
1200 RETURN
1210 PRINT
1220 PRINT"YOUR SCORE IS ABOVE AVERAGE."
1230 PRINT"THERE IS A POSSIBILITY THAT YOU"
1240 PRINT"ARE CLAIRVOYANT."
1250 RETURN
1260 REM DELAY
1270 FOR Z=1TO500
1280 NEXTZ
1290 RETURN
```

CHAPTER 31

Parapsychology Test 2: Precognition

Precognition is defined as the ability to perceive events before they occur. This program tests for precognition using five each of the symbols *, +, −, =, and 0 stored in the computer. The subject will try to guess the symbol card in order from 1 to 25. The deck is shuffled after all 25 guesses are entered. After the test is completed, a score is given. A score of 6 or more, after at least five consecutive tests, may be an indication of precognition. The program is written in BASIC for your microcomputer. See Program 31-1 for the program listing.

THE PROGRAM

After you run the program, enter your name, or the subject's name, and the date (MM/DD/YY). Then the precognition test number is displayed along with the date, the subject's name, and CARD# 1. You are then requested to enter the symbol guess.

Before entering your guess of the symbol, try to imagine yourself looking into the computer's memory at some future time, after the cards have been shuffled (the cards will not be shuffled until all symbol guesses are entered). Imagine seeing the first symbol which will appear in the shuffled deck. This first symbol will be stored in array C$(1), the second will be in C$(2), and so on through the twenty-fifth card. Enter the first symbol that appears in your mind. The program will advance to card No. 2. Continue entering the symbols in this manner until all 25 guesses are entered. Then the cards will be shuffled. You may now take another test, by entering a Y, or end the testing with an N.

Entering an N will cause the computer to display your test data including your score out of 25, for each test, the average score out of G tests taken, and the percent score. Then an analysis is given. If your average score is 6 or above, the program will indicate that there is a possibility that you have precognition abilities. If your average score is 5 or less, the program will indicate that you have an average score and there is no indication of precognition.

It is recommended that at least five tests are taken to ensure an accurate analysis of your test data. The program allows a maximum of 25 consecutive tests.

PLOT

After your test scoring is complete, you may see a plot of the test data. The total score for each test is plotted horizontally, using the TAB function. A period (.) is displayed, along with the test number, at TAB(GG) on the horizontal line, where GG is the test score for each test as taken from the array T(A).

See Fig. 31-1 for a sample run.

```
PARAPSYCHOLOGY TEST 2: PRECOGNITION
COPYRIGHT (C) 1980 BY HOWARD BERENBON

THIS IS A TEST FOR PRECOGNITION. USING
FIVE EACH OF THE SYMBOLS *, +, -, =,
AND 0, THE SUBJECT WILL TRY TO GUESS
THE SYMBOL CARD IN ORDER FROM 1 TO 25.
THE DECK IS SHUFFLED AFTER ALL 25
GUESSES ARE ENTERED. AFTER THE TEST IS
COMPLETED, A SCORE IS GIVEN. A SCORE OF
5 OR LESS IS AVERAGE. A SCORE OF 6 OR
MORE, AFTER AT LEAST 5 TESTS, MAY BE AN
INDICATION THAT THE SUBJECT CAN
PREDICT THE FUTURE.


ENTER SUBJECT'S NAME
? BRUCE

ENTER DATE (MM/DD/YY)
? 05/07/80



PRECOGNITION TEST  1

DATE :  05/07/80
SUBJECT: BRUCE

CARD#  1          TEST  1

ENTER SYMBOL GUESS
(* + - = 0)
? =


CARD#  2          TEST  1

ENTER SYMBOL GUESS
(* + - = 0)
? +


CARD#  3          TEST  1

ENTER SYMBOL GUESS
(* + - = 0)
? *


CARD#  4          TEST  1

ENTER SYMBOL GUESS
(* + - = 0)
? *


CARD#  5          TEST  1

ENTER SYMBOL GUESS
(* + - = 0)
? 0

CARD#  24         TEST  1

ENTER SYMBOL GUESS
(* + - = 0)
? =


CARD#  25         TEST  1

ENTER SYMBOL GUESS
(* + - = 0)
? -


ENTRY COMPLETED AND RECORDED

STAND BY . . .
THE CARDS ARE BEING SHUFFLED

SHUFFLING COMPLETED


NOW SCORING


TEST  1   SCORE RECORDED

ANOTHER TEST?
Y=YES  N=NO
? N


PRECOGNITION TEST SCORING
DATE:  05/07/80
SUBJECT:  BRUCE

CORRECT SCORE OUT OF 25
TEST #  1
 5
AVERAGE SCORE OUT OF  1
TEST(S) IS  5
THAT'S  20  PERCENT CORRECT


YOU HAVE AN AVERAGE SCORE.
AT THIS TIME, THERE IS NO
INDICATION OF PRECOGNITION
ABILITIES.

WOULD YOU LIKE A PLOT
OF THE TEST SCORES
Y=YES  N=NO
? Y


PLOT OF PRECOGNITION TEST DATA
SUBJECT:  BRUCE    DATE: 05/07/80

0    5    10   15        25
++++++++++++++++++++++++++
         TEST #  1
```

Fig. 31-1. Parasychology Test 2: Precognition sample run.

Program 31-1. Parapsychology Test 2: Precognition Program Listing

```
100 CLS:PRINT"PARAPSYCHOLOGY TEST 2: PRECOGNITION"
110 PRINT"TRS-80 LEVEL II"
120 PRINT"COPYRIGHT (C) 1980 BY HOWARD BERENBON"
130 PRINT
140 CLEAR 500
150 DIM A(25),C$(25),T(25),D$(25)
160 PRINT"THIS IS A TEST FOR PRECOGNITION. USING"
170 PRINT"FIVE EACH OF THE SYMBOLS *, +, -, =,"
180 PRINT"AND 0, THE SUBJECT WILL TRY TO GUESS"
190 PRINT"THE SYMBOL CARD IN ORDER FROM 1 TO 25."
200 PRINT"THE DECK IS SHUFFLED AFTER ALL 25"
210 PRINT"GUESSES ARE ENTERED. AFTER THE TEST IS"
220 PRINT"COMPLETED, A SCORE IS GIVEN. A SCORE OF"
230 PRINT"5 OR LESS IS AVERAGE. A SCORE OF 6 OR"
240 PRINT"MORE, AFTER AT LEAST 5 TESTS, MAY BE AN"
250 PRINT"INDICATION THAT THE SUBJECT CAN"
260 PRINT"PREDICT THE FUTURE."
270 GOSUB1250
280 GOSUB1250
290 PRINT
300 PRINT"ENTER SUBJECT'S NAME"
310 INPUT N$:PRINT
320 PRINT"ENTER DATE (MM/DD/YY)"
330 INPUT D$
340 PRINT
350 CLS:G=0:T=0
360 T=T+1
370 CLS
380 PRINT"PRECOGNITION TEST ";T
390 PRINT:PRINT"DATE :  ";D$
400 PRINT"SUBJECT: ";N$
410 PRINT
420 FORA=1TO25
430 PRINT"CARD# ";A,"TEST ";T
440 PRINT
450 PRINT"ENTER SYMBOL GUESS"
460 PRINT"(* + - = 0)"
470 INPUT C$:CLS
480 D$(A)=C$
490 NEXTA
500 PRINT:PRINT"ENTRY COMPLETED AND RECORDED"
510 GOSUB1250:GOSUB1250
520 GOSUB1320
530 PRINT"ANOTHER TEST?"
540 PRINT"Y=YES  N=NO"
550 INPUT A$
560 IF A$="Y" THEN 360
570 CLS
580 PRINT"PRECOGNITION TEST SCORING"
590 PRINT"DATE:  ";D$
600 PRINT"SUBJECT:  ";N$
610 PRINT
620 PRINT"CORRECT SCORE OUT OF 25"
```

```
3280 CLS:PRINT"YOU HAVE ";H1;" 'HIT-POINT(S)' LEFT"
3290 GOTO1120
3300 W=RND(4)+30
3310 FORAA=1TOW
3320 READMS$,HP,HM
3330 NEXTAA
3340 RESTORE
3350 PRINT
3360 PRINT"THERE IS SOMETHING LURKING"
3370 PRINT"IN THIS CORRIDOR . . .":GOSUB460
3380 PRINT:GOTO3680
3390 TE=1:TL=1
3400 IFK=1THEN3460
3410 K=1:PRINT:PRINT"YOU NOTICE A SHINY OBJECT . . . ."
3420 PRINT". . . . AT YOUR FEET":GOSUB460
3430 PRINT"YOU PICK IT UP AND FIND THAT . . ."
3440 PRINT"IT IS THE ENCHANTED KEY . . . . .":GOSUB460
3450 PRINT:PRINT"BUT YOU WEREN'T CAREFUL . . . .":GOSUB460
3460 PRINT"YOU ACTIVATED SOME SORT OF TRAP . . .":GOSUB460
3470 C=RND(8):D=RND(8):BB=5:GOSUB470:CLS
3480 PRINT"SUDDENLY YOU FEEL DIZZY, AND PASS OUT"
3490 PRINT:BB=2:GOSUB470:GOSUB3540
3500 PRINT"WHEN YOU WAKE UP . . . YOU FIND"
3510 PRINT"THAT YOU WERE . . . . TELEPORTED"
3520 PRINT"TO AN UNKNOWN LOCATION . . . ."
3530 BB=5:GOSUB470:RETURN
3540 FORAA=1TO300
3550 PRINT"*        %";
3560 NEXTAA
3570 GOSUB460:CLS:RETURN
3580 IFA=4THEN3600
3590 W=RND(15):GOTO3610
3600 W=RND(15)+15
3610 FORAA=1TOW
3620 READMS$,HP,HM
3630 NEXTAA
3640 RESTORE
3650 PRINT
3660 PRINT"THERE IS SOMETHING LURKING . . . "
3670 PRINT". . . . IN THIS CHAMBER . . . .":GOSUB460
3680 PRINT". . . . . . . . . . . BEWARE":GOSUB460
3690 PRINT
3700 PRINT"IT IS A . . . . . ";MS$;" . . ":GOSUB460
3710 GOTO4510
3720 DATA"LARGE DRAGON",6,12
3730 DATA"HIDIOUS GHOUL",5,10
3740 DATA"LIZARD MAN",4,8
3750 DATA"MANTICORE",6,12
3760 DATA"PURPLE WORM",6,12
3770 DATA"DEADLY COBRA",5,10
3780 DATA"MAD ELF",5,10
3790 DATA"CLAY MAN",4,8
3800 DATA"HAIRY BEAST",5,10
```

```
1160 PRINT"INDICATION OF PRECOGNITION"
1170 PRINT"ABILITIES."
1180 PRINT
1190 RETURN
1200 PRINT"YOUR SCORE IS ABOVE AVERAGE."
1210 PRINT"THERE IS A POSSIBILITY THAT YOU"
1220 PRINT"HAVE PRECOGNITION ABILITIES"
1230 PRINT
1240 RETURN
1250 REM DELAY
1260 FOR Z=1TO500
1270 NEXTZ
1280 RETURN
1290 PRINT
1300 PRINT"YOUR SCORE IS LESS THAN AVERAGE."
1310 GOTO1150
1320 PRINT
1330 PRINT"STAND BY . . ."
1340 PRINT"THE CARDS ARE BEING SHUFFLED"
1350 GOSUB800
1360 PRINT:G=G+1
1370 PRINT"SHUFFLING COMPLETED"
1380 GOSUB1250
1390 PRINT:GOSUB1250:GOSUB1250
1400 PRINT"NOW SCORING"
1410 GOSUB1250:GOSUB1250
1420 FORA=1TO25
1430 IFC$(A)=D$(A)THENT(G)=T(G)+1
1440 NEXTA
1450 CLS:PRINT"TEST ";T;"  SCORE RECORDED"
1460 GOSUB1250
1470 PRINT
1480 RETURN
```

SECTION V

A Fantasy Game

This last section includes a complete fantasy game called The Dungeon of Danger. It is the longest program in the book, requiring almost 16K of RAM to run.

Here, you may choose your fantasy character's name and boldly roam the chambers and corridors of the dungeon, with your magic sword, seeking out monsters and gold. Your goal is to find your way out, unharmed, with as much gold as possible. Good luck.

CHAPTER 32

The Dungeon of Danger

The Dungeon of Danger is an adventure fantasy game in which the player must fight monsters as he or she wanders through the chambers and corridors of the dungeon. It's a two-level dungeon, based on the fantasy role-playing game Dungeons and Dragons.* It's written in BASIC for your microcomputer, and it requires 16K of RAM to run. See Program 32-1 for the program listing.

THE PROGRAM

You are given 500 gold pieces and are teleported to a random location in the lower level of this 128-chamber, two-level (64 chambers per level) dungeon. Your goal is to find your way out, with as much gold as possible. Gold pieces are acquired by finding and killing monsters that occupy the dungeon. Each time you kill a monster, you will find a random amount of gold in the chamber. But, monsters fight back, and if you're not careful you can be killed and lose the game. There are other places in the dungeon where gold may be found, but this will be discussed later.

ACTIONS OR MOVES

In your trip through the dungeon you will encounter monsters (up to 37 types), thieves, empty chambers, trap doors, secret doors leading to north-south or east-west corridors, caverns, vials (filled with liquids that can heal), teleportation traps, maps, enchanted keys, and stairways leading up.

See Fig. 32-1 for a sample run.

After you run the program, enter your name or your favorite fantasy character's name, for your trip into the Dungeon of Danger. Then enter the difficulty level; enter a 1 for moderate or a 2 for difficult. The computer will then generate your "hit-point" value for combat. A typical hit-point value for difficulty level 1 is about 26, and for difficulty level 2 is about 15. When fighting, if a monster scores a "hit" on you, then this number is subtracted from your current hit-point value. If your hit-point value is depleted to zero, then you will die and lose the game. Each monster has a different strength, and may be difficult to kill, depending on its hit-point number.

After your hit-point value is generated, you will be teleported to a random location in the lower level of the dungeon.

You now have a choice of eight actions. Enter the letter in parentheses for the following actions or moves in the dungeon:

(N)ORTH movement	(up)
(E)AST movement	(right)
(S)OUTH movement	(down)
(W)EST movement	(left)
(U)P movement	(when at a stairway, and have the enchanted key)
(M)AP display	(if found-when encountering thieves)
(G)OLD pieces left	
(H)IT POINTS left	

North Movement (UP)

Entering an N allows you to move north through the dungeon. You may not move north under the following conditions:

1. If you reach the North Wall, you cannot pass through it.
2. If you enter an east-west corridor (through

* Dungeons and Dragons is a registered trademark of TSR Hobbies, Inc.

```
THE DUNGEON OF DANGER
COPYRIGHT (C) 1980 BY HOWARD BERENBON

A FANTASY GAME




YOU WILL BE TELEPORTED TO . . .

THE DUNGEON OF DANGER

ENTER DIFFICULTY LEVEL?
1=MODERATE  2=DIFFICULT
? 1

ENTER YOUR CHARACTER'S NAME?
? FRODO




YOU CARRY A MAGIC SWORD
AND 500 GOLD PIECES WITH YOU.
YOUR 'HIT-POINT' VALUE IS  21
IF IT REACHES ZERO, YOU WILL DIE
. . . . . . . . . SO BE CAREFUL

FRODO . . . YOU ARE ON YOUR WAY



YOU HAVE ARRIVED AT . . . .

THE DUNGEON OF DANGER . . . LEVEL 2

YOU WILL ENCOUNTER MONSTERS AND
THIEVES, AND GOLD . . . GOOD LUCK




YOU ARE IN A DAMP AND MISTY
. . . . . . . EMPTY CHAMBER

FRODO,  WHAT IS YOUR ACTION OR MOVE?

(N)ORTH, (E)AST, (S)OUTH, (W)EST
(U)P, (M)AP, (G)OLD, (H)IT POINTS
? N




THERE IS SOMETHING LURKING . . .
. . . . IN THIS CHAMBER . . . .
. . . . . . . . . . . . BEWARE

IT IS A . . . . . VAMPIRE BAT . .


WILL YOU (F)IGHT OR (R)UN ?
? F



YOU ATTACK THE . . . VAMPIRE BAT
WITH A SWING OF YOUR SWORD
YOU DO  2  HIT POINT(S) OF DAMAGE

IT HAS . .  4  'HIT-POINT(S)' LEFT

. . . . . . . IT ATTACKS YOU
AND IT DOES  2  'HIT-POINT(S)' OF DAMAGE

YOU HAVE . . .  19  'HIT-POINT(S)' LEFT


WILL YOU (F)IGHT OR (R)UN ?
? F

YOU ATTACK THE . . . VAMPIRE BAT
WITH A SWING OF YOUR SWORD

YOU HAVE KILLED THE VAMPIRE BAT

YOU SEARCH THE AREA . . . .
AND FIND . . .  229  GOLD PIECES

FRODO,  WHAT IS YOUR ACTION OR MOVE?

(N)ORTH, (E)AST, (S)OUTH, (W)EST
(U)P, (M)AP, (G)OLD, (H)IT POINTS
? E



YOU ENTER AN . . . EAST-WEST CORRIDOR
THRU A . . . . . . . SECRET DOOR

THE DOOR CLOSES AND LOCKS BEHIND YOU

FRODO,  WHAT IS YOUR ACTION OR MOVE?

(N)ORTH, (E)AST, (S)OUTH, (W)EST
(U)P, (M)AP, (G)OLD, (H)IT POINTS
? E



THERE IS A THIEF IN THIS CHAMBER

. . . . . . . . HE SURPRISES YOU
AS HE QUICKLY PASSES BY YOU HE
SNATCHES . . .  65  GOLD PIECES

FRODO,  WHAT IS YOUR ACTION OR MOVE?

(N)ORTH, (E)AST, (S)OUTH, (W)EST
(U)P, (M)AP, (G)OLD, (H)IT POINTS
? N




YOU STUMBLED ONTO . . . . .
A HIDDEN CAVERN

YOU LOOK AROUND . . .
ON THE GROUND, AT YOUR FEET, IS A VIAL

YOU PICK UP THE VIAL . . AND SEE THAT
IT CONTAINS . . . A MILKY LIQUID

WOULD YOU LIKE A DRINK?
ENTER (Y)ES  OR  (N)O
? Y


YOU TAKE A DRINK . . .


IT WAS A WHITE MAGIC POTION . . .
WHICH INCREASED YOUR 'HIT-POINTS' BY  12

THE CAVERN SEEMS EMPTY . . .

FRODO,  WHAT IS YOUR ACTION OR MOVE?

(N)ORTH, (E)AST, (S)OUTH, (W)EST
(U)P, (M)AP, (G)OLD, (H)IT POINTS
? W



YOU ARE IN A DAMP AND MISTY
. . . . . . . EMPTY CHAMBER

FRODO,  WHAT IS YOUR ACTION OR MOVE?

(N)ORTH, (E)AST, (S)OUTH, (W)EST
(U)P, (M)AP, (G)OLD, (H)IT POINTS
? W
```

Fig. 32-1. The Dungeon

```
THERE IS SOMETHING LURKING . . .
. . . . IN THIS CHAMBER . . . .
. . . . . . . . . . . . BEWARE

IT IS A . . . . . BLACK CAT . .


. . . . . . . IT ATTACKS YOU
AND IT DOES  2  'HIT-POINT(S)' OF DAMAGE

YOU HAVE . . .  36  'HIT-POINT(S)' LEFT


WILL YOU (F)IGHT OR (R)UN ?
? F



YOU ATTACK THE . . . BLACK CAT
WITH A SWING OF YOUR SWORD

YOU HAVE KILLED THE BLACK CAT

YOU SEARCH THE AREA . . . .
AND FIND . . .  126  GOLD PIECES

FRODO,  WHAT IS YOUR ACTION OR MOVE?

(N)ORTH, (E)AST, (S)OUTH, (W)EST
(U)P, (M)AP, (G)OLD, (H)IT POINTS
? S



THERE IS A THIEF IN THIS CHAMBER

. . . . . . . HE SURPRISES YOU
AS HE QUICKLY PASSES BY YOU HE
SNATCHES . . .  135  GOLD PIECES

YOU SEARCH THE CHAMBER AND
YOU . . . . . FIND A MAP

FRODO,  WHAT IS YOUR ACTION OR MOVE?

(N)ORTH, (E)AST, (S)OUTH, (W)EST
(U)P, (M)AP, (G)OLD, (H)IT POINTS
? S



YOU ARE AT A STAIRWAY
 . . . . . . GOING UP


FRODO,  WHAT IS YOUR ACTION OR MOVE?

(N)ORTH, (E)AST, (S)OUTH, (W)EST
(U)P, (M)AP, (G)OLD, (H)IT POINTS
? U



YOU WALK UP THE STAIRWAY
THE ENCHANTED KEY . . . OPENS THE LOCK

YOU ARE AT . . . . . LEVEL 1



THERE IS SOMETHING LURKING . . .
. . . . IN THIS CHAMBER . . . .
. . . . . . . . . . . . BEWARE

IT IS A . . . . . DEADLY COBRA . .


WILL YOU (F)IGHT OR (R)UN ?
? F



YOU ATTACK THE . . . DEADLY COBRA
WITH A SWING OF YOUR SWORD

YOU HAVE KILLED THE DEADLY COBRA

YOU SEARCH THE AREA . . . .
AND FIND . . .  571  GOLD PIECES

FRODO,  WHAT IS YOUR ACTION OR MOVE?

(N)ORTH, (E)AST, (S)OUTH, (W)EST
(U)P, (M)AP, (G)OLD, (H)IT POINTS
? E



YOU ACTIVATED A . . . TRAP DOOR

BUT . . . YOU CAUGHT YOURSELF
FROM FALLING

FRODO,  WHAT IS YOUR ACTION OR MOVE?

(N)ORTH, (E)AST, (S)OUTH, (W)EST
(U)P, (M)AP, (G)OLD, (H)IT POINTS
? S



THERE IS SOMETHING LURKING . . .
. . . . IN THIS CHAMBER . . . .
. . . . . . . . . . . . BEWARE

IT IS A . . . . . BERSERKER . .


. . . . . . . IT ATTACKS YOU
AND IT DOES  11  'HIT-POINT(S)' OF DAMAGE

YOU HAVE . . .  25  'HIT-POINT(S)' LEFT


WILL YOU (F)IGHT OR (R)UN ?
? F



YOU ATTACK THE . . . BERSERKER
WITH A SWING OF YOUR SWORD

YOU HAVE KILLED THE BERSERKER

YOU SEARCH THE AREA . . . .
AND FIND . . .  126  GOLD PIECES

FRODO,  WHAT IS YOUR ACTION OR MOVE?

(N)ORTH, (E)AST, (S)OUTH, (W)EST
(U)P, (M)AP, (G)OLD, (H)IT POINTS
? N



YOU ARE AT A STAIRWAY
 . . . . . . GOING UP


FRODO,  WHAT IS YOUR ACTION OR MOVE?

(N)ORTH, (E)AST, (S)OUTH, (W)EST
(U)P, (M)AP, (G)OLD, (H)IT POINTS
? U



YOU WALK UP THE STAIRWAY
THE ENCHANTED KEY . . . OPENS THE LOCK
YOU FOUND YOUR WAY . . .
. . . OUT OF THE DUNGEON OF DANGER

YOU HAVE ACQUIRED  2708  GOLD PIECES

GAME RATING IS  556  = WARRIOR

YOU TOOK  48  TURNS TO FIND THE WAY OUT,
AND KILLED  12  MONSTERS.

ANOTHER GAME?
ENTER (Y)ES  OR  (N)O
? Y
```

of Danger sample run.

a secret door), movement north is not allowed.

East Movement (RIGHT)

Entering an E allows you to move east. You may not move east under the following conditions:

1. If you reach the East Wall, you cannot pass through it.
2. If you enter a north-south corridor (through a secret door), movement east is not allowed.

South Movement (DOWN)

Entering an S allows you to move south. You may not move south under the following conditions:

1. If you reach the South Wall, you cannot pass through it.
2. If you enter an east-west corridor (through a secret door), movement south is not allowed.

West Movement (LEFT)

Entering a W allows you to move west. You may not move west under the following conditions:

1. If you reach the West Wall, you cannot pass through it.
2. If you enter a north-south corridor (through a secret door), movement west is not allowed.

Up Movement

Entering a U, when you are at a stairway and have found the Enchanted Key, allows you to go up to the next level. If you haven't found the key or you are not at a stairway, you cannot go up the stairway. To find the Enchanted Key, you must kill a random number of monsters for each level. Also, there is a different key for each level.

Map Display

Entering an M, when you have found a map, will display the map for that level. Each level has a different map, and they may be found when encountering thieves. The 64-chamber dungeon is displayed using the following symbols:

M = monster
0 = empty chamber
? = unknown contents (either a thief or a trap door)
C = cavern
UP = stairway up
NS = north-south corridor (entered through secret doors)
EW = east-west corridor (entered through secret doors)
=P= = your location in the dungeon

See Fig. 32-2 for a sample map.

```
THE DUNGEON OF DANGER-MAP:  LEV   1

M   EW  NS  M   0   C   M   UP
EW  EW  EW  C   0   M   0   M
NS  EW  EW  ?   0   M   M   UP
M   C   UP  NS  0   NS  C   C
NS  ?   0   ?   0   M   0   NS
?   UP  ?   NS  0   P1  M   0
?   M   NS  NS  0   0   0   M
NS  EW  EW  0   C   0   EW  ?

FRODO,  WHAT IS YOUR ACTION OR MOVE?

(N)ORTH, (E)AST, (S)OUTH, (W)EST
(U)P, (M)AP, (G)OLD, (H)IT POINTS
? N
```

Fig. 32-2. The Dungeon of Danger sample map.

A question mark (?) indicates either a thief or a trap door. There is no way of knowing which is there, unless you enter the chamber. If you encounter a thief, either you surprise him and he drops some of his gold, or he surprises you and steals some of your gold. This is randomly determined, but it's in favor of the thief. After you encounter a thief, the chamber becomes empty.

If you activate a trap door, you can either fall through or catch yourself from falling. If you fall through, you will lose most of your gold pieces, when playing at difficulty level 1 (moderate). But you can die if you are playing at difficulty level 2 (difficult). There is a 25-percent chance that you will fall through, when your difficulty level is 1, and a 50-percent chance when your difficulty is 2. If you are at level two of the dungeon, then you will fall into a deep pit. If you made it up to level one, then you will fall back down to level two. Avoid these traps, if possible.

When displaying the map, your location in the dungeon is identified with the symbol =P=.

Gold Pieces Left

Entering a G will display the number of gold pieces you have with you. You will start out with 500 and can gain or lose gold during your trip. The more gold you acquire, the better your game rating will be.

Hit-Points Left

Entering an H will display the number of hit-points you have left. Also, each time you fight a monster, your number of hit-points left is displayed.

MONSTERS AND FIGHTING

When you are entering into a chamber occupied by a monster, the monster may or may not attack you. Then, you have the option of fighting, by entering an F, or running, by entering an R.

Fighting

If you choose to fight, then enter an F. Your character will swing at the monster with his magic sword, always making contact, and damaging it by depleting some of its hit-points. But then the monster will attack you and possibly score a hit, depleting some of your hit-points. There is a chance that the monster will miss you, if you are lucky. You may now continue fighting until the monster is killed, it kills you, or you run out.

Each monster has a different hit-point number, depending on its strength. A weak monster (easy to kill) will have a hit-point value of between 1 and 3. A monster with a hit-point value of 4 or greater is considered strong and more difficult to kill. The stronger the monster, the harder it can hit you. Each of the 37 monsters have two hit-point numbers. The first number is the maximum it can hit you with, at one time, and the second is the number of hit-points required to kill it. The DATA statements in program lines 3720 through 4050 hold the names and hit-points of most of the monsters in the dungeon. This data may be changed, or modified, for different monsters with different strengths. The last four monsters in the data list are the corridor monsters. They are the weakest and easiest to kill.

Each hit on a monster will deplete its hit-point value, until it reaches zero, then it is killed. Each time you kill a monster, you will find a random amount of gold in the chamber, and then the chamber becomes empty.

Running

When fighting a monster, you have the option of running away, by entering an R. This option should be used if your hit-point value is low and you may not survive the next attack. This choice depends on the strength of the monster. Use your own judgment. Entering an R will send you back to the chamber that you previously occupied, but the monster can attack you, with one or two hit-points, as you leave.

Your Strength at Different Levels

The number of hit-points that you deplete from a monster increases with the number of monsters you have killed. So, generally, the more monsters you kill, the easier it will be to kill the next monster that you encounter.

Generally, monsters are more difficult to kill at level one of the dungeon. But if you have killed a large number in finding your way up from level two to level one, then they should be easier to kill, due to your experience. Also, your reward for killing a monster at level one is generally higher than at level two.

CAVERNS

There are several things that can happen to you when you enter into a cavern. Often you will find vials filled with liquids. These liquids can heal wounds, two-thirds of the time, by increasing your hit-point value after you drink them. But sometimes the liquids have no effect, or even decrease your hit-point value slightly. It is recommended that you drink the liquid, if your hit-point value is low.

You may run into giant spiders or the Dark Wizards. They can hit hard and are difficult to kill, so be careful. But fortunately there are the Ancient Wizards that you may encounter. They will increase your hit-point value and give you gold.

Pools of Water

On the lower level of the dungeon (level two), there are pools of water that you may fall into. The following three things can happen when you fall into a pool:

1. You may be attacked by a Gill Monster; and he's not easy to kill.
2. The water will feel warm and soothing; and nothing happens.
3. The water will be steaming hot; and you will lose a random number of gold pieces in the pool.

NORTH-SOUTH AND EAST-WEST CORRIDORS

North-south and east-west corridors may be entered from any direction (through secret doors), but will limit your next move to the direction displayed.

Three things can happen when entering into a corridor:

1. You can activate a teleportation trap and be teleported to an unknown location (at your present level) in the dungeon.
2. You can encounter corridor monsters that may or may not attack you.

3. Or, the corridor can be empty.

There are four types of monsters that you may encounter in the corridors. They are among the weakest of the monsters in the dungeon and can be killed quite easily. They are as follows:

1. Gelatinous Cube
2. Giant Centipede
3. Giant Rat
4. Shadow

No other monsters can appear in the corridors.

WINNING

To win the game you must sucessfully make it up through the two levels and then exit the dungeon.

LOSING

You will lose the game if your hit-point value is depleted to 0. But in some cases (about 50 percent of the time) you will get a second chance. Your hit-points will be restored, and then you will be allowed a random number of moves (based on the number of monsters previously killed) to find your way out. If you die again, you won't get another chance.

GAME RATING

After you complete the game, a game rating is displayed along with the number of gold pieces acquired, the number of monsters killed, and the number of turns (moves) taken. The rating is a number from approximately −600 to +2000, depending on the statistics above. The higher the rating number, the better is the game rating.

Along with the number rating, there is a title rating. The following is a list of ten possible title ratings, and their scores:

−401 or less	Incompetent Serf
−101 to −400	Weakling
−100 to −1	Apprentice
0 to 99	Halfling
100 to 199	Foot Soldier
200 to 599	Warrior
600 to 899	Great Warrior
900 to 1499	Swordsman
1500 to 2499	Magic Swordsman
2500 and above	Dungeon Master

After the game is completed, you may play another game by entering a Y for yes, or end the game by entering an N for no.

THE MONSTER LIST

The following is a list of monsters that appear in the dungeon, with their hit-point values. The first number is used to generate its hit on you. The second number is its strength:

Gill Monster	8	14
Dark Wizard	8	14
Giant Spider	6	12
Large Dragon	6	12
Hideous Ghoul	5	10
Lizard Man	4	8
Manticore	6	12
Purple Worm	6	12
Deadly Cobra	5	10
Mad Elf	5	10
Clay Man	4	8
Hairy Beast	5	10
Mad Dwarf	4	8
Zombie	4	8
Berserker	5	10
Giant Scorpion	6	12
Giant Cockroach	4	8
Doppleganger	5	10
Giant Fire Beetle	1	2
Giant Ant	1	2
Giant Tick	2	4
Mummy	3	6
Nasty Orc	2	4
Skeleton	1	2
Troll	3	6
Goblin	3	6
Vampire Bat	3	6
Creeping Blob	3	6
Mad Dog	2	4
Large Spider	3	6
Black Cat	2	4
Man-Eating Plant	1	2
Hydra	3	6
Gelatinous Cube	2	4
Giant Centipede	1	2
Giant Rat	2	4
Shadow	2	4

Program 32-1. The Dungeon of Danger Program Listing

```
100 CLS:CLEAR 500:DEFINTA-D
110 PRINT"THE DUNGEON OF DANGER"
120 PRINT"TRS-80 LEVEL II"
130 PRINT"COPYRIGHT (C) 1980 BY HOWARD BERENBON"
140 PRINT
150 PRINT"A FANTASY GAME"
160 BB=2
170 GOSUB470
180 CLS:DIMA(9,9,2)
190 PRINT"YOU WILL BE TELEPORTED TO . . . "
200 PRINT
210 PRINT"THE DUNGEON OF DANGER"
220 PRINT:DY=0:MD=1
230 RANDOM:GOSUB5530
240 MA=0:CA=0:G=500:M1=1:K=0:HI=20+RND(15):HI=INT(HI/PL)
250 H1=HI:PRINT"ENTER YOUR CHARACTER'S NAME?"
260 INPUTA$
270 GOSUB460
280 PRINT:PRINT"YOU CARRY A MAGIC SWORD"
290 PRINT"AND 500 GOLD PIECES WITH YOU."
300 PRINT"YOUR 'HIT-POINT' VALUE IS ";H1:GOSUB460
310 PRINT"IF IT REACHES ZERO, YOU WILL DIE"
320 PRINT". . . . . . . . SO BE CAREFUL"
330 PRINT:GOSUB460:PRINTA$;" . . . YOU ARE ON YOUR WAY"
340 BB=5:GOSUB470
350 GOSUB500
360 CLS
370 PRINT"YOU HAVE ARRIVED AT . . . ."
380 PRINT
390 PRINT"THE DUNGEON OF DANGER . . . LEVEL 2"
400 PRINT
410 PRINT"YOU WILL ENCOUNTER MONSTERS AND"
420 PRINT"THIEVES, AND GOLD . . . GOOD LUCK"
430 BB=6
440 GOSUB470
450 GOTO1030
460 BB=1
470 FORZZ=1TO400*BB
480 NEXTZZ
490 RETURN
500 FORX=1TO8
510 FORY=1TO8
520 FORZ=1TO2
530 A(X,Y,Z)=RND(7)
540 NEXTZ
550 NEXTY
560 NEXTX
570 H=RND(3)
580 FORA=1TO2
590 FORN=1TOH
600 X=RND(8)
610 Y=RND(8)
620 A(X,Y,A)=8
```

```
630 NEXTN
640 NEXTA
650 S=RND(4)+2
660 FORA=1TO2
670 FORN=1TOS
680 X=RND(8)
690 Y=RND(8)
700 A(X,Y,A)=9
710 NEXTN
720 NEXTA
730 RETURN
740 L1=L1-1
750 PRINT"YOU WALK UP THE STAIRWAY"
760 GOSUB460
770 PRINT"THE ENCHANTED KEY . . . OPENS THE LOCK"
780 GOSUB460
790 IFL1=0THEN890
800 MA=0:K=0:K4=RND(4)+1:IFH1<HITHEN820
810 GOTO 850
820 H1=HI
830 PRINT"YOU FEEL STRONGER . . . . .":GOSUB460
840 PRINT"YOUR 'HIT-POINTS' ARE RESTORED TO ";HI
850 PRINT:CB=CA+K4
860 PRINT"YOU ARE AT . . . . . LEVEL 1"
870 BB=4:GOSUB470
880 GOTO1070
890 PRINT"YOU FOUND YOUR WAY . . . "
900 PRINT". . . OUT OF THE DUNGEON OF DANGER"
910 PRINT
920 PRINT"YOU HAVE ACQUIRED ";G;" GOLD PIECES"
930 GOSUB950
940 GOTO1810
950 GG=G+100
960 R=INT((GG*CA-7000+1)/M1)
970 PRINT
980 PRINT"GAME RATING IS ";R;" = ";:GOSUB5620
990 PRINT:IFG<=0THEN3210
1000 PRINT"YOU TOOK ";M1;" TURNS TO FIND THE WAY OUT,"
1010 PRINT"AND KILLED ";CA;" MONSTERS."
1020 RETURN
1030 C=RND(8)
1040 D=RND(8)
1050 A(C,D,2)=1
1060 L1=2:K4=RND(4)+1
1070 F$=" ":CLS
1080 A=A(C,D,L1)
1090 GOSUB460
1100 ON A GOSUB 2100,4060,3580,3580,2210,2510,2560,2610,2870
1110 IFTE=1THENTE=0:GOTO1070
1120 PRINT:IFH1<=0THEN1700
1130 IFDY=1THENMD=MD-1
1140 IFDY=1ANDMD=0THEN1700
1150 IFF$="R"THEN1070
```

```
1160 PRINTA$;",  WHAT IS YOUR ACTION OR MOVE?"
1170 PRINT
1180 PRINT"(N)ORTH, (E)AST, (S)OUTH, (W)EST"
1190 PRINT"(U)P, (M)AP, (G)OLD, (H)IT POINTS"
1200 INPUTM1$
1210 M1=M1+1:TL=0
1220 C1=C:D1=D
1230 IFM1$="N"THEN1320
1240 IFM1$="E"THEN1360
1250 IFM1$="S"THEN1400
1260 IFM1$="W"THEN1440
1270 IFM1$="U"THEN1480
1280 IFM1$="M"THEN1570
1290 IFM1$="G"THEN1600
1300 IFM1$="H"THEN3280
1310 PRINT:GOTO1120
1320 IFA=7THEN1620
1330 IF(D-1)=0THEN1880
1340 D=D-1
1350 GOTO1070
1360 IFA=6THEN1660
1370 IF(C+1)=9THEN1930
1380 C=C+1
1390 GOTO1070
1400 IFA=7THEN1620
1410 IF(D+1)=9THEN1950
1420 D=D+1
1430 GOTO1070
1440 IFA=6THEN1660
1450 IF(C-1)=0THEN1970
1460 C=C-1
1470 GOTO1070
1480 CLS:IFA<>9THEN1540
1490 IFK=1THEN740
1500 PRINT
1510 PRINT"YOU CANNOT GO UP THE STAIRWAY"
1520 PRINT"YOU DON'T HAVE THE KEY"
1530 GOSUB460:PRINT:GOTO1120
1540 PRINT"YOU ARE NOT AT A STAIRWAY"
1550 GOSUB460:GOTO1120
1560 GOTO 1120
1570 CLS:IF MA=1THEN1990
1580 PRINT"YOU DON'T HAVE THE MAP"
1590 PRINT:GOSUB460:GOTO1120
1600 CLS:PRINT"YOU HAVE ";G;" GOLD PIECES WITH YOU"
1610 PRINT:GOTO1120
1620 PRINT
1630 CLS:PRINT"YOU ARE IN AN EAST-WEST CORRIDOR"
1640 PRINT"YOU CAN ONLY GO EAST OR WEST"
1650 PRINT:GOTO1120
1660 PRINT
1670 CLS:PRINT"YOU ARE IN A NORTH-SOUTH CORRIDOR"
1680 PRINT"YOU CAN ONLY GO NORTH OR SOUTH"
```

```
1690 GOTO1650
1700 BB=2:GOSUB470:CLS:IFDY=1THEN5510
1710 PRINT"YOUR 'HIT-POINTS' HAVE BEEN DEPLETED,"
1720 PRINT:G=0:PRINT"AND UNFORTUNATELY . . . YOU JUST DIED"
1730 BB=5:GOSUB470
1740 PRINT:W=RND(6):IFDY=0ANDW>=3THEN5370
1750 CLS:PRINT"YOU LOST ALL YOUR GOLD AND YOU WERE"
1760 PRINT". . . UNABLE TO MEET THE DEMANDS OF"
1770 PRINT". . . . . THE DUNGEON OF DANGER"
1780 PRINT:PRINT
1790 PRINT"BETTER LUCK NEXT TIME"
1800 GOSUB 950
1810 PRINT
1820 PRINT"ANOTHER GAME?"
1830 PRINT"ENTER (Y)ES  OR  (N)O"
1840 INPUTF$
1850 IFF$="Y"THEN1870
1860 END
1870 CLS:GOTO210
1880 CLS:PRINT"YOU ARE AT THE NORTH WALL"
1890 PRINT"YOU CANNOT PASS THROUGH"
1900 PRINT
1910 PRINT"TRY ANOTHER DIRECTION?"
1920 GOTO 1120
1930 CLS:PRINT"YOU ARE AT THE EAST WALL"
1940 GOTO1890
1950 CLS:PRINT"YOU ARE AT THE SOUTH WALL"
1960 GOTO1890
1970 CLS:PRINT"YOU ARE AT THE WEST WALL"
1980 GOTO1890
1990 CLS:PRINT"THE DUNGEON OF DANGER-MAP:  LEV  ";L1
2000 PRINT
2010 FORQ=1TO8
2020 FORN=1TO8
2030 IFC=N AND D=Q THEN PRINT"P1  ";:GOTO2060
2040 S1=A(N,Q,L1)
2050 ON S1 GOSUB 2910,2970,2930,2930,2950,2990,3010,3030,3040
2060 NEXTN
2070 PRINT
2080 NEXTQ
2090 GOTO1120
2100 W=RND(2):IFW=2THEN2160
2110 PRINT
2120 PRINT"YOU ARE IN A COLD AND DARK"
2130 PRINT" . . . . . . EMPTY CHAMBER"
2140 PRINT
2150 RETURN
2160 PRINT
2170 PRINT"YOU ARE IN A DAMP AND MISTY"
2180 PRINT". . . . . . . EMPTY CHAMBER"
2190 PRINT
2200 RETURN
2210 CLS:PRINT"THERE IS A THIEF IN THIS CHAMBER"
```

```
2220 A(C,D,L1)=1
2230 GOSUB460
2240 G4=RND(500/L1):IF(G-G4)<0THENG4=G
2250 Y=RND(8)
2260 IFY<=3THEN2420
2270 PRINT
2280 PRINT". . . . . . . HE SURPRISES YOU"
2290 GOSUB460
2300 PRINT"AS HE QUICKLY PASSES BY YOU HE"
2310 PRINT"SNATCHES . . . ";G4;" GOLD PIECES":PRINT
2320 G=G-G4
2330 IFMA=1THEN RETURN
2340 MA=RND(4):IFMA<=2THENMA=1
2350 IF MA=1THEN2380
2360 RETURN
2370 GOSUB460
2380 PRINT"YOU SEARCH THE CHAMBER AND"
2390 GOSUB460
2400 PRINT"YOU . . . . . FIND A MAP"
2410 RETURN
2420 PRINT:PRINT"YOU SURPRISED THE THIEF . . . ."
2430 GOSUB460
2440 PRINT"AS HE RUNS OUT HE DROPS . . . ."
2450 G4=RND(400/L1):PRINT" . . . ";G4;" GOLD PIECES."
2460 PRINT"YOU PICK UP THE GOLD PIECES":G=G+G4
2470 PRINT:IFMA=1THENRETURN
2480 MA=RND(4):IFMA<=2THENMA=1
2490 IFMA=1THEN2380
2500 RETURN
2510 CLS:PRINT
2520 PRINT"YOU ENTER A . . . NORTH-SOUTH CORRIDOR"
2530 PRINT"THRU A . . . . . . . SECRET DOOR"
2540 PRINT:GOSUB3240
2550 RETURN
2560 CLS:PRINT
2570 PRINT"YOU ENTER AN . . . EAST-WEST CORRIDOR"
2580 PRINT"THRU A . . . . . . . SECRET DOOR"
2590 PRINT:GOSUB3240
2600 RETURN
2610 PRINT"YOU ACTIVATED A . . . TRAP DOOR"
2620 GOSUB460
2630 TD=RND(4)*PL:IFTD>4THENPRINT"YOU FELL THRU . . .":GOSUB460:GOTO1720
2640 IFTD=4THEN2690
2650 PRINT
2660 PRINT"BUT . . . YOU CAUGHT YOURSELF"
2670 PRINT"FROM FALLING"
2680 RETURN
2690 IFL1=2THEN2800
2700 L1=L1+1:PRINT:K=1
2710 PRINT"YOU FELL THRU TO LEVEL 2 . . . AND"
2720 G=0
2730 GOSUB460
2740 PRINT
```

```
2750 PRINT"YOU . . . . . . . . LOST"
2760 PRINT"ALL OF YOUR GOLD PIECES"
2770 PRINT:IFPT=1THENPT=0:RETURN
2780 PRINT"BUT . . . YOU STILL HAVE YOUR KEY"
2790 RETURN
2800 PRINT"YOU FELL INTO A DEEP . . . PIT":PT=1
2810 GOSUB460
2820 PRINT"LUCKILY . . YOU DIDN'T GET HURT"
2830 PRINT
2840 GOSUB460
2850 PRINT"BUT IN CLIMBING OUT . . ."
2860 GOTO2720
2870 PRINT"YOU ARE AT A STAIRWAY"
2880 PRINT" . . . . . . GOING UP"
2890 PRINT
2900 RETURN
2910 PRINT"O    ";
2920 RETURN
2930 PRINT"M    ";
2940 RETURN
2950 PRINT"?    ";
2960 RETURN
2970 PRINT"C    ";
2980 RETURN
2990 PRINT"NS   ";
3000 RETURN
3010 PRINT"EW   ";
3020 RETURN
3030 GOTO2950
3040 PRINT"UP   ";
3050 RETURN
3060 H=1:O=9:W=8
3070 B=0:E=5:R=14
3080 C=0:PR=0
3090 GOTO1030
3100 RETURN
3110 GOSUB460
3120 K=1
3130 PRINT:PRINT"YOU LOOK TO THE GROUND . . . . . ."
3140 PRINT"AND FIND THE ENCHANTED KEY"
3150 GOSUB460
3160 RETURN
3170 GOSUB3120
3180 GOTO1230
3190 IFCA=CBTHEN3110
3200 RETURN
3210 PRINT"YOU KILLED ";CA;" MONSTERS "
3220 PRINT". . . . . IN ";M1;" TURNS."
3230 RETURN
3240 PRINT"THE DOOR CLOSES AND LOCKS BEHIND YOU":GOSUB460
3250 W=RND(8):IFW>=7THEN3300
3260 W=RND(8):IFW=8THEN3390
3270 RETURN
```

```
630 J=0
640 FORA=1TOG
650 PRINT"TEST # ";A
660 PRINT T(A):J=T(A)+J
670 NEXTA
680 GOSUB1250
690 PRINT"AVERAGE SCORE OUT OF ";G
700 PRINT"TEST(S) IS ";J/G
710 PRINT"THAT'S ";(J/G)*4;" PERCENT CORRECT"
720 GOSUB1250:GOSUB1250
730 GOSUB1250:GOSUB1250:GOSUB1100:GOSUB1250
740 PRINT"WOULD YOU LIKE A PLOT"
750 PRINT"OF THE TEST SCORES"
760 PRINT"Y=YES  N=NO"
770 INPUT A$
780 IFA$="Y" THEN 940
790 END
800 FORN=1TO25
810 A(N)=0
820 NEXTN
830 FORN=1TO25
840 M=RND(25)
850 FORA=1TOM
860 READ B$
870 NEXTA
880 RESTORE
890 IF A(M)=1THEN840
900 A(M)=1
910 C$(M)=B$
920 NEXTN
930 RETURN
940 CLS:PRINT"PLOT OF PRECOGNITION TEST DATA"
950 PRINT"SUBJECT:  ";N$;"   DATE: ";D$
960 PRINT
970 PRINT"0    5    10   15        25"
980 PRINT"++++++++++++++++++++++++++"
990 FORA=1TOG
1000 GG=T(A)
1010 PRINT TAB(GG)".    TEST # ";A
1020 GOSUB1250
1030 NEXTA
1040 END
1050 DATA"*","*","*","*","*"
1060 DATA"+","+","+","+","+"
1070 DATA"-","-","-","-","-"
1080 DATA"=","=","=","=","="
1090 DATA"0","0","0","0","0"
1100 PRINT
1110 IF J/G>=6THEN1200
1120 IFJ/G<4THEN1290
1130 PRINT
1140 PRINT"YOU HAVE AN AVERAGE SCORE."
1150 PRINT"AT THIS TIME, THERE IS NO"
```

```
3810 DATA"MAD DWARF",4,8
3820 DATA"ZOMBIE",4,8
3830 DATA"BERSERKER",5,10
3840 DATA"GIANT SCORPION",6,12
3850 DATA"GIANT COCKROACH",4,8
3860 DATA"DOPPLEGANGER",5,10
3870 DATA"GIANT FIRE BEETLE",1,2
3880 DATA"GIANT ANT",1,2
3890 DATA"GIANT TICK",2,4
3900 DATA"MUMMY",3,6
3910 DATA"NASTY ORC",2,4
3920 DATA"SKELETON",1,2
3930 DATA"TROLL",3,6
3940 DATA"GOBLIN",3,6
3950 DATA"VAMPIRE BAT",3,6
3960 DATA"CREEPING BLOB",3,6
3970 DATA"MAD DOG",2,4
3980 DATA"LARGE SPIDER",3,6
3990 DATA"BLACK CAT",2,4
4000 DATA"MAN EATING PLANT",1,2
4010 DATA"HYDRA",3,6
4020 DATA"GELATINOUS CUBE",2,4
4030 DATA"GIANT CENTIPEDE",1,2
4040 DATA"GIANT RAT",2,4
4050 DATA"SHADOW",2,4
4060 PRINT"YOU STUMBLED ONTO . . . . ."
4070 PRINT"A HIDDEN CAVERN":GOSUB460
4080 PRINT:GOSUB4210:IFH1<=0THENRETURN
4090 W=RND(9)
4100 GOSUB460:IFW>3THENPRINT:PRINT"THE CAVERN SEEMS EMPTY . . .":RETURN
4110 BB=2:GOSUB470:GOSUB4500
4120 GOSUB460:PRINT"BUT WAIT . . BEFORE YOU PROCEED":GOSUB460:PRINT
4130 PRINT"YOU HEAR A NOISE OFF IN THE DISTANCE"
4140 BB=2:GOSUB470
4150 PRINT"CAUTIOUSLY YOU WALK TOWARDS THE SOUND"
4160 BB=3:GOSUB470:W=RND(4):IFHI<H1THEN4180
4170 IFW=1THEN5040
4180 IFW=2THEN5170
4190 IFW=4ANDL1=2THEN5720
4200 GOTO5230
4210 PRINT:PRINT"YOU LOOK AROUND . . . ":GOSUB460
4220 V=RND(7)
4230 IFV>=5THEN4250
4240 RETURN
4250 PRINT"ON THE GROUND, AT YOUR FEET, IS A VIAL"
4260 PRINT:BB=2:GOSUB470
4270 PRINT"YOU PICK UP THE VIAL . . AND SEE THAT"
4280 PRINT"IT CONTAINS . . . A MILKY LIQUID"
4290 PRINT
4300 PRINT"WOULD YOU LIKE A DRINK?"
4310 PRINT"ENTER (Y)ES  OR  (N)O":DL=RND(6)
4320 INPUTD$
4330 IFD$="Y"THEN4350
```

```
4340 RETURN
4350 PRINT:PRINT"YOU TAKE A DRINK . . .":BB=2:GOSUB470:CLS
4360 IFDL>=3THEN4440
4370 IFDL=2THEN4480
4380 H3=RND(6)*PL:H1=H1-H3
4390 PRINT"YOU FEEL A LITTLE FUNNY . . .":GOSUB460:GOSUB460
4400 IFH1<=0THENRETURN
4410 PRINT:PRINT"IT WAS A BLACK MAGIC POTION . . ."
4420 PRINT"WHICH DECREASED YOUR 'HIT-POINTS' BY ";H3
4430 RETURN
4440 H3=RND(10/PL)+(6/PL):H1=H1+H3
4450 PRINT"IT WAS A WHITE MAGIC POTION . . ."
4460 PRINT"WHICH INCREASED YOUR 'HIT-POINTS' BY ";H3
4470 RETURN
4480 PRINT"THE LIQUID HAD NO EFFECT ON YOU"
4490 RETURN
4500 GOSUB460:PRINT:RETURN
4510 PRINT:W=RND(4)
4520 IFW<=2THEN4540
4530 GOSUB460:GOSUB4780
4540 IFH1<=0THENRETURN
4550 PRINT:PRINT"WILL YOU (F)IGHT OR (R)UN ?"
4560 INPUTF$:CLS
4570 IFF$="F"THEN4600
4580 IFF$="R"THEN4700
4590 GOTO4540
4600 CLS:PRINT:GOSUB460
4610 PRINT"YOU ATTACK THE . . . ";MS$:GOSUB460
4620 PRINT"WITH A SWING OF YOUR SWORD"
4630 N=RND(5)+RND(INT(CA/2+1)):HM=HM-N
4640 IFHM<=0THEN4890
4650 PRINT"YOU DO ";N;" HIT POINT(S) OF DAMAGE"
4660 PRINT:GOSUB460
4670 PRINT"IT HAS . . ";HM;" 'HIT-POINT(S)' LEFT"
4680 PRINT:GOSUB460
4690 GOTO4530
4700 W=RND(4):C=C1:D=D1
4710 PRINT"YOU QUICKLY RUN OUT . . .":IFTL=1THEN5560
4720 N=RND(2):BB=2:GOSUB470:IFW>=3THEN5330
4730 H1=H1-N
4740 PRINT"AS YOU LEAVE . . . THE ";MS$;" ATTACKS":GOSUB460
4750 IFH1<=0THENRETURN
4760 PRINT"AND IT DOES ";N;" 'HIT-POINT(S)' OF DAMAGE"
4770 BB=3:GOSUB470:RETURN
4780 PRINT:W=RND(7)
4790 PRINT". . . . . . . IT ATTACKS YOU":IFW<=2THEN5350
4800 W=RND(6):IFW>=3THEN4830
4810 N=RND(INT(HP/L1+1))+RND(INT(HP/L1+1))
4820 GOTO4840
4830 N=RND(HP*PL)
4840 IFHM<=2THENN=1
4850 H1=H1-N:GOSUB460:IFH1<=0THENRETURN
4860 PRINT"AND IT DOES ";N;" 'HIT-POINT(S)' OF DAMAGE"
```

```
4870 PRINT:PRINT"YOU HAVE . . . ";H1;" 'HIT-POINT(S)' LEFT"
4880 PRINT:RETURN
4890 PRINT:GOSUB460
4900 PRINT"YOU HAVE KILLED THE ";MS$
4910 PRINT
4920 IFA(C,D,L1)>=6THEN4950
4930 IFA(C,D,L1)=2THEN4950
4940 A(C,D,L1)=1
4950 G8=500:IFA(C,D,L1)>=6THENG8=250
4960 G4=RND(G8/L1)+75:IFA=2THENG4=G4*2
4970 G=G+G4:GOSUB460
4980 PRINT"YOU SEARCH THE AREA . . . ."
4990 GOSUB460:PRINT"AND FIND . . . ";G4;" GOLD PIECES"
5000 CA=CA+1:IFK=1THENRETURN
5010 IFL1=1THEN3190
5020 IFCA=K4THEN3110
5030 RETURN
5040 GOSUB460:GOSUB460
5050 GOSUB5290
5060 PRINT"HALT . . . I AM THE ANCIENT WIZARD"
5070 PRINT"I WILL NOT HARM YOU . . . . . .":GOSUB460:GOSUB460
5080 PRINT:G4=RND(300)+100:G=G+G4:PRINT
5090 PRINT"I GIVE YOU . . . ";G4;" GOLD PIECES"
5100 PRINT"OUT OF GOOD WILL AND FRIENDSHIP"
5110 PRINT
5120 H4=RND(10/PL)+(6/PL):H1=H1+H4
5130 PRINT"ALSO, I WILL INCREASE . . . "
5140 PRINT"YOUR 'HIT-POINTS' BY . . . ";H4
5150 GOSUB460
5160 RETURN
5170 GOSUB5290
5180 MS$="GIANT SPIDER":HP=6:HM=12
5190 PRINT"IT'S A HUGE MAN-SIZED CRAWLING"
5200 PRINT". . . . . . . SPIDER . . .":GOSUB460
5210 PRINT". . . . . AND . . . . ."
5220 GOTO4530
5230 GOSUB5290
5240 MS$="DARK WIZARD":HP=8:HM=14:CLS
5250 PRINT"DO NOT PASS . . . I AM THE ";MS$:GOSUB460
5260 PRINT"AND I WILL HACK YOU TO PIECES . . ."
5270 BB=2:GOSUB470
5280 GOTO4530
5290 CLS:PRINT"SUDDENLY . . . SOMETHING JUMPS . . ."
5300 PRINT"IN FRONT OF YOU . . . . . . . ."
5310 BB=3:GOSUB470:CLS
5320 RETURN
5330 GOSUB460:PRINT"AS YOU LEAVE . . . ";
5340 PRINT"THE ";MS$;" ATTACKS . .":GOSUB460
5350 GOSUB460:PRINT"BUT . . . . . . . . . IT MISSES":BB=2:GOSUB470
5360 RETURN
5370 BB=2:GOSUB470:GOSUB3540:DY=1:H1=HI
5380 PRINT"YOU HAVE ENTERED . . A ZONE"
5390 PRINT"BETWEEN . . LIFE AND DEATH"
```

```
5400 PRINT:BB=3:GOSUB470
5410 PRINT:PRINT"I . . . . THE ANCIENT WIZARD"
5420 PRINT"WILL RESTORE YOUR 'HIT-POINTS' TO ";HI
5430 PRINT"AND . . . . YOU HAVE ONE MORE"
5440 PRINT"CHANCE IN THE DUNGEON"
5450 PRINT:MD=RND(15)*CA+10:H1=HI
5460 PRINT"YOU SHALL HAVE ";MD;" MOVES"
5470 PRINT"LEFT TO FIND YOUR WAY OUT"
5480 PRINT"OF THE DUNGEON OF DANGER"
5490 BB=9:GOSUB470
5500 GOSUB3540:GOTO1110
5510 PRINTA$;", YOU HAVE DEPLETED YOUR MOVES"
5520 GOTO1720
5530 PRINT"ENTER DIFFICULTY LEVEL?"
5540 PRINT"1=MODERATE  2=DIFFICULT"
5550 INPUTPL:PRINT:RETURN
5560 TL=0:BB=2:GOSUB470
5570 PRINT"YOU REACTIVATED THE TELEPORTATION TRAP"
5580 BB=2:GOSUB470:GOSUB3540
5590 PRINT"YOU END UP BACK IN THE AREA WHERE"
5600 PRINT". . . YOU LAST TELEPORTED FROM":GOSUB460
5610 BB=2:GOSUB470:RETURN
5620 IFR<-400THENPRINT"INCOMPETENT SERF":RETURN
5630 IFR<-100THENPRINT"WEAKLING":RETURN
5640 IFR<0THENPRINT"APPRENTICE":RETURN
5650 IFR<100THENPRINT"HALFLING":RETURN
5660 IFR<200THENPRINT"FOOT SOLDIER":RETURN
5670 IFR<600THENPRINT"WARRIOR":RETURN
5680 IFR<900THENPRINT"GREAT WARRIOR":RETURN
5690 IFR<1500THENPRINT"SWORDSMAN":RETURN
5700 IFR<2500THENPRINT"MAGIC SWORDSMAN":RETURN
5710 IFR>=2500THENPRINT"DUNGEON MASTER":RETURN
5720 CLS:PRINT"YOU FALL INTO A DEEP . . DARK":GOSUB460
5730 PRINT". . . POOL . . OF MURKY WATER":BB=4:GOSUB470
5740 W=RND(6):PRINT:IFW>=5THEN5780
5750 IFW>=3THEN5860
5760 PRINT"IT IS WARM AND SOOTHING . .AND":BB=2:GOSUB470
5770 PRINT"YOU CLIMB OUT . . FEELING RELAXED":PRINT:RETURN
5780 MS$="GILL MONSTER":HP=8:HM=14:CLS
5790 PRINT"THE WATER IS . . . ICY COLD":BB=5:GOSUB470:PRINT
5800 PRINT"SUDDENLY . . YOU FEEL SOMETHING WARM"
5810 PRINT" . . . RUB AGAINST YOUR LEGS . . . .":BB=4:GOSUB470:PRINT
5820 PRINT"IT THEN SURFACES NEXT TO YOU . . ."
5830 PRINT" AND YOU SEE THAT IT IS A SLIMY . ."
5840 PRINT". . .  ";MS$;" . . READY TO ATTACK":BB=2:GOSUB470
5850 PRINT:PRINT"AS YOU CLIMB OUT . . .":GOSUB460:GOTO4530
5860 PRINT"THE WATER IS STEAMING . . . . HOT":BB=3:GOSUB470
5870 PRINT:PRINT"AS YOU QUICKLY JUMP OUT . . . ."
5880 G4=RND(500)+100:IF(G-G4)<0THENG4=G
5890 G=G-G4:PRINT"YOU DROP . . . ";G4;" GOLD PIECES"
5900 PRINT"WHICH FALL INTO THE POOL . . LOST":BB=5:GOSUB470:RETURN
```

NOTES

NOTES

NOTES

NOTES

TO THE READER

Sams Computer books cover Fundamentals — Programming — Interfacing — Technology written to meet the needs of computer engineers, professionals, scientists, technicians, students, educators, business owners, personal computerists and home hobbyists.

Our Tradition is to meet your needs and in so doing we invite you to tell us what your needs and interests are by completing the following:

1. I need books on the following topics:

____
____
____
____
____
____
____
____

2. I have the following Sams titles:

____
____
____
____
____
____
____
____

3. My occupation is:

_____ Scientist, Engineer
_____ Personal computerist
_____ Technician, Serviceman
_____ Educator
_____ Student
_____ D P Professional
_____ Business owner
_____ Computer store owner
_____ Home hobbyist
Other ______________________
____

Name (print)____
Address____
City ______________________ State __________ Zip __________

Mail to: **Howard W. Sams & Co., Inc.**
Marketing Dept. #CBS1/80
4300 W. 62nd St., P.O. Box 7092
Indianapolis, Indiana 46206

21865